WORLD COME OF AGE

WORLD
COME OF AGE

Edited and
with an Introduction by
Ronald Gregor Smith

CONTRIBUTORS
Karl Barth
Eberhard Bethge
Rudolf Bultmann
William Hamilton
Hanfried Müller
Regin Prenter
Hans Schmidt

Fortress Press   Philadelphia

Portions of this book are translated from 'Die Mündige Welt', volumes I–IV, published in 1955–1963 by Chr. Kaiser Verlag in Munich, Germany

Printed in Great Britain

Contents

Acknowledgements

'The Challenge of Dietrich Bonhoeffer's Life and Theology', being the Aldin Tuthill Lectures delivered at Chicago Theological Seminary in January 1961, is reprinted (in a revised form) by kind permission of the Editor of the *Chicago Theological Seminary*, where it appeared in February 1961 (vol. LI, 2). 'The Letters are a particular Thorn', by William Hamilton, is reprinted (in a somewhat longer form) by kind permission of the Editor of *Theology Today*, where it appeared in January 1962 (vol. XVIII, 4). The essay by Professor Rudolf Bultmann, 'The Idea of God and Modern Man' first appeared in its German form in *Zeitschrift für Theologie und Kirche*, in December 1963 (vol. LX, 3), and acknowledgements are due in the first place to the Editor of that journal and to the publisher, Messrs. J. C. B. Mohr (Paul Siebeck), Tübingen, for permission to make use of it here. The Editor's Introduction repeats in somewhat different form some pages of his book, *Secular Christianity*, 1966, and thanks are due to the publisher, Messrs. Collins, for their complaisance in this matter. The other contributions all appeared in *Die Mündige Welt*, 1955–63, a four-volume collection of essays on Bonhoeffer, edited by Eberhard Bethge: Karl Barth's Letter in vol. I, Regin Prenter's 'Dietrich Bonhoeffer and Karl Barth's Positivism of Revelation' in Vol. III, and the others in vol. IV. Thanks are due to the publishers, Messrs. Kaiser Verlag of Munich, for permission to pick out these pieces for English publication.

For the work of translation the help of the following is acknowledged with gratitude from the Editor: the Revd. Martin Rumscheidt, of McGill University, for the translation of 'Dietrich Bonhoeffer and Karl Barth's Positivism of Revelation'; Mr. Ronald A. Carson of Colgate Rochester Divinity School and Glasgow University, for the translation of 'The Cross of Reality?'; Mr. Nick Fenger of Louisville Theological Seminary for a first draft of 'Bonhoeffer and the Young Luther', and similarly Dr.

Acknowledgements

Antony Phillips of Stephens College, Columbia, Missouri, for a draft of 'The Problem of the Reception and Interpretation of Dietrich Bonhoeffer'. For these last two, and for the translation of Karl Barth's Letter, the Editor takes special responsibility. Lastly, it is a pleasure to record the helpfulness with which Dr. Robert W. Funk of Drew University, Madison, N.J., placed at our disposal his translation of Professor Bultmann's essay. This translation was made for the English *Yearbook* prepared from the notable pages of the *Zeitschrift für Theologie und Kirche*, and Herr Siebeck of Messrs. J. C. B. Mohr (Paul Siebeck) showed in this too his customary magnanimity.

In the quotations from Bonhoeffer's own writings the published English versions have been used; but occasionally – and especially in the *Letters and Papers from Prison* – it has been found necessary to make some alterations. Sometimes the same passage appears in different versions, but it is hoped that such variations will be an aid rather than a hindrance to the reader.

The Contributors

Ronald Gregor Smith is Professor of Divinity at Glasgow University.

Eberhard Bethge is Director of the Pastoral College of the Rhineland at Rengsdorf.

Karl Barth is Professor Emeritus of Basel University.

Regin Prenter is Professor of Theology at Aarhus University.

William Hamilton is Professor of Theology at Colgate Rochester Divinity School, Rochester, N.Y.

Hanfried Müller is Professor of Systematic Theology at the Humboldt University, Berlin.

Hans Schmidt is Lecturer in the Theological Faculty at Hamburg University.

Rudolf Bultmann is Professor Emeritus of Marburg University.

Abbreviations

AB = *Act and Being*, 1962, Collins and Harper and Row (*Akt und Sein*, 1956, Kaiser Verlag, Munich)

C   = *Christology*, 1966, Collins (*Gesammelte Schriften*, III, pp. 166ff.)

CD = *The Cost of Discipleship*, 1959, SCM Press and Macmillan Co. (*Nachfolge*, 1955, Kaiser Verlag, Munich)

CF = *Creation and Fall*, 1959, SCM Press (*Schöpfung und Fall*, 1955, Kaiser Verlag, Munich)

E   = *Ethics*, 1964, Collins Fontana Library and Macmillan Co. (*Ethik*, 1949, Kaiser Verlag, Munich)

GS = *Gesammelte Schriften*, I–IV, 1958–61, Kaiser Verlag, Munich

LPP = *Letters and Papers from Prison*, 1963, Collins Fontana edition and Macmillan Co. (*Widerstand und Ergebung*)

LT = *Life Together*, 1955 SCM Press and Harper and Row (*Gemeinsanes Leben*, 1955, Kaiser Verlag, Munich)

MW = *Die Mündige Welt*, 1955–63, Kaiser Verlag, Munich

NRS = *No Rusty Swords*, Letters, Lectures and Notes from the Collected Works, vol. I, 1965, Collins and Harper and Row

SC = *Sanctorum Communio*, 1963, Collins and Harper and Row (title in USA: *The Communion of Saints*) 1954, Kaiser Verlag, Munich)

WE = *Widerstand und Ergebung*, 1955, Kaiser Verlag, Munich (*Letters and Papers from Prison*)

I

Introduction

by Ronald Gregor Smith

Dietrich Bonhoeffer is without any doubt one of the rare creative spirits in theology in our time. And because he is really creative he has broken out of the theological ghetto, and beckons others to follow him. At the same time he has found among those who are innocent of theological nuances, but open to the realities with which theology is concerned, a response which is almost embarrassing to his more professional companions. For example, to my mind the immense popularity of a book like Bishop John Robinson's *Honest to God* – for which of course other adventitious reasons, as well as some imponderables, may be adduced – is due in the main to the revolutionary powers in Bonhoeffer's thought, from which it so freely draws.

This is not to say that Bonhoeffer himself is a clear and unambiguous figure. On the contrary, it is the very ambiguities, both in his life and his ideas, which offer such immense stimulus to the theologian and the non-theologian alike. The watchwords, which have now almost become clichés, which rise out of his thinking, owe at least some of their attraction to their ambiguous and enigmatic nature. The 'world come of age', 'religionless Christianity', and 'the man for others', are among the best known of his coinages.

Sometimes it seems that such phrases have liberating and revolutionary power in inverse proportion to their clarity of

9

meaning. In consequence, a cult of Bonhoeffer is in danger of forming.

It is one of the purposes of this symposium to demonstrate the variety in the exposition of Bonhoeffer's thought, and to guard against too facile a conclusion about his significance.

It is mainly on the continent of Europe, as might be expected, that the discussion has been waged – has, indeed, at some points raged furiously. A congenial starting-point for this discussion has been the letter written by Karl Barth to Superintendent Herrenbrück, the relevant portion of which is given below (p. 89 *ff*.). Parallel with Barth's shoulder-shrugging and somewhat wistful dismissal of Bonhoeffer's whole concern is the acute and diligent exposition of Barth's theology by Regin Prenter (p. 93 *ff*.). Prenter, for all his anxiety to do justice both to Barth and Bonhoeffer, does not, it seems to me, succeed in being entirely convincing. It is doubtful whether Bonhoeffer can really be understood on the basis that he is one of Barth's school. More convincing, it seems to me, is the equally acute and helpful analysis, also by Prenter, of the kinship between Bonhoeffer and the young Luther (p. 161 *ff*.).

The issue at this point, like the whole issue in Continental theology in general, is in danger of being shrouded in the smoke of battle round the two towering figures of Karl Barth and Rudolf Bultmann. It is one of the pities of our time that Bonhoeffer himself did not live to go his own way. It is, however, relevant to take note of a letter which he wrote on 25 March 1942, in which he speaks more clearly and positively of Bultmann than in the slight and unguarded references to be found in the *Letters and Papers from Prison*. As this letter has not hitherto appeared in English, and indeed is not even to be found in the collected works in German, but has only appeared in Eberhard Bethge's introduction to the German version (*Gott ist Anders*) of Robinson's *Honest to God*, I give the relevant portion now:

Introduction

. . . Now as to Bultmann, I am one of those who welcomed his essay ['New Testament and Mythology']; not because I agreed with it, I regret the twofold point of departure in it (the argument from John I. 14 and from the radio ought not to be confused, though I consider the second too to be an argument – it's just that the separation must be clearer). To this extent I have perhaps remained a pupil of Harnack's. To put it crudely, Bultmann has let the cat out of the bag, not only for himself, but for very many (the Liberal cat out of the Confessing Church bag), and this is what pleases me. He has dared to say what many repress in themselves (I include myself), without having overcome it. In this way he has done intellectual purity and integrity a service. The pharisaism of faith which on the other hand is being offered by many of the brothers strikes me as unfortunate. Now we have to speak and to answer. I should be glad to speak with Bultmann about it, and expose myself to the draught which blows from his direction. But then the window will have to be shut again. Otherwise the susceptible will too easily catch cold.

If you see Bultmann, please give him my greetings . . . tell him that I should like to see him, and how I see things . . .

It is not my purpose here to analyse this letter further than to draw attention to its open welcome to Bultmann's 'intellectual purity and integrity'. The real speaking and answering which Bonhoeffer desired are better served by the presentation of a recent essay by Bultmann himself (p. 256*ff.*). Here we find, I believe, though more by implication than by direct treatment, the common concern of the two men. It is the more important to stress this in view of the tendency to be noted in Eberhard Bethge's standpoint to see Bonhoeffer as ranged in the Barthian camp over against Bultmann. And undoubtedly Bethge's Chicago lectures, which are the *pièce de résistance* of this symposium, provide us with the richest and most comprehensive effort so far made to see the whole complex of Bonhoeffer's life and thought as a substantial, if mysterious, unity.

Of the other essays in this volume it is good to have a contribution from America: William Hamilton of Colgate Rochester Divinity School typifies the best that can happen to a lively and open-minded scholar when faced with the 'enigmatic utterances' (the phrase is Barth's) of the letters:

he gathers the relevant material together, gives it some systematic form, and does not foreclose the issue. Hanfried Müller works from a very different position: he sees the outcome of Bonhoeffer's thought in 'a rational and optimistic atheism which is founded upon the freedom of faith', in 'a new picture of history' which Müller locates quite undialectically in the socialist society, which for him is adumbrated in the East German state where he lives and teaches.

The subtlest and most original critique of Bonhoeffer comes in the essay by Hans Schmidt. His main contention is that the problem of history in all its depth was concealed from Bonhoeffer. If this is correct, then the whole range of Bonhoeffer's thought is bound to lose its impetus, and to be consigned to limbo – much as Barth has suggested in his letter.

But is this really so? I should like to make some observations about what seems to me to be Bonhoeffer's chief concern, whose continued vitality for our time is indisputable. But first, it is perhaps useful for those who come to him for the first time to know the essential outlines of his life.

He was born in Breslau in 1906, where his father was professor of neurology and psychiatry. He was brought up in Berlin, to which the family moved in 1912 when the father began to teach at the university there. On both his father's and his mother's side Bonhoeffer came of families distinguished in the life of Germany. It was a great liberal tradition which he inherited, and this liberalism extended deep into all his views, giving to his theology both breadth and humanity. He was a precocious student, and by the age of twenty-one he had completed a dissertation for his licentiate, *Sanctorum Communio*. A few years later, in 1930, he was habilitated at the university of Berlin with a dissertation entitled *Act and Being, Transcendental Philosophy and Ontology in Systematic Theology*. Thus he was launched on what looked like being a straightforward career in academic theology. There was an interval in Union Seminary, New York, and another interval as pastor in London to the German-speaking

Introduction

congregation there. But the rise of the Nazis to power in 1933 changed all that. Bonhoeffer was early associated with the resistance church movement, the 'Confessing Church'. He led a new, special and illegal seminary of the Confessing Church for ordinands in Finkenwalde in Pomerania, and went on teaching even after the seminary was officially suppressed. In turn he lost the right to teach at a university, the right to speak in public, and the right to publish. By 1940 he was involved in illegal activities, though under the excellent cover provided by the *Abwehr*, the Counter-Intelligence Service under Admiral Canaris, which aimed at the assassination of Hitler and the overthrow of the Nazi régime. After various journeyings abroad, and other activities which are still obscure (but which we may hope to have unveiled by Eberhard Bethge's full-scale study, shortly to be published) – though they include a meeting in Sweden, which we know a fair amount about, with Dr. Bell, then Bishop of Chichester, to whom Bonhoeffer conveyed possible peace terms from the conspirators for the Allies – he was arrested on 5 April 1943, and after two years in prison was finally hanged by the Nazis at Flossenbürg. He was only thirty-nine years of age.

His published work during his lifetime did not, it seems to me, carry any clear indication of what was to come. It is in his two posthumous works, one the unfinished and fragmentary volume of his *Ethics*, and the other the letters and short pieces, especially those to his friend Eberhard Bethge, which he wrote during his two years in prison, and was able to smuggle out, that we find the Bonhoeffer who has caused such a ferment during the last fifteen years. Nevertheless, the earlier writings cannot be ignored, and it is a sign of the deepening understanding of Bonhoeffer's significance for our time that a writer like Hans Schmidt does not ignore them. Highly sophisticated theological writing, for the most part, and deeply involved in the inner concerns of Christian teaching, they are a warning that Bonhoeffer's last thoughts are not so naïve and unguarded as is sometimes supposed. In

13

particular we have to recall that not only in these earlier writings, but also throughout his time in prison, Bonhoeffer was a sober and realistic practitioner of what he later called 'the secret discipline'. It is precisely in virtue of this discipline of prayer and Bible study that no straightforward explanation of his views is possible. The tension between the 'world' and creative discipleship is all the more marked because at the same time Bonhoeffer was directly sensitive to the autonomy of the world. His problem, both in theology and in his life, was how to maintain simultaneously both the reality of the world and the reality of God.

It was only after a year in prison that he broached this problem in the terms which have become so bound up with his name. I quote from the letter of 30 April 1944 (making my own translation, but cf. LPP, p. 91):

I am constantly moved by the question what Christianity really is, or who Christ really is, for us today. The time in which everything could be said to men by means of words, whether theological or pious, is over. So too is the time of inwardness and conscience, which means the time of religion in general. We are moving towards a completely religionless time. Men as they now are simply cannot be religious any more . . . Our entire 1900-year-old Christian preaching and theology are based upon the religious *a priori* of men

– and that *a priori*, he goes on to say, no longer exists as a viable historical possibility. Now he has a great deal more to say of what he means by religion, but it is important to see that what he is chiefly concerned about is not just a self-contained view of the world (namely as one without religion), but what Christianity and Christ really mean today. And as I understand this concern, it is above all a question of understanding and interpreting what faith is, or – what is the same thing – how we may speak of God, how we may use God-language at all. (The connection here not only with the somewhat sensational ideas of Paul van Buren, but also with the more straightforward and comprehensive hermeneutical concern of Rudolf Bultmann, is clear enough; but into these connections I will not go here.)

Introduction

Bonhoeffer goes on to define what he means by religion in a bewildering variety of ways. Religion means calling in God when human resources, intellectual or moral, are at an end: so we have the God of the stop-gaps, the *deus ex machina*, to solve insoluble problems. It means a metaphysical view of transcendence, what he also calls (in the *Ethics*) thinking 'in two spheres', the sphere of nature and the sphere of supernature. It means individualistic piety, what he also calls methodism. It means thinking of religion as a special compartment of life, or 'being religious in a particular way, by means of some method or other making something of oneself (a sinner, a penitent, or a saint)' (18 July 1944). It is not simply identical with the law in the biblical sense. Rather, religion – if I may attempt to summarize Bonhoeffer's view – means an attitude which regards man's life as being somehow completed by the addition of God. And this addition of God is variously regarded as an individual experience, an experience at the boundaries of human need, or the boundaries of human thought, or as some other extension of the world or of the self. (In this connexion the analysis by Gerhard Ebeling, in his essay on 'The Non-religious Interpretation of Biblical Concepts' in *Word and Faith*, p. 148*ff*., is the most reliable exposition known to me.)

Now if we were to look at all this from a simply empirical standpoint we should have to modify Bonhoeffer's view considerably. *Homo religiosus* is still with us, and in us, in many different ways. But even beyond the empirical evidences of religiosity there is still an important sense in which man is not free of religion today: in the sense that he wishes to extend himself, his idea of himself, into some supposed absolute which is really once again an extension of the world. This may be seen in the fascination which ideologies have over men: nationalism, racism, Marxism, the reduction of man to some abstraction, such as the economic man, the political man, the American man or the Soviet man or the practical man. All these extensions of man's view of himself into some

15

would-be summary of his self-understanding are all to be characterized as ideologies with their own religious paraphernalia. They are ideologies with a religious cast, in that they seek to establish security for man by manipulating his future: they wish to anticipate the future, regarded as manageable and disposable, and thus to circumvent the appalling reality of man's essential nature as involving the unpredictability of the future. Thus they are all alike in their effort to make man secure by substituting for man as man a view of the world. In this effort they support themselves by an immense religious apparatus.

For Bonhoeffer this misses the point. His prime concern is the meaning of Christ and Christianity today. So he recognizes man's movement towards religionlessness in terms which are utterly opposed to those blatant movements of repristination of religiosity. Along with his assertion of our movement to a time of no religion at all, we are presented with a conception of man's autonomy which is again both an empirico-historical judgement and something more. The something more I should define as a shift in the view of transcendence. The autonomy of man is at first sight a historical simple judgement. Thus on 8 June 1944 (LPP, p. 106) he writes:

The movement beginning about the 13th century . . . towards the autonomy of man (under which head I place the discovery of the laws by which the world lives and manages in science, social and political affairs, art, ethics and religion) has in our time reached a certain completion. Man has learned to cope with all questions of importance without recourse to God as a working hypothesis . . . As in the scientific field, so in human affairs generally 'God' is being more and more driven out of life, losing more and more ground . . .

This is the adulthood or coming of age of the world. But there are various indications that even in a straightforward empirical sense Bonhoeffer by no means regarded this autonomy as simply analogous to an individual's maturity. Thus in the following passage, from a letter of 21 August 1944, we have a different perspective on 'these turbulent times',

Introduction

which unites a theological judgement with a personal discipline of a remarkable kind:

Once more I have started reading the *Losungen* [an annual volume of biblical texts published by the *Herrnhuter*] and meditated upon them (Numbers 11. 23) ['And the Lord said to Moses, Is the Lord's hand shortened? Now you shall see whether my word will come true for you or not'] and 11 Corinthians 1. 23 ['For all the promises of God find their Yes in him. That is why we utter the Amen through him, to the glory of God']. Surely everything depends on the 'in him'. All that we may rightly expect and pray for from God is to be found in Jesus Christ. All that a God as we think of him ought to do and could do – with this the God of Jesus Christ has nothing to do. We must again and again sink ourselves, at length and in quietness, in the life, sayings, deeds, suffering and death of Jesus, in order to know what God promises and fulfils ... Again and again in these turbulent times we lose sight of why it is really worth living. We think that life only has meaning for us because this or that man is living. But the truth is that if the earth deserved to have the man Jesus Christ, if a man like Jesus lived, then and only then is there any meaning in life for us men ...

What are the implications of this intense christocentric faith for Bonhoeffer's view of the maturity of the world, the world come of age? There is a twofold implication. First, the autonomy of the world is given in Christian faith. And second, the world cannot properly understand itself in its autonomy unless it recognizes its relation to Christian faith.

First, the autonomy of the world is given in Christian faith. What does this mean? It means that while Bonhoeffer's empirical and historical assessment places the movement towards the world's coming of age somewhere towards the end of the middle ages, his understanding of Christian faith enables him, indeed compels him, to place the ultimate source of this movement in the very heart of Christianity. That is to say, it is the life of Christ himself which liberates the world. Man, that is, the man of faith, 'may live in a "worldly" way, that is, he is freed from false religious bonds and inhibitions'. Or again, 'the only way to be honest is to recognize that we have to live in the world *etsi deus non daretur*' (16 July 1944). This does not point to a straight-forward autonomy or independence of the world at all. It is not to be understood as an objective entity, standing by itself, as it were, simply the self-contained and sovereign reality of the world. It is a mere misreading of Bonhoeffer simply to write off the whole movement of Christian faith in the world as being merely the occasion for establishing the world in its maturity. Faith is not so to speak the scaffolding by which we have been able to rise to this point, which may then be knocked away, leaving the structure of the world in solitary power over itself. A good deal of misunderstanding clusters round this complex of Bonhoeffer's ideas. It is at this point that even Hans Schmidt seems to me to miss the subtlety of the dialectic with which Bonhoeffer seeks to hold together the reality of the world and the reality of God.

It is true that Bonhoeffer vacillates in his thought, and more so if we follow the development through the *Ethics* as well – not to mention the earlier writings. He never made clearly enough the distinctions which must be made. But the distinctions are implicit, all the same, in what he does say. For secondly, the world cannot properly understand itself in its autonomy unless it recognizes its relation to Christian faith. Certainly, as he says, 'the world's coming of age is no longer an occasion for polemics and apologetics' (8 June 1944), and the 'driving of God out of life' (*ibid.*) is wrongly seen as 'a great defection from God'. But as he also says, this 'maturity of the world is really better understood than it understands itself, namely, from the standpoint of the gospel, of Christ' (*ibid.*).

In other words, the crux of the matter for Bonhoeffer lies in the way in which we recognize our maturity. We do not simply have to live in the world *etsi deus non daretur*, as though God were not given. But we live in this way – '*before God*'. His letter of 16 July 1944 (LPP, p. 122) contains what is perhaps the most significant of all Bonhoeffer's remarks:

Introduction

God himself compels us to recognize this. So our coming of age leads us to a true recognition of our situation before God. God gives us to know that we must live as men who manage our lives without God. The God who is with us is the God who forsakes us. [And here he refers us to Mark 15. 34: Christ's words from the cross, 'My God, my God, why hast thou forsaken me?'] The God who lets us live in the world without the working hypothesis of God is the God before whom we are ever standing. Before God and with God we live without God. God lets himself be driven out of the world on to the cross. God is powerless and weak in the world, and that is precisely the way, the only way, in which he is with us and helps us. Matthew 8. 17 ['Himself took our infirmities and bare our sicknesses'] makes it quite clear that Christ does not help in virtue of his omnipotence, but by his weakness and suffering.

With these words Bonhoeffer points to the source of the movement towards the liberation of the world, and to the present actuality of that source in the hidden presence of God. It is this hidden presence, this presence in absence and absence in presence, which is the reality of Christ's being. It is not possible to weaken the tension, or to simplify the consequent dialectic, by suggesting (as Prenter does in his essay on 'Bonhoeffer and the young Luther', p. 169) that the God 'without' whom we live 'before God and with God' is merely the false God, the God who has been turned into a principle and made an object of thought and of religious aspirations. On the contrary, it is the one God before whom and with whom we live who is at the same time the God we are without.

It is thus impossible to suggest that Bonhoeffer is attempting just a restoration of the traditional material of Christianity. Unfortunately he himself never had the time to present his reinterpretation of biblical concepts. He planned to do it, and one of the last things he wrote was a few pages which he entitled 'Outline of a Book' (LPP, p. 163*ff*.). Some of the outstanding points from that sketch must be quoted:

Man is once more cast upon himself. He has managed to deal with everything, only not with himself . . . What is God? Not in the first place a general belief in God, in his omnipotence, etc. This is not a genuine experience of God, but a piece of extended world. Meeting

19

with Jesus Christ. The experience that a transformation of all human life is given in the fact that Jesus 'is there only for others'. Jesus 'being there for others' is the experience of transcendence . . . Faith is the participation in this being of Jesus . . . Our relation to God is not a 'religious' relation to some supreme, almighty, best of all beings – this is not genuine transcendence – but our relation to God is a new life in 'being there for others', in participation in the being of Jesus. Transcendence is not infinite and unattainable tasks, but it is the accessible neighbour, who is given to us again and again . . . God in human form . . . the man for others, and hence the Crucified. The man who lived from transcendence.

Here, it seems to me, we have something different from the old forms of religion, as well as different from the old styles of theology. Of course it is inchoate, and elusive, and enigmatic, and it leaves us with a host of questions. But it points in a most promising direction. It is subtle in its dialectic, and radical in the kind of Christianity which it sees as most nearly expressing the reality from which it comes – the two-fold reality of God and of the world, which is given to us in the unity of Christ. It is a thoroughly historical faith which is suggested here. The analysis of man is made with the utmost freedom, but it does not relapse into an ideology which would remove man, historical, actual, living man, from the centre of the picture. At the same time we are offered a view of transcendence which is not identical with a particular metaphysic, but which leaves man in free play within the reality of his historicity. Transcendence is here recognized as an event which happens to us. It is essentially a givenness: we are confronted by the other, by 'the accessible neighbour, who is given to us again and again'. We do not go outside of our own personal history in order to be met by the other. Transcendence, therefore, is the way in which the historical reality of life comes to us, comes upon us. It is the way in which we believe, therefore, that all being is. The clue to this way of being is the historical Jesus – that is, the Jesus who is believed in as the Lord.

These reflections, we hope, will encourage the reader to go

further, both in this volume of essays, and then beyond. For clearly Bonhoeffer with such thoughts has set the whole traditional structure of theology, and with it the traditional styles of Christianity, trembling and moving. What sort of a God is this on whom Bonhoeffer depends? Have we to abandon the metaphysical tradition of the aseity of God? Have we to abandon any attempt to talk of God at all, as Paul van Buren and others are suggesting? If we do that, are we not left merely with a tragic figure, the figure of the suffering Jesus?

One thing is clear: Bonhoeffer did not relapse into a sentimental Jesusology. Consequently, he did not restrict his theology till it was indistinguishable from a naïve variation of liberal humanism. It is a humanism, certainly, of which he is speaking, the humanism of a liberated humanity in a world which has its own way to go in self-responsibility. But it is at the same time a humanism which is human only in the relation with others, a relation whose reality is both released and confirmed in the being of God for the world in his suffering in Christ. 'Only a suffering God can help.'

I I

The Challenge of Dietrich Bonhoeffer's Life and Theology

by Eberhard Bethge

The titles of my three lectures – 'Foundation: The Quest for the Concrete Nature of the Message'; 'Concentration: The Narrow Pass for Christianity'; and 'Liberation: Christianity without Religion' – mark the three periods in which Bonhoeffer acted and thought. One cannot say 'taught', for the officially licensed professorial chair was his for only two years. At the age of thirty he was barred from his academic post; when he was thirty-four, the pulpit was closed to him; at thirty-five, written publication was forbidden; and, with his imprisonment at thirty-seven, even conversation with his friends was denied him. Yet, each time this narrowing circle came closer, his acting and thinking gained power and stretched into new dimensions. When he was silenced for good at thirty-nine, he began to speak more loudly than ever before.

During his lifetime Bonhoeffer was never in the headlines of a newspaper either in his country or abroad, as were Niemöller, Barth, or Dibelius. Only twice did he enjoy the excitement of being a speaker at great meetings: in 1934, when he addressed the famous ecumenical meeting at Fanö, and in 1936, when he spoke to the crowded meeting of the Confessing Church at the Olympic Games in Berlin.

Bonhoeffer did not care for publicity. He did not attempt the skilful handling of the means of mass communication. While many of his colleagues accepted small compromises in order to continue reaching and teaching the crowds, he did not seek to reach mass audiences. Yet there was that self-confidence in his cause which he ascribes to Luther, Lessing, Hugo Wolf, and also to Karl Barth – the *hilaritas* ('serenity'), which 'might be described as confidence in their own work, a certain boldness and defiance of the world and of popular opinion, a steadfast certainty that what they are doing will benefit the world, even though it does not approve, a magnificent self-assurance' (LPP, p. 97). That is the atmosphere around him, which you felt on meeting him and which you feel now when you read his last letters.

The first challenge Bonhoeffer's life represents comes through our confrontation with his own high standard. It is a standard of long waiting for one's hour; a standard that is aristocratic in disdaining cheap results and humble in its judgement of real priorities, the standard of sacrifice. Rosenstock-Huessy says: 'If anyone makes a complete sacrifice, history goes forward one millimetre.'

Today, in contrast, Bonhoeffer is receiving great public attention. He transcends the boundaries of his denomination and of his country. What is more, he transcends the unbridgeable gap made by guilt and suspicion: each time a new volume of the *Gesammelte Schriften* appears, the first review is to be found in the paper of the *Jüdische Lehrhaus* (Zürich) and in the *Allgemeine Wochenzeitung der Juden in Deutschland*. Bonhoeffer now transcends boundaries as vigorously as he confined himself to his own spiritual and bodily roots in his lifetime. But no clear-cut formula has yet appeared defining his contribution. The many voices have not yet been tuned into a harmonious chord. He is felt to be a great stimulant stirring up the waters. This is precisely what he has always been. He was never the convenient analyst who addressed people from an easy chair. He was not the comfortable contemporary. He was usually moving on to a new playing-field just when the others turned up for the game. When the multitude in 1933 put all their efforts into developing the doctrine of God's orders of creation (*Schöpfungsordnungen*), which seemed to give Christian support to Hitler's racial legislation, he ignored it completely and preached an irritant eschatology. When the others finally discovered all their comfort in eschatology in the late Nazi years, he had already turned back to 'this-worldliness' – at the same moment when there was no room left for him in this world.

There is a certain justification, then, for not coming too easily to terms with Bonhoeffer's challenge. Perhaps the Bonhoeffer who becomes acceptable and comfortable ought always to be at once replaced by the disturbing one. I think we must leave it open as to whether the different forms of witness in the three periods of Bonhoeffer's life are such that a later one neatly and finally replaces an earlier one. To accept the witness of one period and to stay with it might become the means to escape from the challenge and make the living Christ a mere object for our religious desires. It might happen that 'concentration' alone leads to deadly narrowness or that 'liberation' alone results in blasphemous cheapness.

The difficulty of grasping the meaning of Bonhoeffer's challenge could already be seen in Germany just after the war. Lutheran church representatives refused to accept him as a Christian martyr when they made the unpleasant discovery that this biblical scholar was a political plotter, but they eagerly reprinted and distributed his eschatological church writings in camps all over the country. What about abroad? The ecumenical representatives immediately honoured Bonhoeffer as a modern Christian martyr precisely because the German theologian died as an active resister, but they let the shadow of ignorance prevail as to whether or not Bonhoeffer was a theologian of some stature. Rouse and Neill's great *History of the Ecumenical Movement* (1954) does not even mention Bonhoeffer's heated theological discussions

24

with Geneva and with Faith and Order in 1934 and after-
wards – discussions which would make a good and penetrating
textbook for our judgement of the present crisis between the
churches in South Africa and the relation of Geneva to this
crisis. The answer still has to be given to the question:
Admitting that the life of this man has spoken – can his
theology make any impact?

The rather formalistic headings for these lectures –
'Foundation', 'Concentration', and 'Liberation' – cover,
chronologically, roughly the periods 1927–33, 1933–40, and
1940–5. Theologically, these same periods might be called
the dogmatic, the exegetical, and the ethical; or, again, the
theoretical period in which he learned and taught at Berlin
University, the pastoral period in which he served the Confessing Church in a preachers' seminary, and the political
period in which his life became ambiguous.

In the first period Bonhoeffer laid the foundations while
still clinging to the traditional lecture desk. He seemed born
for the academic life, since his father was a famous figure in
psychiatry and his brothers and brothers-in-law distinguished
professors in law, science, and theology. The family had at
their disposal the connexions to the self-contained German
academic world. There was ease of entrance and promotion
when a gifted scholar moved into the familiar exclusive
academic circle with its members ready to speed him on his
way. But in Bonhoeffer's case only one question mattered:
whether the claim of Christianity could be met by this
traditional privileged life of research and teaching. The
second period started with the gloomy stumbling-block of
discrimination against some of his colleagues. Bonhoeffer
concentrated by paying the price for the foundations he had
laid theoretically, and moved to serve the pulpit exclusively –
at that time not a traditional step at all. But he enjoyed it
when the unprivileged church became a new spirited outlet
for theology. His famous colleague from Berlin University,
Professor Lietzmann, wrote with some disappointment to a

Swedish friend in 1936, 'Now our most gifted young teacher has turned into a fanatic; he declares now, "there is salvation only in the Confessing Church".' In the third period Bonhoeffer broke through the limitations of his bourgeois and Lutheran heritage by walking into the dark corner of conspiracy. It not only made him an outcast; it also robbed him of the spiritual protection of his beloved Confessing Church and set him in complete moral loneliness. In November 1943 he wrote, in his first smuggled letter: 'At first I wondered a great deal whether it was really for the cause of Christ that I was giving you all this heartbreak, but I soon put that out of my head as a temptation, and I became quite sure that it was my special call to put this borderline case into practice and see it through to its end, no matter how problematic its nature might be' (LPP, p. 40; I have emended the translation. Ed.).

THE FIRST PERIOD

Foundation : The Quest for the Concrete Nature of the Message

October, 1931: This invisibility smashes us indeed . . . this madness being thrown back again and again on the invisible God himself – who can stand that any more? (GS, I, p. 61).
Sermon (1932): A proper sermon should be of the kind that holds out to a child a shining red apple or to a thirsty man a glass of fresh water and asks them: do you want it? In this way we should be able to speak about the things of faith so that hands are stretching out faster than we can fill them (GS, IV, p. 51).

These two quotations show the state of mind of the young Bonhoeffer and indicate the two points I wish to present: the character of concreteness and the way the message opened up. The first quotation was written when Bonhoeffer got back from America feeling that his hopes of encountering the visibility of the Christian God, at least in that country, had perhaps not been confirmed. He thinks it possible, he continues, that 'the great dying hour has come for Christianity.

Our time seems to have passed and the gospel might be given to another people, presented in quite different words and deeds.'

The other words were spoken in an agitated Berlin, when in the midst of many prophets Hitler's clever agent Joseph Goebbels was already offering his poisoned fruits to the hungry unemployed. At this time Bonhoeffer lived for months in the worst slum district, giving confirmation classes to proletarian children. Though rising in the academic world Bonhoeffer did not shut himself off in the theological ghetto but faced extensively and intensively the concrete problems of Christianity of that time. Before we try to see whether there is any concreteness in his abstract theology of this period, let us have a look at his biographical relations, the influences upon him, and the things which played a determinative part in his life.

Biographica

Bonhoeffer never studied with Karl Barth. As a student he was practically confined to Berlin and its peculiar intellectual atmosphere. During this period he gained some command of the tools of sociology through heated discussions with his elder brothers who were familiar with the two Webers, Max and Alfred – the last a close friend of Bonhoeffer's father – and also with Tönnies and Troeltsch. It was still the time of the German Youth Movement (*Jugendbewegung*), with its anti-rationalistic philosophy of life. Dilthey and Simmel were the philosophers; Dostoevski, Soloviev, Berdyaev, the heroes of literature. Bonhoeffer read all of Nietzsche very carefully, and Nietzsche's tremendous plea for the earth and for loyalty to its creatures never left his mind. The giant Antæus, who retained his strength so long as he had his feet on the earth, appears in a speech of Bonhoeffer's as early as 1928, and is present again in a draft of a play written in prison in 1944. When Bonhoeffer assumed that Barth's philosophical background was neo-Kantianism, then his own was certainly coloured by the terminology of the 'philosophy of life'.

When Bonhoeffer took up theology in Berlin (after a year at Tübingen), Troeltsch had just died. Karl Holl was still lecturing, and his Luther seminar gave Bonhoeffer a magnificent introduction which led him to love Luther above anyone else, though he soon criticized Holl's interpretation. Old Adolf von Harnack was still giving seminars. He liked the young theologian, whom he had known for a long time through family connexions. Bonhoeffer was permanently influenced by these great liberal modernist teachers. The Union Seminary teachers would not have believed that this young man, whom they found to be an absolutely fanatic Barthian, had spoken in 1930 at the grave of Harnack on behalf of his pupils: 'Harnack was concerned with nothing but the truth of his answer [to his pupils]. But it became clear to us through him that truth is born only of freedom. We saw in him the champion of the free expression of a truth once recognized, who formed his free judgement afresh time and time again, and went on to express it clearly despite the fear-ridden restraint of the majority' (NRS, p. 30).

We might remember Bonhoeffer's strong plea for intellectual honesty in the prison letters! His special teacher in systematic theology and the sponsor of his promotion and license to lecture was Reinhold Seeberg, the mediating spirit between idealism, orthodoxy, and modernism. Under him Bonhoeffer became a Hegelian specialist, and many of the terms in his thesis, *Sanctorum Communio*, came out of the workshop of Hegel and Seeberg. These were the formative influences of Bonhoeffer's contemporaries: Troeltsch's interest in the sociological realities of Christianity, Holl's reawakening of the genuine Luther, Harnack's intellectual incorruptibility, and Seeberg's philosophical openness.

But all this was the foil, rather than the real substance of Bonhoeffer's own foundations. In spite of the conservative Berlin faculty, he soon linked himself with the great upheaval against the Schleiermacher-Ritschl-Troeltsch tradition. Although he had not yet met any of the leading dialectical theologians personally, and although he met Barth only after returning from the United States in 1931, his first two books were shaped by the early dialectical theology. He accepted the new direction, although he used his own Berlin terminology. What he gave was in fact very much his own.

The thesis *Sanctorum Communio* he wrote when he was twenty-one (published 1930; republished 1954; English translation, *Sanctorum Communio*, 1963). There was not much response at the time, but in 1955 Barth was to write:

'If there is any justification for Reinhold Seeberg, here it is: out of his school came this man and this dissertation which gains our deepest respect in the breadth and depth of its vision: not only for its relation to the time when it was written but also because even now it can instruct, stimulate, illuminate and edify, far more than many more famous works about the problem of the church which have come out since. . . . I admit that I myself have difficulty in keeping up the standard which Bonhoeffer set in those days, and in not saying less from my own perspective and in my own language, or speaking more weakly than this young man did at that time' (KD, IV, 2, p. 725, cf. CD, IV, 2, p. 641).

After a year as a curate for Germans in Barcelona, Bonhoeffer wrote his thesis, *Act and Being* (published 1931; republished 1956; English translation, 1962), in order to qualify as a university teacher. In it he formulated his own critical questions to the Barthians. But he dropped these criticisms completely when, as Sloane Fellow at Union Theological Seminary in 1930–1, he presented Barth's case to John Baillie's seminar: 'I confess that I do not see any other possible way for you to get into real contact with Barth's thinking than by forgetting, at least for this one hour, everything you have learned before' (NRS, p. 362).

Back in Berlin he accepted four jobs. First, he gave full courses of lectures in systematic theology. Secondly, he

29

ministered as student chaplain at the Technical University at
Berlin-Charlottenburg and preached regularly. Thirdly, he
took over a confirmation class in the slum area and subsequently founded a settlement house (*Jugendstube*). Fourthly,
he became one of the three secretaries of the Youth Commission of the World Alliance for International Friendship
through the Churches and of the Universal Christian Council
for Life and Work. He ran international and local conferences. In those days ecumenical enterprises were extremely
unpopular, especially in Germany where, even before the
Nazis, ecumenism was ostracized as 'internationalism', an
invective not only used by rising nationalists but also supported by a fanciful and snobbish Lutheranism. (Remember
the famous, notorious statement by Althaus and Hirsch in 1932
against all ecumenical activities just as the big World Alliance
meeting in Hamburg started, which showed a characteristic
mixture of the nationalistic and Lutheran elements: 'They dis-
own the German fate and perplex consciences at home and
abroad.') Bonhoeffer mastered these jobs without ever giving
the impression of being an overworked and nervous man.
He combined an extraordinary capacity for concentration
and relaxing – many evenings, even at that time, were given
over to music and games, and these he seldom missed.

Literary access to this period of Bonhoeffer's life is much
more difficult than to the next two. Only one of his lectures,
Creation and Fall, is preserved in the original (winter, 1932–3;
published 1933; several reprints since 1955; English translation, 1959). Another on *Christology* (summer, 1933) can now
be read in the form of compiled student notes (GS, III, p. 166;
English translation, *Christology*, 1966). But anyone who reads
German may get a vivid impression of his literary activity
from his correspondence, papers, and sermons of that period,
collected in the *Gesammelte Schriften*.[1] There are even several

---

[1] Now appearing in generous selection in English: vol. 1, *No Rusty
Swords*, 1965; vol. II, *The Way to Freedom* 1966, both published London,
Collins and New York, Harper and Row.

English pieces: his papers at Union Theological Seminary, struggling with Professors Lyman and Reinhold Niebuhr, and some of his ecumenical contributions.

Before moving into the search for the concrete in the abstract, let me give one more biographical observation of the Barth–Bonhoeffer relation, which will crop up again and again. There is one interesting point where they differ. Karl Barth began as a Swiss pastor, involved in the social struggle of his congregation, moving later into the academic world. Bonhoeffer, born into highly bourgeois academic surroundings, started as the obvious future professor, living in the distinguished company of scholars; later he strove after the practical involvement of the ministry, to the slight disappointment of his father and to the bitter regret of his colleagues. Without discounting Barth's most vivid and helpful involvement during the early days of Nazism – there would have been no Barmen Synod and Declaration without Barth – one still might come to the general conclusion that he went from practical involvement into the mere battle of minds and became the great critical spectator of events. But with Bonhoeffer, in his so much shorter life, it is definitely the reverse, not the way from the pulpit to the lecture-room but from the lecture-room to the pulpit. Barth, though highly systematic, started with sermon and biblical exegesis and moved on, though remaining highly exegetical, into dogmatics. Bonhoeffer started as a wholly dogmatic theologian and moved into a period of nearly exclusively exegetical interests. (This interest, it should be mentioned, was not the interest of the historian who wants to clarify objectively the old sources as such, but the personal commitment of the exegetical preacher who, in accepting the claim of the authority of Scripture, bears witness to the biblical truth for contemporary minds.) This means that a comprehensive study of the relationship of the two men would show that the story of the meeting of their minds and interests was not a very lucky one. Look at the most exciting correspondence

31

between them (GS, II, pp. 39*ff*., 126*ff*., 283*ff*.; NRS, pp. 204*ff*., 230*ff*.). Usually one was busy with a topic which the other had just left behind or had not yet arrived at. Bonhoeffer, being much younger, did not get his answers from Barth when he asked for them, and did not get the praise he might have liked in time. But there is no doubt that as far as this independent and creative mind opened itself to contemporary influence, Bonhoeffer sided with none more readily than with Karl Barth.

Summing up the biographical influences: Bonhoeffer was first challenged by the careful agnosticism of his father and his brothers; he was then affected by the uncommitted mild teaching of the great old men of the Berlin faculty; but he found his first liberating independence in encountering the theology of revelation of the twenties.

The Concrete Nature

In facing the first of the two points I want to make regarding Bonhoeffer's quest for the concrete nature of the message, I will put up a danger signal. It concerns the term 'concrete' itself. We usually think of concreteness in terms of the application after the explanation of the text. But this separation into two additional activities in order to grasp the revelation is precisely what Bonhoeffer was fighting. To be fair to Bonhoeffer, it must be clear that we are dealing not with a pastoral category but with a dogmatic one. 'Concrete nature' describes not an expedient tool but a basic fact. We would completely miss Bonhoeffer's point if we said 'the quest for *making* the message concrete'. No, we are dealing with the concrete nature of the message. When he is most certainly and passionately longing and looking for the concrete nature of the message, he turns his eyes not to the messengers and to their poor or rich gifts, their worth-while education and equipment – that he will do later – but keeps them entirely on the revelation in Christ, in order to discover and describe its concreteness. Much later he calls it 'this-worldliness'. Concreteness is to be understood not as an addition or second activity but as a genuine attribute of revelation itself. Otherwise, we would split the revelation into two parts; first, a more or less hidden treasure-box – fifteen years later Bonhoeffer might call it the religious chemist's shop – and, second, the art of the religious magicians in making the treasure shiny and palatable to the audience. For Bonhoeffer, there are not two parts. There is no treasure at all, except the one which, at the moment of being discovered, also presents its own application. Therefore the danger signal: Do not think now in terms of modernization of the message. Do not think of an attempt to save Christianity by a new dressing-up in appearance and vocabulary, by a better translation, by skilful study of the speech and sociology of audiences. Keeping this in mind will deepen our understanding later on of Bonhoeffer's outlook on the mysterious 'non-religious interpretation of biblical terms' in the prison letters, which we will then discover to be based on a deeper and more comprehensive motive than demythologizing. I repeat: we are dealing not with a mere pastoral category of expediency but with the dogmatic unfolding of revelation itself.

My first thesis therefore reads: *Concreteness is the attribute of revelation itself.*

The theme and argument of *Sanctorum Communio* forcibly illustrate the quest for this concreteness. The subtitle is 'A systematic Inquiry into the Sociology of the Church'. It was a unique and unparalleled enterprise, in those days, to take into account both aspects, the *Offenbarungstheologische* (revelational) one and the sociological one. It found its concise expression in the key phrase of the book: *Christus als Gemeinde existierend* ('Christ existing as a community'). When the book appeared, a friend pitied Bonhoeffer: 'Not many will really grasp and accept your concern: not the Barthians because of your sociology – and not the sociologists because of your

Barth'. Troeltsch had unmasked the church by putting all his searchlights on its historico-sociological shapes and conditions – the non-theological factors. But Troeltsch soon became taboo with the theologians of revelation for his purely anthropological disposition. Bonhoeffer grasps the nettle firmly. He uses sociology for interpreting the shapes of this pretentious and mysterious body, the church. He brings together phenomenology and theology of revelation. But Bonhoeffer takes his stand within the church and rejects the possibility of grasping her sociological facts from outside. Thus he tries to overcome historico-sociological relativism. Our point here is that for Bonhoeffer revelation means nothing beyond, but an entity in, this historically and sociologically shaped world. Becoming and being a part of it belong to it essentially. This claim is the theme of his first work.

This leads a great step further. Bonhoeffer says you must, and you actually can, think revelation only in social relations. All the great old dogmatic terms and *loci* – grace, justification, etc. – have a genuinely social sphere. They *are* social facts. Revelation exists in the fellowship of persons: 'Christ existing as the community of men.' Here Bonhoeffer brings in what he had learned from the contemporary philosophers of personalism, of the 'I-Thou' relation. The 'Thou' is claim, is limitation, is incomprehensible, is transcendence. Each human 'Thou' is the image of God's 'Thou' under which we experience God (sc, pp. 35–7). It is here that he coins 'ethical' or 'social' transcendance over against philosophical transcendence. Fifteen years later this notion appeared to some to be utterly new in the prison letters. Revelation, even in Bonhoeffer's first writing, is opposed to any philosophical idea of transcendence or metaphysics called God. In Christ the human 'Thou' is where God meets us. In this concept of revelation are dormant all the explosives which will catch fire again and again in Bonhoeffer's life.

Incarnation is thus at the heart of Bonhoeffer's theology. There cannot be any speculation about a God before or outside this concreteness. The incarnate God is the only one we know. We cannot even think of concreteness as an addition God made later to his being. All we know, and this is breathtaking, is that incarnate concreteness is *the* attribute as far as we can think.

Here it becomes obvious how much Bonhoeffer develops his Lutheran heritage, as he presents his case in criticizing Barth's neo-Kantian transcendentalism – God, the *ganz Andere*, the negation of all we know and do. Bonhoeffer fully accepted and recognized the great contribution of Barth in his uncompromising emphasis on the contingency of revelation, so that it might never become an object for our handling, in his interest in the *unverdingliche* majesty of God, which is never 'at our disposal'. But this interest Bonhoeffer sees as safeguarded not in the beyond but in the Christ 'existing as the community of men'. There, in persons, the claim of God remains outside and does not come into our possession, its limits condemn and edify us, but it meets us continually *extra nos, pro nobis*. There Christ is and exists for others. The striking formula – 'Christ being the man for others' (cf. also LPP, p. 165) – is here already. Of course, in the prison letters the realm for this Christ is everybody, and here it is thought of as the realm of the church. If Bonhoeffer says here, 'Christ existing as the church', then he says fifteen years later, much more consciously, 'Christ, the man existing for others'. Bonhoeffer holds that Barth cannot secure the continuity and the concern for existence by his emphasis on contingency. Barth describes his revelation all the time with negations, and the revelation is atomized in pure acts. The church, in the early Barth, becomes merely the hint of something absolutely different. There is no God, Bonhoeffer emphasizes, other than the incarnate One known to us and meeting and claiming us in the 'Christ existing as the community of men', the church. This, he thinks, secures both the contingency and the continuity or concern for existence.

This criticism arising out of Bonhoeffer's Lutheranism

comes out best in a very fine and important quotation from
Act and Being, the book which in its very theme puts a
question mark over the actualism of the dialectical theology
of the time. Bonhoeffer accuses Barth of formalism in his
grand attempt to secure God's freedom. Here again we have
the quest for concreteness. It reads:

'In revelation it is a question less of God's freedom on the
far side from us; i.e. his eternal isolation and aseity, than of
his forth-proceeding, his *given* Word, his bond . . . God is not
free of man, but *for* man. Christ is the Word of his freedom.
God *is there*, which is to say: not in eternal non-objectivity,
but (looking ahead for the moment) "haveable", graspable
in his Word within the church. Here a substantial comes to
supplant the formal understanding of God's freedom' (AB,
pp. 90–1).

Bonhoeffer completely agrees when Barth opposes Schleiermacher in unmasking religiosity coming from below and
differentiating faith from it as coming from above. But, by
staking everything on the *Unverfügbarkeit* (eternal 'non-
objectivity'), Bonhoeffer cannot see how Barth can solve the
problem of present faith and obedience which Barth only
hints at. Bonhoeffer assumes that this concept of having the
new ego only as non-ego puts a dangerous element of reflection into faith, which is fatal. The believing ego must not
reflect on its non-ego, Barth says. That kills faith. Faith must
not have any intention directed to itself, it must be directed
totally to Christ; that means it must be saved from deadly
reflection. Reflection is loneliness and allows abstraction.
Faith is sociality and experience of the concreteness of the
incarnate One.

In arguing against Barth's attempt to save God's free
majesty by using neo-Kantian transcendentalism, Bonhoeffer
suspects here the old Extra-Calvinisticum which does not
allow the glory of God to enter entirely into this world. *Finitum
incapax infiniti*, the Calvinists say. Bonhoeffer vigorously
protests with Luther against this all his life. *Finitum capax*

infiniti – God's glory is total freedom not from, but for, man. God's free majesty we do know in the assuming and accepting of man in Christ, known today in the church. Bonhoeffer knows very well that the church is not the incarnation or the continuation of it, but it is the body of the incarnate One. Whether there might be some different majesty of God we do not know, and we should even refrain from interesting ourselves in it in order to worship the real and concrete majesty of God. Bonhoeffer can even say: '*Einen Gott, den es gibt, gibt es nicht*' ('A God who "is", isn't'!) (cf. AB, p. 126). The God we know has bound himself socially in vicarious acting. The ontological idea of God and the transcendental idea are replaced and overcome by the sociological idea and this term 'God' is thought of as referring to the historical faithfulness of God. One may generalize: while Barth, in order to save God's majesty, started by pushing God away, Bonhoeffer starts by drawing him in – in order to save the same majesty of God.

The preceding analysis, though still rather abstract, might give us a picture of Bonhoeffer's concept of concreteness as the essential attribute of revelation itself. But I must not finish this first point before admitting that there is a certain vagueness in the title of the lecture. Just now I talked about 'revelation'; but there I said 'message'. In this first section I could have said 'revelation', but I hesitated. One of the reasons, besides another which covers my second point, is that the term 'revelation' might suggest that we are still with Barth. But Bonhoeffer is not Barth even when he refuses to be a critic from outside, preferring to question from inside the camp. Bonhoeffer comes much more quickly to the church and to Christology than Barth did. Barth started with a theology of revelation; Bonhoeffer started with ecclesiology, which from the beginning was attached to Christology. Many years before, Barth made the famous change from his *Christian Dogmatics* to a *Church Dogmatics* (1932); Bonhoeffer proposed in *Sanctorum Communio* to start dogmatics not with a doctrine of God but with a doctrine of the church. But his Christology took many years to achieve systematic shape. He confessed it to be the most difficult lecture he prepared. In that form (1933) it was one great confirmation of what we tried to say earlier: the theology of incarnation and humiliation, the fullness of God to be found in that limited, weak, and humiliated man Jesus, who took the risk of utter human concreteness.

Concrete Message to the World?

Concreteness, being essential to and a genuine attribute of revelation, includes temporality, historicity, involvement, and the realities of the day. The question soon arose: where do you meet this 'Christ existing as the church'? Where is this church speaking the word of authority; where do you hear her voice? If there is not such a word of authority to be heard, is the concept wrong? In the apparent difficulty of verifying this presupposition Bonhoeffer did not waver one moment. The difficulty was just another challenge to confirm the presupposition and get an even deeper understanding of God's humiliation. The result was not only rejoicing in the presence of Christ but grim judgement of the actual church by that presence. You feel a tantalizing restlessness in Bonhoeffer's correspondence of this period, an ardent severity in the sermons. The call for repentance is addressed to the church which does not accept the presence of its Head but prefers the transcendent God far away. Bonhoeffer's criticism is as sharp and uncompromising as possible, but it is not destructively cynical in its nature. The presupposition gives the call the positive power of *metanoia*. He preached on Reformation Day in 1932 in the presence of President von Hindenburg:

The trumpets of these glorious Reformation festivities are the trumpets for a funeral. Reformation-day is a bad day. With the thousands of trumpets today, which sound to testify for a mortally sick Germany,

38

the other trumpet has joined in to sound loud the dying of the church into the world. . . . The church of the Reformation has not yet realized that each time she says 'God' this God is turning against her. Today we loudly sing 'A safe stronghold our God is still . . .' but God speaks 'Nevertheless I have somewhat against thee' (the text of the day, Revelation 2. 4*ff.*). . . . The church of the Reformation does not allow Martin Luther to rest. He must stand the racket for all the evil which today is taking place in the church. . . . One lets him say again with all the pomposity of self-reliance: 'Here I stand, I cannot otherwise!' This is not true, it is utter frivolity and unforgivable pride to hide behind this man: we *can* otherwise (GS, IV, p. 93*f.*).

In June of the same year he asks at the end of a sermon:

Should we be surprised if again days come for our church in which the blood of martyrs will be demanded? If some of us really should have the faith and the honour and the loyalty to shed this blood, then indeed it will not be the innocent and shining blood of the first witnesses. Our blood will be heavily burdened with our deep guilt; the guilt of the unprofitable servants (GS, IV, p. 71).

This was concreteness indeed, but still prophetic.

With the second point we move into the second half of the first period of Bonhoeffer's life. On returning from the United States, he had to preach regularly. This was painful enough to remind him not to speak cheap, non-binding comments on daily life. Equally important, he had to contribute to or to protest against the resolutions of ecumenical meetings which he understood must contribute a word in the name of Christ to the turmoil of those days. (It is, by the way, an interesting story: he first protested regularly against resolutions, accusing them of being just marginal notes on contemporary events. He held to the necessity of prior theological clarifications as to what the gathering stood for and what it could testify in the name of Christ; he often argued that to remain silent, doing without a resolution, and to declare in repentance, 'We do not know what to do, but our eyes are upon thee' (II Chronicles, 20. 12), would be a more fruitful and better pointer to the real helper, better than a resolution not spoken in the name of God. Curiously enough, after 1933 Bonhoeffer changed completely and eagerly desired resolutions

World Come of Age

coming from the *Oekumene* – for much the same reason that he had been against them before: now everybody knew exactly what the church would say in the name of Christ. Unfortunately, some of the same resolution-lovers he opposed now opposed him, saying, 'Don't interfere in other churches' affairs.') The time of the first two books had passed, and with it the time of pure learning and teaching. The atmosphere had changed, and Bonhoeffer's question, too. He writes in a letter: 'I do not like this product [*Act and Being*] any more' (GS, I, p. 26). He states his question in August, 1932: 'It is the problem of concretion (*der Konkretion*) in proclaiming the word (*Verkündigung*) in preaching, which is driving me at present' (GS, I, p. 34).

The thesis for the second point reads: *Only the message which becomes a specific concrete word is the eternal word of authority.*

With the quest for the message, Bonhoeffer's searchlight spots new ground, and, as he examines it, the conceptual tools are overhauled. The term 'reality' (*Wirklichkeit*) which is so decisive much later in his *Ethics* and which played a big role in *Act and Being*, emerges from philosophical paleness into the real world. The 'world' comes in, in its fullness and in its fragility. Before, the church was over-emphasized and the world in its vivid historicity had suffered under-emphasis. As a result, the Lordship of Christ gets a much wider range. The *regnum Christi*, which formerly seemed just the realm of the church, is now explicitly recognized as ruling in its different ways through the church and through the state.

The link between the two entities, *church* and *world*, is the proclamation of the word. It has the twofold form of law and gospel. The concretion of the commandment especially alarms Bonhoeffer. The tool he develops in this respect for the time being is his doctrine of the *Erhaltungsordnungen* ('orders of preservation'). All this is no renunciation of his basic teaching in *Sanctorum Communio* and *Act and Being*. Its terms come back again and again, but they are widened and developed. In Bonhoeffer's own terms of 1941, after the

40

enchantment of the ultimate (*das Letzte*), the notion of the penultimate comes forth for consideration.

With Bonhoeffer we asked: where and when is the church speaking the word of authority? He answers: only when and where it does not lack concreteness. He makes an interesting but short-lived attempt to work out this view. The same intention was renewed in his later ethics. In an ecumenical conference paper in 1932, he says that the concreteness of the gospel is present and safeguarded in the sacraments – but where is the specific sacramental concreteness of God's commandment? He answers: 'What the sacrament is for the preaching of the gospel, the knowledge of concrete reality is for the preaching of the command. Reality (*Wirklichkeit*) is the sacrament of command (GS, I, p. 147; NRS, p. 164 [translation altered]).

Following up this suggestion and working it out were soon overshadowed by the other necessities of the day. It was too difficult a task to combine the claim of acquiring full knowledge of the complex reality of world affairs with the urgent need and commission for Christianity to speak without delay. From every angle he faced that problem and struggled – how long has one to wait before speaking in order to be sure of full knowledge? And it was here that he hoped for the renewal of a Protestant ecumenical council which did not simply make statements but delivered the word with authority in the name of Christ. This word, he hoped, would come out of the best knowledge of the complexity, but it fulfilled its commission with the unavoidable element of hazard. The word he thought of was that of peace.

The difficulty of combining one supposition and purpose did not alter Bonhoeffer's intention: 'The church must be able to say the Word of God, the word of authority, here and now, in the most concrete way possible, from knowledge of the situation. The church may not therefore preach timeless truths, however true, but only commandments which are true today. God is "always" *God* to us "*today*"' (GS, I, p. 145;

41

NRS, p. 162). Otherwise, it is better not to speak at all, and to confess in repentance: 'We do not know what to do, but our eyes are upon thee.' This text meets us again and again in Bonhoeffer's mind in 1931 and 1932.

What interests us now is that we see Bonhoeffer coping with the term 'reality', struggling with its dangers of sheer positivism or even more of idealism. It seems that he would rather fall into positivism than into idealism, in order not to lose contact with the earth. But it is not positivism, because reality is never something in itself. It is only reality under the Lordship of Christ. This Lordship is proclaimed by the church in words. And this Lordship is asserted by Christ's vicarious suffering and reconciling men in the world. And this Lordship is working in the acts of preservation which at the same moment point to the great break-up of this world and to new creation in every possible action. The commission of this Lordship extends to the church, which must know it, and to the state which may or may not know it. The *regnum Christi* is now clearly the creation, preservation, and salvation of all (cf. 'Dein Reich komme', GS, III, p. 270*ff.*).

At this point in 1932 Bonhoeffer developed his doctrine of *Erhaltungsordnungen* ('orders of preservation'). With them he tried to grasp this world, but he opposed the Lutherans, especially Erlanger and Brunner, with their *Schöpfungsordnungen*, which are good in themselves apart from Christ. In spite of tending towards reality, Bonhoeffer wanted in this to remain christological and eschatological. He saw already the misunderstanding which allowed the Nazis to worship the creator of race alongside the Lord of reconciliation. The notion of orders of preservation was meant to avoid such misunderstanding; it involves recognition of God's good activities in history, and a confession of its character of breaking-up. In 1933 the term was adopted by others (Künneth and Schreiner), and Bonhoeffer dropped it for ever. Much later he tried to deal with the same problem with the concept of 'mandates'.

In concluding this section, I repeat that the specific concretion of the message is not a problem of *how* to say what we know anyway but of knowing *what* to say, of knowing *the* message for the day. It is the same in the prison letters, where the main point, too, is not how to present Christ but *who* Christ is for us today. Is that not precisely our own problem, much more than the problem of modern sermon illustration? We will have the means and the authority to speak when we are sure what the word in the name of God *is*. 'We do not know what to do, but our eyes are upon thee!' And the other reaffirmation: we will know only when we let Jesus speak to us.

The next period seems to be the opposite of concretion. But when this turning is really a turning to him and not to an object of religious worship, then it should lead us to a concreteness and widening of fields Bonhoeffer himself might not have expected. Concreteness is still not the aim or the result of the explorer on his tour; it is in Bonhoeffer's sense always the presupposed equipment for the tour, which waits with surprising discoveries. The real concreteness derives from grasping the essential concreteness of Christ.

We have followed Bonhoeffer's development in his youth, and we have seen that it represents an overture to the drama of the next two periods, where it will be enlarged and deepened. The overture has accentuated the themes. We keep it in our ears: ethical transcendence; the man for others. It is still all in the classroom and sounds academic when we say it here: the message is concrete in itself, not 'beyond': it is the incarnate One actualized in the person next to me. The community of Christ is not the meeting-place of those removed from life, but the centre of life; the centre of men 'who persevere together in the midst of the world, in the depths of it, in its trivialities and bondages'. This reads like a quotation from one of the prison letters, but it was said in November 1932 (GS, III, p. 276). The seeds are sown; we are on the road where 'Christianity without religion' will meet us, everything loaded with experience and involvement.

43

World Come of Age

Concentration: The Narrow Pass for Christianity

In describing the second period of Bonhoeffer's life and theology, we could, for neatness, re-phrase the theme: 'The quest for the costly nature of the message'. But then the term 'quest' would better be replaced by 'affirmation' or 'assertion'. Bonhoeffer's quests had not the wistful tone of the half-hearted man who does not really believe he will get what he is asking for. Bonhoeffer's quests were always vehemently on the way towards positive discoveries which he was quick to formulate in destructive criticism as well as in demanding practical steps. On the other hand, such a re-phrasing would show that the concrete nature of the message means costliness in the first place. At least it is this costliness that Bonhoeffer is now going to establish by his living and writing.

The two books he wrote in this period were actually the ones well-known in his lifetime, comprising and fixing all notions associated with his name for nearly twenty years: *The Cost of Discipleship*, (Munich, 1937; E.T. 1959), characteristically the first to be translated into English, and *Life Together* (Munich, 1939; E.T., 1955). And the very same books are now held by some students of Bonhoeffer to mark a detour in his life, an unpleasant pietistic and legalistic narrowing of the pass, producing fundamentalists of a sort. The liberals think so, finding in the late Bonhoeffer a great confirmation for their cause but overlooking the Christology which leads to Bonhoeffer's 'new liberalism'. Behind the Iron Curtain some theologians think so, basing everything on Bonhoeffer's Christology and making him the liberator not only from religion but from a Christian *Weltanschauung* as well. In giving way to a Marxist *Weltanschauung*, they overlook his view of the church. Therefore neither can make much use of this second period.

44

Bonhoeffer's Life and Theology

The planned path of Bonhoeffer's life seems to have been robbed of its own initiative by Nazi history. Besides the well-known dates, some special ones must be remembered as determining the course of Bonhoeffer's way. In April 1933, the 'law for the restitution of the civil service' was instituted, which dismissed Jewish people, including university pro-fessors, from all public offices; this law applied to two of Bonhoeffer's relatives by marriage. In July 1933, church elections were held all over Germany, which, with the inter-ference of Hitler, returned more than seventy per cent of the *Deutsche Christen* (the Nazi followers in the church) into the governing bodies under the notorious National Bishop, L. Müller. This led to the so-called 'Brown Synod' in September, which put the Aryan legislation of the state into effect for the church as well. But it called forth, too, the first small nucleus of organized stubborn opposition (the Pastors' 'Emergency League'). In May and October 1934 the two synods of Barmen and Dahlem solemnly declared the *deutschchristliche* church government to be heretical, and set up an Emergency Church Government (the Brethren Councils of the Confessing Church). At the end of 1935 Reichsbischof Müller was dethroned, a fact which seemed to be a success for the opposition. Hitler's minister for church affairs appointed the *Kirchenausschüsse* ('church committees'), consisting mainly of neutrals but also of some Confessional men. This split and hopelessly weakened the Confessing Church for the future. In 1937 these church committees, under the leadership of the well-known General Superintendent, Zoellner, abandoned the attempt to restore the old order. The ruins of the church were left victims of rigid, purely administrative bodies who in the name of the state ruled by means of money restrictions and with the help of the Gestapo.

Even now the small remaining groups of the organized Confessing Church could not be crushed. The main burden of the struggle was on the shoulders of the so-called 'destroyed churches' in the Church of the Union of Prussia – that means on their Brethren Councils – while most of the Lutheran provinces (Bavaria, Württemberg, Hannover, etc.) were able to keep their old church governments intact and uncorrupted. These Lutheran provinces organized themselves, departing from the resolutions of Barmen and Dahlem, and in 1935 set up the 'Lutheran Council'. This action meant an unhappy and debilitating split in the general opposition, which was skilfully exploited by Hitler's church minister and his appointees. This split is not a forgotten event today between those Lutherans and the Lutherans of the Union in Germany, and it is useful to know this story in order to understand present groupings in German Protestantism. Politically, there is one more important date which greatly affected Bonhoeffer throughout this period. Hitler introduced conscription in March 1935, and Bonhoeffer was faced with the likelihood that he would be actively drawn into the war preparations by being conscripted. Bonhoeffer's personal history must be seen in this larger framework.

In February 1933, whole companies of brown-shirted storm troops were led into church services both to please and to frighten the churches. Some churchmen regarded this as a unique evangelistic opportunity. It was then that Bonhoeffer chose for his first sermon under Hitler the text of the Gideon story: Gideon says, 'O my Lord, wherewith shall I save Israel?' God answers, 'The people that are with thee are too many!' Bonhoeffer finished by saying to his own church: 'Do not listen, do not wish to be strong, powerful, honoured and esteemed, let God be thy strength, thine honour, thy glory. . . . With us Gideon is kneeling before the altar of the one, the one and only God: Gideon who was brought to believe by fear and doubts. There he prays with us: O Lord, crucified, be thou our only Lord!' (GS, IV, p. 117).

Disappointed with the reaction of his superiors after the events of July and September, Bonhoeffer, of his own will,

left the university and the Berlin church and became pastor
of two very small German-speaking independent congregations in London. There he established his lasting and most
important friendship with Bishop G. J. A. Bell. In 1934 in
Fanö he was made a co-opted member of the Ecumenical
Council for Life and Work. As a result he was in 1937 a
member of the German Oxford delegation, which in the end
was forbidden to travel. In April 1935, Bonhoeffer gladly accepted the call back to Germany from the recently established
emergency church government of the Confessing Church of
the Union. He was to lead a newly founded, small seminary
for ordinands in Finkenwalde (Pomerania). In connexion
with the seminary, he founded a community, the *Bruderhaus*
('Brethren House'). The seminary and the community were
forcibly dissolved in October 1937. Bonhoeffer then continued to teach the ordinands in the hidden form of a
Sammelvikariat. The ordinands, spread out in a diocese as
appointed curates, were taught by him several days a week
in a remote vicarage. He himself accepted a curacy as well
(*Hilfsprediger*) in order to be properly registered with the
police, but in fact he did not have a real home up to the
time of the second dissolution in April 1940. In order to get
out of the conscription dilemma, he managed to get an
invitation to the United States from Reinhold Niebuhr. Paul
Lehmann arranged the lecture tour. It was in vain. Bonhoeffer cancelled everything as soon as he arrived, so that he
could return to his own country. The decisive character of
this action for him is reflected in a most moving diary of his
time in the States (GS, I, p. 291*ff.*).

This decision brought to naught an apparently promising
career. It would have been possible for Bonhoeffer to retreat
into purely theological science at the university and survive
there as some professors did. Some developed a theology
which had room for that – if they had not had one like that
before. Although Bonhoeffer was never prepared to compromise with the authorities, he was not altogether free from

painful deliberations to try a new start somewhere else in order to satisfy his intellectual ambitions. The period therefore began and ended with such an attempt. The retreat in 1933 was undertaken because he would no longer serve a church corrupted by the new privileges; but he came back to serve an unprivileged, outcast church. The retreat in 1939 was undertaken because he would not serve a fatherland heading towards war; but he came back to serve a fatherland of the past and of the future. Both times it meant losing his good name and stepping into anonymity, the first time being branded as an instigator, the second time being ostracized as a traitor.

In the thirties the tempting argument against men like Bonhoeffer by the church majority was always that by their stubbornness and rigidity they spoiled the ready occasions for reaching and evangelizing the multitudes. Why, they argued, spoil these opportunities by quarrels between groups of church leaders which nobody really can understand as vitally necessary? Why not try to save the *Volkskirche* (the established national church) by accepting small compromises? Bonhoeffer had no ear for these arguments. As early as July 1933, he wrote: 'Now back into the small conventicles!' Nor did he believe in the evangelistic usefulness of being in the headlines during the first years of the struggle. He wrote in April 1934:

Though I join with all my strength the opposition in the church, I am quite aware of this opposition being just a preliminary transit station for quite a different opposition. The men of this first skirmishing will be partakers of the second battle only in smallest numbers. . . . Fencing, striking, pricking, this might possibly go on in the skirmish – but the main battle which might approach us later, will simply be believing and loyal suffering. Then it might occur that God with his word may turn back to his church. But until that time there must be much believing, much praying, much suffering (GS, I, p. 40).

In the summer of 1933 very few saw the necessity of fighting the battle on the front of the race issue. The good bourgeois Christians were tainted with their own small portion of anti-Semitism – as in other countries, too. Even men like Niemöller hesitated to start the opposition just on this ground. Why protest on behalf of the ridiculously small number of pastors of Jewish origin and jeopardize reasonable privileges of the church? Bonhoeffer jumped to the rostrum, arguing that if you make Aryan birth conditional to the ministry, you are adding to all the other privileges that fatal one which will finally kill its spiritual authority. The Gospel would lose all its concreteness even if the smoothest compromise and the help of the government brought the masses into this privileged church.

It is obvious that these events in German history had decisive and formative effects on Bonhoeffer's views. It would be astonishing if this were not so; yet did not his theological development make him a master of the situation rather than merely a victim of these events?

The Turn to the Narrow Path

There is no question but that there is a turning-point in Bonhoeffer's thought. Perhaps it is even a kind of intellectual tragedy that the path, described in the first lecture, was interrupted just at this point – to be taken up again ten years later, when he had only two more years to live. And Bonhoeffer himself in those two last years recognized limitations in the *Cost of Discipleship*, although he was unwilling to withdraw a single word. Yet this book and what it stands for is not simply the result of 1933. Although it was to serve as one of the strongest answers in Christendom to the challenge of 1933, originally and essentially it answered earlier questions. For, parallel to the widening trend in 1932, the movement towards concentration was already in full swing. We must study this period of 'concentration', so that the contrast with the period of 'liberation' in the prison letters may be clearly disclosed.

By insisting on the social character of the body of Christ,

Bonhoeffer had to test the Reformers' strong rejection of faith as a *habitus*, to find out whether this really could mean that faith must as a result not be concerned for its earthly existence and that 'new creation' excluded any bodily appearance. Bonhoeffer always added to the two classical notions of the church in the Lutheran Confessions – word and sacrament – a third, the fellowship of men. 'The church is not the fellowship of "souls"; the church is not only proclamation of the Gospel, not just pulpit; she is the real body of Christ on earth' (GS, II, p. 327). It is Bonhoeffer's old quest for the concrete nature of the message which sets him on the path of discipleship.

What in the *Cost of Discipleship* comes from the earlier period, and what is new? Where lies the detour? The actual work on the book itself started in 1933–4 with meditations and preaching on the Sermon on the Mount. The Sermon on the Mount finds no mention in *Sanctorum Communio* and *Act and Being*. In a talk as curate in 1928, Bonhoeffer is still the traditional Lutheran who has learned his lesson of how to escape the directness of the Sermon on the Mount; the literal understanding makes it law, and the law is abolished in Christ. In the United States, however, the encounter with the social gospel faced him again with the Sermon on the Mount. The theology underlying the American version of the social gospel did not impress Bonhoeffer, but its actualization left marks on him. The full force of the question of faith and obedience was on him when the period of preaching and ecumenical activity came. In his lectures he dealt with it in terms which come very close to his later terminology. Other foreshadowings are to be found in his theological evaluation of the child at the end of *Act and Being*, in the long treatment of the innocent simplicity of the believer and the bedevilled nature of reflection in *Creation and Fall*. Finally, there exists a Bible study in student notes in 1932 where the nucleus of Bonhoeffer's characteristic terms appears: faith is true only in the concrete following of Jesus. Here in 1932 we trace for the first time the challenging terms of 'cheap and costly grace'.

These observations show that the turn of the theme of the second period is not the result of the tremendous concentration caused by the church struggle. Though the book was published only in autumn 1937, its theme emerges fully much earlier and is rooted in Bonhoeffer's own theological foundations. We cannot therefore move quickly to 'liberation', by-passing the period of concentration as a temporary aberration in Bonhoeffer's thinking. To be sure, our generation wants the results and not the process by which these results are produced. Modern man lives from fruits, not knowing the tree they come from; but still there will be no fruits without the tree. The *Cost of Discipleship* is important because it represents Bonhoeffer's first great authentic unfolding of the christological concept.

But what is new? After stating the genuine continuity, one is free to discover the tremendous impact of historical events. First of all, they certainly promoted the energetic exclusiveness of the theme which made its presentation at the same time both confined and grandiose. Bonhoeffer became much surer of himself, sure that his theme was not just his own any more, but that of his church in a most existential way. Therefore he dropped the further development of his doctrine of Christ's Lordship over the world just after he had launched it. Positive statements about the state (see GS III, p. 279ff.) disappear. The clever notion of the *Erhaltungsordnungen* ('orders of preservation') he never mentions again. He drops it at the same moment as some prominent Lutherans (Künneth) take it up to develop their own concept of the two realms on this basis. He lost in 1933 any interest in discussing with Brunner, Gogarten, and their friends the doctrine of *Schöpfungsordnungen* ('orders of creation'), which gave a good scheme for providing a place in the Christian catechism for a tamed version of the German 'spring doctrine' of a pure race (*Blut und Boden*, national 'blood and soil').

51

To the extent that the cry for a new theology of creation filled the periodicals and Sunday papers, to the same extent Bonhoeffer became contemptuously silent. He would have agreed with Gogarten, Althaus, Elert, and Hirsch that these complex Christian doctrines had not been treated satisfactorily. But the hour for doing so had been missed. To look at them closely now, however seriously, seemed to lead to the smell of incense offered at the Nazi altar. Bonhoeffer could have said in his terms: now is the time to engage not in *Ordnungstheologie* ('theology of the orders') but in *Durchbrechungstheologie* ('theology of breaking through' orders and creation), i.e. eschatology over against creation theology. Walking the easy way in picking out Luther's statements about world, state, and creation seemed now to Bonhoeffer the opposite of clinging to the concreteness of the message. Concreteness was now its 'otherness'. There might come another hour for a theology of creation, but only after the hour for an eschatological one had been endured.

In the abandoning of these interests, the role of the world in his thought changes considerably. And this is what worries the 'detourists' most. The world becomes the threatening jungle which must be passed by. The world has not disappeared, it is not suspended; on the contrary, the world rules. But with Bonhoeffer there can be no *Weltflucht* ('withdrawal from the world'). This would be a gross misinterpretation. Discipleship is all call for fight. Bonhoeffer's ghetto of discipleship is far from being the peaceful corner of the pietist or the beyond of the enthusiast, both of whom are disloyal to the earth. On the contrary it is all attack, for no other reason than to save the creative openness and earthly breadth of the message. Expressed in Bonhoeffer's later terminology: when the penultimate pushed into the front of the queue, when it wanted to be glorified, languishing for worshippers and victims – and it got its legion of honour in the church indeed – in that moment, Bonhoeffer turned to the ultimate for the sake of the penultimate itself.

The turn was not easy or done boldly. Nobody can stay alone near the ultimate for long. Bonhoeffer yearned for help and endorsement by friends, for corrective and critical discussion with colleagues. In reshaping the doctrine of faith and works, or justification and sanctification, he was aware of stepping into *the* great battlefield of theology, full of thorns and traps. His students did not quickly encourage him. It sounded much too unfamiliar when he shook the old holy Lutheran priority of faith over obedience and made them dialectical and exchangeable entities. For Barth it took nearly twenty years to come out in high praise of Bonhoeffer's conception. For the time being, Barth answered anxiously:

Now I hear from you that you are busy with the inexhaustible theme of justification and sanctification, theoretically and practically. . . . You cannot expect it otherwise from me than that I am looking forward to the matter with an open mind, but not indeed without uneasiness . . . I can see already, especially in the midst of the young theologians of the Confessing Church, that there is approaching another wave of this kind [Barth means resignation of the christological and eschatological disposition in favour of some concretion and realizations in a realm belonging to man] in which all the past is revived. It might well be that you are just the one, called and able to be the speaker and leader in this sphere. . . . I will have to look, very carefully, which way the cat is jumping in order to say perhaps – whether it is possible in my opinion to think as you do (14 October 1936: GS, II, p. 288*f.*).

It *was* possible, in Barth's opinion. Ten years after Bonhoeffer's death he wrote:

Far the best that has been written on the subject seems to me the book *The Cost of Discipleship* by D. Bonhoeffer, not in all parts, but so well in some of them in which the matter is grasped so deeply and dealt with so precisely that I would be able simply to insert it here as one long quotation (KD, IV, 2, p. 604; cf. CD, IV, 2, p. 533).

I am afraid we will wait in vain for another word of praise like that about the *Ethics* and *Letters* after another twenty years have passed.

Thus the new phase is one of restriction which is not a matter of methodical expediency alone. Rather, there is a

53

prevailing consistency. In 1927 Bonhoeffer's question concerned the concrete nature of the body of Christ in the church as a sociological unit (*Sanctorum Communio*). In 1929 he transformed the question into the problem of how to combine the earthly continuity of revelation with its free contingency in the church (*Act and Being*). In 1932 he examined the relation of the body of Christ to the world by asking for the concrete proclamation of God's commandment. In 1933 he tried to outline the structure of explicit Christology from an academic deathbed by interpreting faith as the cost of discipleship. This claim of consistency is not a claim of mere logical relationship; rather, we are observing an auspicious synthesis arising out of Bonhoeffer's sensitive perceptiveness as he faced the challenges of his day.

The Book: 'The Cost of Discipleship'

Regarding the book itself, may I make a few points. First, discipleship is for Bonhoeffer the recovery of concrete place and time for the Reformers' misused term 'faith'. The self-limited and self-bound reality of the incarnate, present in faith, means visibility and involvement in history. Discipleship to the incarnate as the form of belief produces different, even opposite, decisions historically and geographically. Believing for Luther meant leaving the monastery; believing for us might mean re-opening the monasteries in places. It might mean also entering politics. As Bonhoeffer said, referring to Kierkegaard: 'If Luther were alive today he would have said the exact opposite of what he said in the sixteenth century' (LPP, p. 31). With this interpretation of faith as discipleship, Bonhoeffer restored its dimension of existence. Bonhoeffer would have understood the recent criticism of H. Schlier, the famous professor of the Confessing Church, who became a convert to Roman Catholicism after the war: 'It is a dangerous abstraction if you see the justification of existence as given in an intellectual principle, such as the principle

54

of belief.' The present heated discussion about the churches' opinion on nuclear rearmament in Germany is an argument about the element of obedience within the faith. 'Only he who believes is obedient and only he who is obedient believes' (CD, p. 54 *ff*.). This key quotation in that forceful first chapter of the book does not mean to dethrone the fullness of Martin Luther's great *sola fide, sola gratia,* but to recover it, giving it back its earthly concreteness.

Secondly, the concept of discipleship as faith in reality is meant not to weaken but to confirm the claim of the social essence of each one of the Christian dogmas. 'He who wants to become a new man as a solitary individual remains the old one . . . it is not the justified and sanctified individual who is the new man, but the church, the body of Christ' (CD, p. 218). Yet the emphasis now lies in the fact that this social involvement is executed only by total involvement of the single individual. Concretion occurs in the realm of the individual. Jesus' call allows no hiding in the multitude. Discipleship does not allow the faith of masses and 'movements'; it is personal engagement. Christ's church is based on single disciples and not on masses. Individual discipleship and individualism exclude each other. Bonhoeffer's latest notion of 'religion' as individualism in the *Letters* is fully in line with this emphasis on the individual.

Thirdly, Bonhoeffer takes pains again to stress the fundamental difference between discipleship and any ideal or ideology. Jesus' call is not to be re-coined into a programme. Doing this is just what 'following' is not. Turning his word into an ideal or programme calls for casuistic materialization. The step into discipleship is the exact opposite. It is a breaking through casuistic and legalistic programmes. Being called, go and follow – that represents the right Christology. Being called, not to follow but to work out a programme to be applied, reveals a wrong Christology. It is to leave Christ outside for occasional use. The call creates the new existence and establishes new relations. Christ, the person, who by his call makes a person, prevents legalism. He creates not just constitutional rules but relations.

To this context belongs the most impressive passage: 'The word is weaker than ideology, so are the witnesses with this word weaker than the propagandists of an ideology . . . yet they are free from that morbid restlessness of the fanatics, they suffer with the world' (CD, p. 166). Christ's word is not a victorious idea, an overriding conviction. It respects the impossible, it has regard for the barriers it meets, it honours the person in the person, especially when this person does not agree; but an idea overrides the person, the term 'impossible' must not exist for a programme. The incarnate word even allows itself to be held in contempt and repudiated. Here again is Bonhoeffer's Lutheran concept of God's freedom which has bound itself to the limitation of a weak and human community of persons. 'The weak Christ, the weak word' – that gives us a foretaste of the later Bonhoeffer. This belongs to his great central teachings in all periods.

Fourthly, this concept of the weak word touches the deepest notion, where Bonhoeffer comes to describe discipleship as sharing in the vicarious suffering of Christ, as fellowship with the crucified. There is an extraordinary richness of experience with Jesus which never approaches the painful self-pitying tone of most of our hymns or the blind exaltation of some mystics. The strong vicarious element safeguards the matter from becoming an end in itself. Disciples are men and women who accept what others want to shake off. On the last page of the book Bonhoeffer says of Christ: 'His life on earth is not finished yet, for he continues to live in the lives of his followers' (CD, p. 274). This is the abundant unfolding of the *Christus praesens* of *Sanctorum Communio*. In a highly concentrated form the same theme appears in the lecture *Temptation*, given in one of the most critical moments of the church struggle. And here is nothing outdated; it remains at the heart of 'Christianity without religion'.

Yet out of the third and fourth points originates the concept of full solidarity with the godless, which some of our brethren try to follow behind the Iron Curtain. Christ does not want to preserve for himself even the refuge of a *Weltanschauung*.

Fifthly, a final observation must be made with respect to a passage concerning the 'first step before you believe' (CD, p. 54*ff.*). Besides the fact that this passage gives a very suggestive hint for counselling – he actually did teach counselling on these lines! – it represents a clear forerunner to his distinction between the ultimate and the penultimate and their relation, conditioning, limiting, qualifying, and enforcing each other. It shows how near to the surface the penultimate was, even when Bonhoeffer turned to the ultimate; and it demands attention. Of course, 'first step' in the realm of the penultimate points here still to its relative unimportance, being just a transit station, not getting the autonomy it gets later! But the basis is there. Bonhoeffer himself testifies to it: 'You cannot and must not speak the last word before you have spoken the next to last . . . In *The Cost of Discipleship* I just hinted at this, but did not carry it any further. I must do so some day' (LPP, p. 50).

We ask again: Did Bonhoeffer betray the Reformation by developing a new doctrine of sanctification? He explicitly opposed such a suggestion. He claims to base what he says upon justification, nothing else. He believes that justification by faith remains the incontestable presupposition and needs no supplement. But it needs re-installation by the preservation of the costliness of the gift. Discipleship is an expression of that preservation, so badly needed to secure justification of the sinner over against the justification of sin. The disciple is precisely he who lives by the renunciation of all his own justice. 'Justification is the new creation of the new man, and sanctification his preservation until the day of Jesus Christ' (CD, p. 250). In addition to scriptural sources Bonhoeffer tries hard to find hints for this view in the Lutheran Confessions. But he found only hints (CD, p. 55). He actually was ploughing new ground or at least ploughing in another climate.

The House of Brethren Life Together

When winning the masses seemed to determine the course of the day, Bonhoeffer concentrated on the very small and reduced circle of interdependent persons. A purely theoretical study of discipleship would have been cheap blasphemy for him.

I must report here the particular attempt to form a kind of monastic order, called the *Bruderhaus* ('Brethren House'). In order to do this I must omit an account of Bonhoeffer's part in the continuing church struggle. This story is important, but at this point it might divert us from following the inner course of his life and thought.

For many years Bonhoeffer had been thinking about the small community, even as he was engaged in the study of the theology of discipleship. Since the first world war there had been pastoral brotherhoods existing alongside official church bodies and conferences. Suddenly these brotherhoods captured the enthusiasm of the young pastors of the Confessing Church when they needed pastoral guidance and regular exchange. They organized themselves under the official leadership of the Brethren Councils in 1934–5. But as yet nobody in German Lutheranism had dared to think of a *vita communis* or of giving up the traditional shape of the ministry and eventually reviving some sort of classical vows. But such a *vita communis* was precisely what was in Bonhoeffer's mind.

Four driving forces or influences contributed to the experiment. First, since about 1932 Bonhoeffer had himself practised daily meditation on a scripture passage. This was not done in order to prepare a sermon or to make a study, say, of the gnostic elements in the Fourth Gospel. Bonhoeffer used to differentiate between the uses of the Bible in the pulpit, in the study, and in private prayer. Sharing in the traditional German zeal for exegetical interpretation which overshadows if it does not extinguish all other uses of scripture (and which makes the Bultmann debate hotter in Germany than in any other country), Bonhoeffer's practical step into another dimension beyond the intellectual wrestling with the Bible could only come out of a theology of the church which learned anew to hear the call of Christ himself through her decision about the canon, the authority of scripture. This meant meditative listening to the voice of the brethren who first listened to and pointed to the sources where Christ was to be heard. Bonhoeffer called his first attempts with the Sermon on the Mount *Exercitien,* spiritual 'exercises' (Loyola) (GS, I, p. 41).

Secondly, the interest in a community had a strong relationship to his response to Gandhi. As a result of his stay in the United States, Bonhoeffer tried hard to go to India. After he succeeded in getting a personal invitation from Gandhi, the call back to lead the seminary meant the final cancellation of the plan. Of course he was eager to study non-violent resistance as a possible pattern for Christian resistance against Hitler, but he mainly wanted to learn from Gandhi's *ashrama.* We find him sometimes calling his idea for the *vita communis* a 'Christian settlement' (*Siedlung*).

Thirdly, the new Anglican monasteries of the nineteenth century in Britain attracted him very much, and he learned there something for his own order of daily life and prayer.

Fourthly, the course of events in Germany helped to further his intentions in so far as there was increased pressure for a change in the education of ministers. For centuries this education had remained nearly exclusively in the hands of the state university faculties. For several decades the church had made attempts to provide her own courses in the *Predigerseminare* before ordination. They never gained their own stature and integrity but turned into repetitions of the university courses on a lower level or into grants for individual research after the pattern of an Oxford fellowship. Bonhoeffer long doubted the fitness of this purely intellectual framework of schooling, unrelated to spiritual education and discipline. These doubts were suddenly confirmed by the dreadful dependence of the professors upon the state, who, in April 1933, were already subjected to the Aryan legislation and were later, by decrees of the Minister for Cultural Affairs, bound not to join the church opposition or write or act for them. (The Ecumenical Movement, by the way – in its traditional esteem for the German scholar and its justified belief that he represented German Protestantism, since he was the first to engage in ecumenical co-operation – made a mistake in continuing to believe in and listen to those who, with some praiseworthy exceptions, became dependent and weak civil servants of Hitler's state.) Bonhoeffer wrote in 1934 to his Swiss friend: 'I am bothered in deciding whether to return to Germany in order to lead a seminary or to go to India or to stay here. I no longer have any faith in the University. . . . The whole of education for the ministry today belongs to the church – monastic-like schools in which pure doctrine, the Sermon on the Mount and the Liturgy are taken seriously. In the University none of these is taken seriously, and it is impossible to do so under present conditions' (GS, I, p. 42). This sounds completely the opposite of what Bonhoeffer later pleaded for, namely, to put theology back into the open air of fierce discussion with philosophy and science. Did he mean to kill everything he said in 1934? Is it a strict either-or? We certainly have not solved the problem today. But open and fierce discussion is not meant to make the church unsure of herself. It is at this point that Bonhoeffer's advocacy of the *Arkandisziplin* ('secret discipline') needs to be understood.

The opportunity for the concrete experiment came with the opening of the ordinands' seminary. It started with six young ordinands at the end of the first term in 1935 living in the building of the seminary. The authorities of the Confessing Church reluctantly gave permission and left the young pastors in Bonhoeffer's care. The outcry everywhere was loud: what sinister re-Catholicization was going on at Finkenwalde! The following reasons were given by Bonhoeffer for the application: (1) preaching with intrepidity comes better out of a brotherhood; (2) the general question of what Christian life is, can be given not in abstract but in a concrete common attempt to live together and reflect in common on the commandments of Christ; (3) there is needed a completely free group of pastors available for the battle outside, who renounce all traditional privileges; (4) lonely pastors need a spiritual refuge, a brotherhood where they can disappear for a while and be refreshed for the ministry. Daily order of prayer, free oral confession of sin, sharing of one's livelihood, a pledge to follow an emergency call by the church at once, were the main rules.

The membership of the small community had a fast turnover because the emergency calls came quickly with the growing rate of imprisonments, especially in 1937. Some of the classical vows are there in nucleus but are deliberately not fixed. 'Not monastic seclusion, but concentration for the life outside, this is the goal,' wrote Bonhoeffer in his application. The enterprise came to a sudden end when the Gestapo dissolved Finkenwalde in the autumn of 1937. The new form of underground teaching did not allow the re-opening of the Brethren House.

The premature abolition of the community resulted in the little book *Life Together* (Munich, 1939; Eng. Tr., 1955), which achieved the biggest distribution of any of Bonhoeffer's books in his lifetime. He probably would never have written the book had not the Gestapo interfered. He did not want to make the experiment public while it was going on, feeling strongly that it was still in its beginning stages. During the years in Finkenwalde he left it to his friends to write the answers when the many questions came in about it. But when all was over, he wanted to fix and preserve the short but condensed experience. For German Lutherans, at least, all was new and opened up new dimensions. The reaction showed that Bonhoeffer had touched a weak point in Protestantism where general helplessness prevailed. Something was regained for the church which had been left to the conventicles and sects. For the first time there was renewed the *vita communis*, not against and not outside the Church of the Reformation (as is still was with Herrenhut) but within the church, and strongly defended on the basis of an understanding of the church.

Visitors, especially from the Oxford Group Movement, which had great success at that time with the neutrals in Germany, came to observe Bonhoeffer's experiment. But he was not in agreement with them at all. Interestingly enough, it was he who worried about their insistence on the 'change'. The man of discipleship, of the first step, of engagement, was repelled by their replacement of the testimony of scripture by the testimony of personal change. He passionately disliked being led into the circle of reflecting about one's own beginnings. This seemed to have been one of the liberating moments in his youth when he found that Christ means the turning-away from deadly reflection about personal beginnings. His view comes out in its universal implications in *Creation and Fall*. He used to remark that the really great men in church history did not look too closely into their own beginnings; they knew too well the lurking abyss. What the *Cost of Discipleship* and *Life Together* certainly are not is a plea for a doctrine of conversion. In the Group movement Bonhoeffer missed the message of the crucified and noted their indifference to the church struggle and Confessions. 'Moved people' (*Bewegte*), he found, always have paralysing effects; 'The Oxford Movement was naïve enough to try to convert Hitler – a ridiculous misunderstanding of what really happens – *we* are to be converted, not Hitler' (GS, I, pp. 42–3).

Life Together is not just piety. Bonhoeffer was alert enough to know the danger of his own very dogmatical basis. Once in 1936 he came across some Zinzendorf writings: 'At the end I was rather depressed. What a mouldy foundation to this piety! . . . And this all in spiritual hymns! This is man! The pious man! I shudder in view of the consequences of the *finitum capax infiniti*. There must be around us the clean and true air of the word. But we cannot and must not escape ourselves. But let us take our eyes away from man!' (GS, II, p. 278). The pietist danger, so near to his own concept, made him sharp and very unfriendly to similar-looking experiments. 'I find,' Bonhoeffer writes to a leader of another brotherhood, 'that in your concept the holy spirit is not a reality alone which is bound to the true and unanimous word of scripture . . . but a principle of formation, of an ideal of Christian life. . . . Behind your explanation lurks an idea of the "Christian" which is derived . . . from our own judgement of human needs *(Befund)*' (GS, II, p. 215).

The fierce opposition which Bonhoeffer first met from his own students against meditation and confession steadily abated, since everything was sanely balanced by hard theological work, by alert response to each turn of the church battle. Nobody acted more quickly and more critically than Bonhoeffer. Soon it became clear what it was all for. The personal Christian engagement had never the signs of remoteness, of mania or mystification. Nobody in Finkenwalde was more eager for games and music than he. His inventive qualities in guessing games equalled that of any American quiz fan. And up to the time of his imprisonment he was unlikely to miss a bridge party.

It is difficult to say what would have happened if the attempt could have been carried on, though this would be important for both the 'detourists' and the liturgists. Anyway the experiment was a proper instrument for the time of great crisis in the privileged established church *(Volkskirche)*. This crisis will certainly come upon us later on a much bigger scale. The legitimate place for these deliberations and experiments is to be found in the late Bonhoeffer in his 'secret discipline', where the Christians who renounce all the privileges they have enjoyed in devotion and study do what is not meant for publicity and posters.

Biographically the self-imposed narrow pass was over. At Christmas 1940, Bonhoeffer was a guest in the Benedictine Monastery of Ettal. Amused, he told that to his surprise the monks at meals read from his *The Cost of Discipleship* and *Life Together*. The utter loneliness of these last two years, the chaotic dissolution of all personal contacts, hit a man with a long-built, deep-rooted framework of individual spiritual discipline in which he was free and open for his agnostic comrades.

As we said before, it would have been attractive to follow up the consequences of this theology of concentration in the ecumenical history of the thirties. The Confessing Church, through its chief spokesman, Bonhoeffer, presented the *Oekumene* with a most delicate demand to accept the condemnation of the heretics, exactly as the Archbishop of Cape Town does today. Bonhoeffer suffered because the majority of the ecumenical bodies maintained better-functioning contacts with the servants of the neutrals or even the German Christians; but he accepted the situation undisturbed, even though this made his own pass narrower.

This second period made Bonhoeffer known to his contemporaries – favourably to the Confessing people, very unfavourably to the neutral majority. His teaching became accepted by the Friends, and Bonhoeffer's 'otherness' from the world was soon preached in many pulpits. Nobody had a presentiment of the turn which led Bonhoeffer in purposeful secrecy to step over each border-line believed to be sacred with him. It came as a tremendous surprise to all when much later the next Bonhoeffer appeared in the open. They had a hard time repainting their picture; some never did. Is that a proof in favour of the second or of the third period?

What happened was that the second period had slowly become acceptable; in the minds of his friends the bellicose ghetto of Bonhoeffer had turned into a self-contained one. And as soon as the Christian life becomes self-contained, even its enemies will not bother about it. Now, the opposite seems to be true. The third period – of Bonhoeffer's solidarity with the world – is favoured in many quarters, and the second is not known or over-looked as a detour. Is it not useful to keep moving in order to experience the costly fullness of grace instead of the palatable cheap one? The self-contained 'otherness' of the second period is cheap, the self-contained 'solidarity with the godless' of the third period is shallow.

Solidarity will give the otherness strength, and otherness will give the solidarity truth. But this is not a dialectical game of the intellect; it is the intelligent and sacrificial way to follow the next step of the concretely present Christ, and not to stay behind.

THE THIRD PERIOD

Liberation: Christianity without Religion

The *Encyclopaedia Britannica* recently asked for the preparation of a 250-word article about Bonhoeffer. In struggling to formulate the main topic under which I thought Bonhoeffer could be included in this expensive treasure-box for eternity, I said: 'Dietrich Bonhoeffer coined the much debated term "non-religious interpretation of biblical concepts in a world coming of age", in battling against the relegation of Christian belief to a separate religious province, either metaphysical or psychological. . . . His fragmentary "non-religious inter-pretation" programme is under discussion together with Bultmann's demythologization.' The English editor rejected this completely because he thought it was just mystified non-sense; he politely dressed his thoughts by saying, 'You cannot know how impossible this sounds in English.' He offered instead: 'Bonhoeffer insists that the Christian's chief concern must be with his behaviour in this world.' Everybody behaves in this world, doesn't he? I will tell you at the end what I managed to get into the article, with the help of Gregor Smith, who, as you may know, is responsible for all the attention now paid to Bonhoeffer in the English-speaking world.

I think you would approve of Gregor Smith's efforts to introduce Bonhoeffer, not because of Bonhoeffer's tragic and uplifting fate as a modern martyr but because of this very thesis, 'Christianity without religion in an adult world', whatever the meaning and consequence may be. This is the gunpowder which exploded with a noise heard in many quarters. Not everything seemed new to Bonhoeffer himself – indeed, the theological background was fully developed before, though not the tremendous positive evaluation of secularization with its repercussions on theology – but he strongly felt he had stepped out into virgin land. He fell after a few miles of travelling. He did not leave behind an official report of the exploration with a neat map of the territory. The land is still dangerous. One might prefer to stay in the familiarly mapped-out homeland of inherited Christianity of good 'behaviour in this world'. If not, one would at least like to have a deposit of ready-made answers to the questions raised, a settled knowledge applicable for use in the pulpit, maybe a dictionary for the 'non-religious interpretation'. But there is not such a dictionary. I am afraid that any exploration in Bonhoeffer's footsteps will not be successfully achieved with books alone. Knowledge will come only through taking risks and through involvement, as with children who repeat the phrases of the grown-ups and only after years of acting with these terms grasp the implications and the context. With Bonhoeffer, actions and life comment on his sayings, and the words on his actions, in an extraordinary degree. Maybe his concept will never become cheaper.

Biographica

The second escape, as we already know, did not work. While travelling to the United States, he wrote on 9 June 1939:

66

'Big programmes [ideas] lead us only where we already are. We should let ourselves be found where he is! . . . Whether you work there [i.e. Germany] or I in the U.S.A., we are both just where he is. He takes us with him. Or – have I yet escaped from where he is? Where he is at least for me?' A few weeks later, on 20 June, came the painful decision to return. He wrote that night in the Prophets' Chamber at Union Theological College, 'Quite obviously one was disappointed, even cross. For me it means more than I can realize at present.' One of the things he did not realize then was how far he would drop out of the immediate church work and how painfully he would have to separate his activities from the church which he knew to be incapable of digesting these embarrassing ambiguities.

When Bonhoeffer returned in July 1939, his brother-in-law, Hans von Dohnanyi, who was always very close to him, entered the inner circle of the German political resistance by becoming assistant to Admiral Canaris and his deputy, General Oster, head of the Military Intelligence Service. Oster and Dohnanyi up to 1943 were the main conspirators. For the time being Bonhoeffer returned to his teaching of ordinands. When the work was dissolved a second time in March 1940, Bonhoeffer became visiting preacher in several provinces in northern Germany, but finally, in the summer of 1940, he was prohibited from preaching any more. Then, partly in order to save him from conscription, partly in order to use his knowledge for the resistance under the disguise of serving the Canaris office, Oster and Dohnanyi claimed him as a V-man (*Verwendungsmann*), i.e. a civilian employed by the Military Intelligence Service. Already officially banned in 1938 from doing church work in Berlin, Bonhoeffer was forced in 1940 to report regularly to the police. The Canaris people, however, still enjoyed certain independent rights and therefore placed Bonhoeffer far away under their Munich department; but they ordered him again and again to come up for them to their Berlin headquarters. That is why

Bonhoeffer lived for a while in southern Germany in the Benedictine Monastery of Ettal and was so often to be found back in Berlin with his parents.

Bonhoeffer was now an official part of Hitler's war machine; he entered 'the great masquerade of evil' (LPP, p. 135), as all the resisters had to do to get the weapons for their plans. This would have had curious results if Bonhoeffer had lived through to the end, since the Canaris office with all its employees, after the failure of the 20 July plot, became an integrated part of the Himmler SS organization. Bonhoeffer – as happened to one of our friends, a man of the Confessing Church – would have been imprisoned for years by the Americans in one of the special camps provided for the re-education of SS men.

In 1941 Bonhoeffer made his first journey in his new capacity as V-man and saw Barth and Visser't Hooft in Switzerland. In 1942 he had that surprise meeting with Bishop Bell in Sweden to give him the information about the plotters' plan, to be conveyed to his government in the hope of obtaining a cessation of hostilities.

In the autumn of 1942 – it was just the time of his engagement to the daughter of a noble family – one of his Munich superiors was imprisoned and became talkative to the Gestapo. Bonhoeffer and his friends therefore had to prepare for their own imprisonment, which took place on 5 April 1943. This interval was a breathtaking race, because two attempts on Hitler's life had been staged and had failed in March 1943. The military court, under Gestapo supervision, could not get any substantial evidence besides suspicions – everything was covered up well – until the discoveries made after the failure of 20 July 1944. This explains the optimistic note in some of his prison letters. At this stage Bonhoeffer was to be tried only for being unjustifiably reserved as a civilian. It was a terrible but successful fight to lie intelligently and to hide the truth boldly in those hearings. When everything was discovered in late September 1944, Hitler had just changed his orders to kill everybody involved at once, in order to get more information about the extent of the plot. Because of this order Bonhoeffer nearly survived. But in a special order of 5 April 1945, his name was put on the death list. The excellent Gestapo apparatus worked well to the last minute. The SS staged a high-treason trial during the night of 9 April, and hanged Bonhoeffer, together with Canaris, Oster, and others, next morning, without the necessary endorsement of the High Command. There is no grave; the ashes were scattered in the wind. There was no religious comfort and ceremony around him. The camp, the stoves, uniforms in a dreary quarry, that was the last setting. No shroud, no hymn, no church.

Bonhoeffer had developed from passive to active resistance. The factual change can be dated in 1940. But it was not a sudden change. First, Bonhoeffer resisted, wrote, and spoke as a churchman against anti-Semitism, disappointed with his own society's reaction, very much hoping for his church to speak out. But the voice of the church slowly became hoarse. Secondly, Bonhoeffer considered giving his testimony as an individual pacifist in the realm of conscientious objection. Here, though fighting for an understanding in his own church he realistically never dared to hope for the cover of that tradition-bound church. Finally, he sacrificed himself quite differently, as a German, as a member of the bourgeoisie, as a Christian, in order to pay the overdue price for the guilt of his class and nation, without asking for ecclesiastical protection any more.

None of the writing of his decisive third period is properly finished. *Ethics*, which he felt to be the task of his life, is as we have it now an absolute fragment, a posthumous compilation. But the uproar was created by a book which was never planned as a manuscript by him, made up mainly of smuggled letters from the more reasonable part of his detention, the result of the impression Bonhoeffer made on his guards by the mixture of his enchanting aristocracy and skilful

bribery (until recently the regular companion of tyranny)!
The illegal part of the letters starts when the first period of
hearings was over and Bonhoeffer was no longer afraid of
disclosing our relationship. That means that the small
sources of this period of vision are not even purposefully
planned epistles. These few letters are the only available
sources for the last stage. Do not hope for later ones; I burned
them when I was myself caught. But has it not happened
before that great letters influenced history just because they
were real letters and not papers?

Ethics

Before giving an account of the doctrinal outcome, I quote
two passages which signify the switch from ardent devotion to
liberating this-worldliness. The one is more personal, the
other more theological. The first quotation, the theological
one, is from *Ethics*: 'The more exclusively we acknowledge
and confess Christ as our Lord, the more fully the wide range
of his dominion will be disclosed to us' (E, p. 58).

The exclusiveness of Christ – that is the claim of *The Cost
of Discipleship*. The expansiveness of Christ's totality – that is
the new departure. Exclusiveness leading to the self-contained ghetto – that was the danger of the first, but legitimately it leads into the comprehending encounter with
reality, with history, and gives full right to secularization.

The second quotation is from June 1942, when Bonhoeffer
was just returning from Stockholm and was travelling south
in order to go soon to the Vatican, where an agreed coded
answer from London might arrive:

Again and again I am driven to think about my activities which are now
concerned so much with the secular field. I am surprised that I live
and can live without the Bible for days. I would say: it is not obedience
but auto-suggestion if I should force myself to the daily meditation. I
know, such auto-suggestion would be of great help – and indeed it is.
But I am afraid that I would in this way falsify a real experience and
that at last I would not get the real help. If I open the Bible again

after such a period, it is new and rewarding as ever and I eagerly want to preach once again. I know very well that I must only open my own books in order to hear all that there is to be said against it. I do not want to justify myself, and I observe that I have gone through much richer spiritual periods. But I feel the resistance growing in me against all religiosity [*das 'Religiöse'*], sometimes reaching the level of an instinctive horror – surely, this is not good either. Yet I am not a religious nature [*eine religiöse Natur*] at all. But all the time I am forced to think of God, or Christ, of genuineness [*Echtheit*], life, freedom, charity – that matters for me. What causes me uneasiness is just the religious clothing. Do you understand? This is no new concept at all, no new insights, but because I believe an idea will come to burst upon me I let things run and do not offer resistance. In this sense I understand my present activity in the secular sector [GS, II, p. 420].

Let us remember: Bonhoeffer says explicitly, There is nothing new invented; the basic concepts were laid out before, yet something is around the corner. There are more dimensions to the foundations which will stand the test than were first thought. What is the new element?

It is fascinating to escort Bonhoeffer on his fragmentary way in his four new and different attempts to approach ethics from 1940 to 1943. He begins rather near *The Cost of Discipleship* and breaks off with the full this-worldliness of the letters on the fourth attempt. The plan to write an ethics was in itself a singular enterprise at that time, since Barth's *Dogmatics* had crushed all efforts in that direction on the Continent for the time being.

The first approach, 'The Love of God and the Decay of the World', speaks the language of *The Cost of Discipleship*, but it stresses in a new emphasis the oneness of the world and of God in Christ. Actually the quotation about the exclusiveness and the totality of Christ comes from this section and shows the direction.

The second approach strides vigorously forward, stepping right into the present and the historical scene of the western world. The catchphrase is 'ethics as formation' or 'conformation'. The christological basis is as strong as ever. Christ as Lord and Redeemer of the world is centre, reason and aim of

71

all human reality, and claims, therefore, all fields of human existence. By Christ's conforming to this world and its preliminaries (*Vorläufigkeiten*), he draws this world into conformation to himself. The time-bound and place-bound Lordship has clear connexions with the shy attempts of 1932. It would be a misinterpretation of Bonhoeffer's intention to think of clericalization of the world, though this danger might be nearest here. The church is a piece of redeemed world, it is the break-through of the figure of Christ into this world. The relation between church and world comes much more positively into the foreground than ever before. In *The Cost of Discipleship* the world was the place just for the first step in believing; now the Lordship of Christ establishes explicit historical responsibilities. The Enlightenment of the eighteenth century has already a positive value. The church, 'while still preserving the essential distinction between herself and the forces [of order] . . . unreservedly allies herself with them' (E, p. 109). In these September days of 1940 the relation between church and world assumes the form of a blessed discovery.

The third approach, written only a few weeks later (in Ettal!) starts with the concept of 'The last things and the things before the last', which turns out to be the most fruitful of Bonhoeffer's creative formulas. It seems unconsciously to have been present in Bonhoeffer's theology for a long time. The last word, as justification by faith embraces beginning and end, both limits and puts into force the penultimate; it is in time and quality the first and the last. The penultimate maintains, prepares the way for, and is before the last, but having its full, free, established autonomous right. The structure of the ultimate and penultimate represents the christological order. In Christ the last 'neither renders the human reality independent nor destroys it', the penultimate 'has become the outer covering of the ultimate' (E, p. 90). In the cross the ultimate became the judgement of and at the same moment the grace of the penultimate. Life as the penultimate is sharing or 'is participation in the encounter of Christ with the world' (E, p. 91). Related to Christ's Lordship, life comes to its relative, but full, autonomy.

Now the way is free for the full refreshing swing into a theology of the 'natural', which had not been done before on a christological basis and was left to the Roman Catholics. The balance of the 'natural' against the 'unnatural', its beauty and vicissitudes, the liberation of reason – that is what strikes most readers in the letters. The martyr Bonhoeffer experienced in the midst of the tyranny of the unnatural the full liberation of the 'natural' and of 'reason' by his very Christology. The artificiality suddenly has gone; no tension but only freedom and joy prevail. 'Life is not only a means to an end but is also an end in itself' (E, p. 150). In its own creativity it has its rights and duties, and Bonhoeffer sets out to describe first the rights – in direct opposition to the German Kantian feeling that there are first of all duties to be faced. No, 'God gives, before he demands' (E, p. 151). The first Intelligence Service journey to Switzerland in 1941 put an end to this chapter, but the concept of ultimate and penultimate remained.

It is the fourth and last new approach of the *Ethics* which really reaches the threshold of the prison letters. We had the 'conformation' of Christ with the world and of the world with Christ; we had the 'natural'; now we have 'the setting-free of life for genuine worldliness' (E, p. 263). The basis for the 'setting-free' is Bonhoeffer's particular interest and preference for the term 'reality'. It had always a rather dominant place, but here it gets its fullest christological treatment. 'All factual reality derives its ultimate foundation and its ultimate annulment, its justification and its ultimate contradiction, its ultimate affirmation and its ultimate negation from the real man whose name is Jesus Christ' (E, p. 198). It is the time in which Bonhoeffer read with new fascination *Don Quixote*, the story of the honourable knight who became isolated from reality fighting for a principle. In

1932 reality was the dimension to preach to. In 1935 reality was the transit station. Reality is now full partner for man shaping his deeds (E, p. 197). Bonhoeffer no longer wants to have the world or the reality of the world without the reality of God (E, p. 62). Reality always is that which is entered into and accepted by Christ. By Christ's entering there is an ontological coherence of God's reality with the reality of the world. There are not two realities, but the one already entered by Christ and in the process of being judged and renewed. Christ is not the absolutized real and outside norm. The worldly real is not the material on which to force a programme or idea – that would be clericalization again. The worldly real in itself is drawn into the action as sharing in the forming of it. Incarnation does not smash the worldly real and does not make the world Christian – that again would be the false idealistic tyranny of the norm outside, dressed in Christian clothing. Bonhoeffer transcends the idealistic devaluation of the real and avoids the positivistic over-valuation. Being in Christ is participating in the world. There is no abstract 'good' standing over against evil. Good is a movement, the movement of constantly entering into and accepting man and world. Ethics consists in learning 'to share in life' (E, p. 237), in its centre and not on its border-line. Christ guides you not beyond but into this daily human reality. Christianity is not an end in itself, but it enables man to live as man before God, not to be a superman but to live for others (E, p. 262). Here we see again the simple formula from *Act and Being*, foreshadowing its treatment in the *Letters*. Christ is not erecting foreign rules but 'setting creation free for the fulfilment of the law which is its own' (E, p. 264). 'The cross of atonement is the setting free for life before God in the midst of the *godless* world' (E, p. 263). The oneness of the reality established by Christ's entering is not a synthesis and not a diastasis (the one the Roman Catholic, the other the enthusiasts' danger), but the biblical one which Christ's vicarious acting sustains.

74

Here we have arrived at the end of Bonhoeffer's fragmentary, yet systematic, work. But we are in the context of the
'non-religious interpretation of biblical terms' of the letters
and we have an idea now where we are when we hear: 'I
should like to speak of God not on the borders of life but at
its centre, not in weakness, but in strength, not in man's
death and guilt, but in his life and his good' (LPP, p. 93). 'It
is not with the next world that we are concerned, but with
this world as created and preserved and set subject to laws
and atoned for and made new. What is above the world is
in the gospel, intended to exist *for* this world' (LPP, p. 94*f.*).
'We should find God in what we *do* know, not in what we
don't. Christ is the centre of life, and in no sense did he
come to answer our unsolved problems' (LPP, p. 104). 'Jesus
does not call men to a new religion, but to life!' (LPP, pp.
123–4).

The New Discovery

At the climax of Bonhoeffer's development, I want to point
out three directions: (1) What actually is the *new* discovery?
(2) What is the term 'religion' pointing to? (3) What might
Bonhoeffer's place be among *contemporary* theologians?

Apparently it was more than the new discovery of the
world in itself which Bonhoeffer felt as the something new
that was emerging. The whole scene started to move. He saw
the coming danger of conservatism, of stagnation and
restoration in the orthodoxy of his own church, as soon as she
dropped out of the first battle line. Having been brought up
in the liberal headquarters of Berlin, and having turned
against liberalism, he now said, 'I feel obliged to tackle this
question myself as one who being a "modern theologian" is
still aware of the debt we owe to liberal theology' (LPP, p. 128).
Church and theology must come under new scrutiny with all
intellectual honesty. The most uncompromising christological theologian, Bonhoeffer asks again the questions of the

tabooed liberal champions – not in rejecting his Christology or by-passing it, but as a consequence of it.

One might render an account of what the 'new' really was for Bonhoeffer and get a clearer vision of what roots nourished the tree. There was, all the time, Bonhoeffer's Lutheran *Kondeszens*-Christology, which separated him from the early Barth and was widened and deepened to the *Christokrator* whose omnipotence is his humanly suffering and being for others – this strikingly simple formula, 'the man for others', not as a simplification but as the reminiscence and the result of a long struggle with Christology and its history: deity not in monstrous almightiness but in weakness and repudiation. The vicarious character of the life of Christ and the participation in this being as faith, this has *its* strong emphasis from the beginning. The 'I-Thou' personalism led him early to the distinction between the philosophical and the ethical or social category of transcendence. Transcendence is 'the nearest *Thou* at hand' (LPP, p. 165; not as in Fuller's translation 'the nearest thing'!). Consequently, the idea of finding Christ not on the boundaries of life but in the midst of life already has its fully developed place in *Creation and Fall*. Bonhoeffer had been an ardent reader of Nietzsche in his youth. His claim for loyalty to the earth and the story of the giant Antaeus, son of Gaea, who was undefeatable as long as he had his feet on the ground, is in his first and last writings (GS, III, pp. 57 and 494; NRS, p. 47). The mockery about religious backwoodsmanship we can read while it is in full swing, as early as 1932. The devaluation of religion in favour of faith was commonplace in the Barthian group. The doctrine of the religious *a priori* is the key of R. Seeberg's (his teacher's) theology and was, as such, soon a target for Bonhoeffer's criticism. Christ as the Lord, and not as the object of a religion, was his presupposition all the time. All this had been said or more or less explained in Bonhoeffer's theology.

If in abbreviation it can be said that Bonhoeffer's peculiar Christology is not what is new in the letters, it is now to be said that the corresponding background, 'the world come of age', is new. It was discovered most impressively when the discoverer was himself a helpless victim of a cruel barbarian world. Of course, secularization had been greeted before Bonhoeffer by many other sons of Christendom, but by none with this Christology as a background, or by doing it in the name of Christ. The new discovery seems to be the full and positive value given to modern secularization accepted as our peculiar Christian heritage, not in spite of, but because of, our faith. Secularization is to be understood not just as defection and guilt but as the necessary business of Christianity. Its promise lies in throwing out all idolatries. Secularization might frighten the present churches, because they have made it a terrible demon or devil. Yet with Bonhoeffer it is no longer the menacing giant but the necessary and positive counterpoint in God's symphony.

One of the liberating consequences is that the burden, which Kant had placed on the shoulders of the churches, has been accepted and integrated. Kant's assertion has been in the Christian subconscious all the time: 'Enlightenment is the departure of man from his self-inflicted immaturity. Immaturity is the inability to use one's own reason without the guidance of someone else' ('Was ist Aufklärung?' *Werke*, viii, 35). Of course the challenge of Kant had been answered before by modernists of the last century by making faith totally an ethic and transforming the Christian heritage into the growth of ethical autonomy of man coming of age (Richard Rothe). But Bonhoeffer accepts and embraces Kant's irrevocable assertion out of the full integration and implication of Christ's cross. The crucified reveals, rejects and confirms and renews, true worldliness, true this-worldliness, true Godlessness, the true man come of age, an adult world, indeed, the heritage of the Enlightenment. This doctrine even protects it against its own unrealistic, unappeasable thirst to deify, glorify, or demonize itself. This concept of Christ even enjoys the optimistic tone of the

77

Enlightenment in protecting this-worldliness against the pessimistic resignation of the agnostics. The christological background gives the courage to let everything be what it is. Bonhoeffer liberates the Christians so that they can listen to Feuerbach and Nietzsche and give them their honest share for their contribution. These people now give us a bad conscience when we make the Christian faith a shop for religious needs or a skilful technique for avoiding this world. It had not been heard before with this emphasis that Christ's Lordship corresponds to secularity, discipleship to participating in this-worldliness. The natural, the profane, the reasonable, the human, the polyphony of real life gets its share not against, but in, Christ.

We might even find, when studying the nineteenth century, that there has already been a disposition to look positively at secularization and to take the man-come-of-age for granted. But it was not done in connexion with this Christology or with this large and poignant concept of the phenomenon of religion. The range of application of religiousness in the name of Christ is new. The old distinction of faith and religion has been related by Bonhoeffer to the whole phenomenon of history and its result positively appraised.

Religion

It is an interdependent triangle in which Bonhoeffer's thoughts are moving: Christ – world come of age – religion. Nothing must be taken apart and made a phenomenology of its own. Trying to do it with the term 'religion' would show that Bonhoeffer's term is unsatisfactory and incomprehensible. He certainly did not give us a scientifically, historically, and systematically full paper on it. Bonhoeffer's treatment of it is strongly related to his primary question – who is Jesus Christ for us today? – and in this context his observations find their true proportion. The time for what he then describes as 'religion' – over against our modern world and over against the figure of Christ – is over. There is, as he says, something in the religious desires and convictions of our time which darkens and hinders the open view and encounter both with Christ and with the adult world. Therefore, we must not use too much time in arguing with Bonhoeffer whether the time for religion is really over or whether everything points to a marvellous rebirth in many countries today. This would not meet his point.

It has already been mentioned that the term 'religion' as distinct from 'faith' was strongly revived by Barth and that Bonhoeffer presupposes this. In this sense religion means human activities to reach the beyond, the postulate of a deity in order to get help and protection if wanted. Bonhoeffer praises Barth in the highest terms for the rejection of religion. Bonhoeffer himself gives in the letters some incidental but guiding definition of features which one had to keep in mind. I see five of them.

First, religion is *individualism*. It cultivates individualistic forms of inwardness. It takes the form of asceticism or concepts of conversion which all abandon the world to itself. One cannot force back the world come of age into such an individualistic inwardness.

Secondly, religion is *metaphysics*. Its transcendence provides the completion which is felt necessary for this world. God or the divine is the superstructure for being. Thus it secures the escape the religious desire wants to have. Religion inescapably leads to thinking in two realms: reality must be completed by the supranatural. It emphasizes Christianity as the religion of salvation.

Thirdly, religion is admittedly a *province* of life, a religious *a priori* besides other *a prioris*, a sector of the whole, more or less interesting, socially and psychologically valuable – a relic of the past, but still to be looked after by the governmental department for cultural affairs. Unfortunately enough, it is still alive in the more remote areas. Is that the Christian God, dwelling in a dark and ever smaller province?

Fourthly, religion is the *deus ex machina* concept. God must be there providing answers, solutions, protection and help. Religion is the spiritual chemist's shop. It is the concept by which the sermon must first produce feelings of terrible need, must hunt for the human weaknesses, and then give out the proper remedies in proper doses. It covers up actual godlessness with piety and religiosity. Has Christ asked for and found the *deus ex machina*? Is he the medicine, answer, and solution?

Fifthly, religion has become perverted into a *privilege*. *Ek-klesia* means in fact not the called-out, but the favoured ones. Religion is gift, physically, psychologically, materially, by law, congenital or not, well deserved or not, the luxury of certain classes. Thus it is a sign of separation, the condition for salvation, law. This leads religion even to acts of violation.

Bonhoeffer now holds that the time for this religion is essentially over. He would not argue with us that human needs and the skilful handling of them again and again produce successful mass meetings and even enlarge the share of religion in private and public life. But it does not matter, and people who matter do not come into it. The main point Bonhoeffer would make is that the Christians themselves give proof every day of this analysis because they are not able to make more out of their religion than a nice little province of their real life. The provinciality of Christian life today speaks loudly for Bonhoeffer's thesis.

Bonhoeffer said all this just when one would have thought religion as the other realm could have been the one great help and answer where no human hope was left. But he joined those who were too honest to escape in their weakness into a pious corner where mean provinciality of worship insults God's majesty.

But who is Jesus? How is he real for us? Bonhoeffer wants to re-check the doctrinal shape of the churches in order to prove that Christ is precisely not all that religion says he is.

He is the man for others against individualistic inwardness. He is lonely and forsaken without transcendent escape. He worships not in provinciality but in the midst of real life. He, though longing for him, does not experience the *deus ex machina*. Thus the time for religion might have gone, but not the time for Jesus, or if you like, for the *theologia crucis*.

Bonhoeffer wanted to work out this view in what he called the 'non-religious interpretation of the biblical terms'. He left us with a tantalizingly short outline. But what I have said provides specific criticism of our sermons and the structure of our churches. The non-religious interpretation does not arise out of any doubts about Christ. Ebeling is right in saying that it is first of all 'christological interpretation' (mw, ii, pp. 21 and 66). Non-religious interpreting must do the opposite of what religious interpretation is doing: not making God the stop-gap of our insufficiencies, not relating the world in its misfits to a *deus ex machina*, but respecting its adulthood. The churches must not fight for the wrong causes, their religious and *weltanschauliche* dressing, for something which is not the cause of Jesus. (As early as 1935 Bonhoeffer said: 'Only those who cry for the Jews are allowed to sing Gregorian chants!') Non-religious interpreting which is christological will not evangelize limitlessly, but will acknowledge and respect limitations when guilt has robbed our words of the power to testify for him. We, as Christians in Germany, for instance, have lost in our generation the right and power to speak the words of faith to the Jews. We are not to evangelize them. Western Christianity might have lost the power to speak words of faith to people behind the Iron Curtain. Christ may not use our present form of proclaiming him. Only he who participates in Jesus' suffering may speak the renewing word of his participation. Non-religious interpretation is not objective translation, and speaking at all costs everywhere and to everybody. It is centrally the involvement in the figure of Christ.

Here the secret discipline comes in, the *Arkandisziplin*. It seems to be on the periphery of Bonhoeffer's letters, but it is not so. This is something which is not a matter of words: the meditation on and participation in the suffering *Christokrator* leading to active intelligent obedience. It would be a great mistake to understand Bonhoeffer as abolishing the worshipping church and replacing service and sacrament by acts of charity. The religionless world in itself is *not* Christianity. The church must not throw away its great terms 'creation', 'fall', 'atonement', 'repentance', 'last things', and so on. But if she cannot relate them to the secularized world in such a way that their essence in worldly life can immediately be seen, then the church had better keep silent. Bonhoeffer himself worshipped and acted vicariously in anonymity and silence, and it is precisely this which enables him to speak loudly now to worldly life. Relating is not advertising profanization: 'The arcanum must be re-established whereby the mysteries of the Christian faith are preserved from profanation' (LPP, p. 95). Bonhoeffer is not at all reducing the content of faith. But they become only religious objects if presented unmotivated. *Arkandisziplin* and non-religious interpretation belong close together. The one without the other is pure 'ghetto', and the other without the one is pure 'boulevard'. The adult in faith in a world come of age knows and keeps the living contact with the foundation of his life, he knows and judges the priorities of his own involvement, he faces the claim of the next to him. The adult in faith is he who answers the question, 'Who is Jesus Christ for us today?' in personal, responsible participation in present life. And the adult church is not the church which exposes its secrets of faith cheaply, but that which exposes itself in its very existence. Living for others is its *raison d'être*.

Contemporaries

A brief comparison with a few other thinkers might throw some more light on understanding the challenge of Bonhoeffer, although the others may not here get the justice they deserve.

Unfortunately, I cannot give a proper analysis of the relation of Bonhoeffer to Tillich, which might interest you most; it would need a careful study which I have never made, and I have not encountered a proper guide to that relationship. There is some criticism by the early Bonhoeffer of the early existentialist Tillich (NRS, 58; SC, pp. 166, 193; AB, pp. 73, 87*n*, 161*n*.). But obviously there is now some similarity in their evaluation of the present world, too. Both can say: Jesus came in order to destroy religion. I ask myself: is it the same when Tillich says 'the courage to be' and Bonhoeffer speaks of loyalty to the earth? Is it the same when Tillich calls being 'God', and Bonhoeffer claims for God all being?

I just cannot omit making a marginal sociological remark. Tillich came from a Christian country vicarage; his way started with the great discovery of other spheres of life and philosophy, determining his alert mind. Bonhoeffer came from a secular doctor's house of high bourgeois standards; his way started with the great discovery of the church and its treasure of theology in spite of its representation in low-middle-class form. Tillich had to struggle and to make a place in his mind for the banned field of philosophy and socialism, and he did. Bonhoeffer had to struggle and to make a place in his mind for the disdained field of church and theology, and he did. The two went in different directions. The one became the apologist, showing the embracing Christian spirit, the liberator of fundamentalists from fundamentalism. The other was always a conqueror, scorning apologetic attitudes; he became the binding champion for newcomers.

The second one to be mentioned must of course be Bultmann. In 1927 and 1929 Bonhoeffer criticized the Heidegger influence, especially the introduction of the term *die Möglichkeit*, the 'deciding possibility', into the category of belief.

Bonhoeffer states: 'Independent of the reality of revelation there is no place for speaking of a possibility' (AB, pp. 73*f.*, 79, 84, 96, 98; NRS, p. 62*f.*). Bonhoeffer's christological 'reality' stands against Bultmann's anthropological 'potentiality'! The famous demythologizing paper was read by Bonhoeffer; he wrote to E. Wolf about his pleasure in reading it: 'I am impressed with the intellectual honesty of his work' (GS, III, p. 45). But in the letter Bonhoeffer sees him rather in line with the old liberals who deduct and subtract to make things palatable. This is not explicitly Bultmann's intention. But it might be that 'interpretation' means different things to each. The non-religious interpretation speaks of a dimension different from Bultmann's existential interpretation. Harbsmeier illuminates that point (MW, II, p. 74*ff.*). First, Bultmann, the professor in the lecture-room, gives an account of the process of interpretation. Bultmann reflects about the phenomenon of understanding and builds up a systematic epistemology of it. Bonhoeffer thinks about the God-forsaken world. Bultmann's problem is that of faith and understanding. This problem is not to be found in Bonhoeffer's letters. Where Bultmann is worried about how the modern man may comprehend, Bonhoeffer is troubled about the man come of age without any religion. The hindrance with Bonhoeffer is not just misunderstanding, but God's absence and hiddenness. Not only are the myths of the New Testament done with: God, also, is done with. Not the miracles, but God, is in question. Therefore Bonhoeffer can say: 'My view of it today would be not that he went too far, as most people seem to think, but that he did not go far enough' (LPP, p. 94). Bultmann's interpretation is undressing and redressing understanding of existence. Bonhoeffer, with his worldly interpretation, means more than hermeneutic, language, vocabulary, terminology, translation. Secondly, Bonhoeffer's accusation of liberalism might mean the obvious distinction which Bultmann draws between appearance and essence. The mythological facts stand for something else behind them. But resurrection for Bonhoeffer is not a clothing for something else behind it. It is the *extra nos* itself, *pro nobis*, and not a signal only for another reality. 'The New Testament is not a mythological garb of a universal truth, this mythology [resurrection and so on] is the thing itself' (LPP, p. 110). This matter itself cannot be replaced by another 'existential'. This 'matter itself' for Bonhoeffer, too, is not a date, accessible and objective for everyone like the battle of Waterloo. Here is the relevance of Bonhoeffer's criticism of *Offenbarungspositivismus* ('posivitism of revelation') which he made of Barth. This 'matter itself' creates faith and remains a date for faith. It is not the ready requirement for orthodoxy.

It appears that Bonhoeffer's non-religious interpretation, if acknowledged and accepted, is somewhat more explosive for the substance and structure of our present church than Bultmann's existential interpretation.

At last back again to Karl Barth. What could have been meant by Bonhoeffer's incidental remark on Barth's 'posivitism of revelation', when otherwise he praises so highly Barth's merits for separating faith from religion? Barth does not like that remark at all. Regin Prenter of Aarhus has made a careful study of this (*see below*, p. 93 *ff.*). Positivism means here the absence of reference (*Beziehungslosigkeit*) of the truths of revelation to the world come of age, and these truths become sheer credal requirements. We remember from *Act and Being* the criticism of Barth's strong dualism, in which the free contingency of God remains worldless actualism and is the negation of all existence. Bonhoeffer's 'non-religious interpretation' establishes the very relation of revelation to the world come of age in discovering their closest reference. Positivism of revelation turns the great themes of revelation again into 'religious units'. It assigns to them a transcendent sphere in the modern world. It provokes again the danger of denying the maturity of the world in making the great themes an additional completion of its own resources.

Yet God is not completion or stop-gap but the Lord of the world come of age. Prenter makes it clear that Barth is not answered by gross simplification and that Bonhoeffer never lost his grateful respect for Barth's re-shaping of the classical dogma of the church, including the parts which are not immediately interpreted for today. But what is meant by positivism stands: 'proclamation of the revelation of God presenting its truth for sheer acceptance without being able to explain its relation to the life of man in a world come of age' (*see below*, p. 103).

Undoubtedly, the ethical parts in the *Kirchliche Dogmatik*, for instance, show most clearly that Barth sees this world as good creation and man as God's partner. There are many hints of Bonhoeffer's terms which can be found in Barth's writings: for instance, the humanity of Christ, the concept of *Mitmenschlichkeit*. The Barth of this period is not answered any more with criticism like that from *Act and Being*. But Prenter holds that Bonhoeffer still might have touched a deep-rooted difference which some day must be worked out. He points to the priority of the element of *cognitio* over against *being* in Barth's work of all periods. Bonhoeffer certainly tends to the opposite order: being as prior to cognition, and not the reverse. Bonhoeffer might have felt the grand speculative trend in Barth's inner Trinitarian movement of love in God. There is with Barth the tremendous and fascinating knowledge of the eternal. His great *summa* includes even an ethic of the worldly life. Yet the passionate interest – or shall we say again the Lutheran education? – of Bonhoeffer sounds another tune. May I quote Prenter here?

With Barth everything points to eternity – undoubtedly in the service of the gospel – in order to anchor man's salvation solidly and un-shakeably in God's eternal decree, even in God's eternal being as self-love. Bonhoeffer moved in another direction. He too wants to guard the mystery of God; as one of Barth's school, so to speak, he too wants to free the gospel from the chains of religion. But he sees the mystery of God and his love, not as the eternal Aseity in its inner-trinitarian relations, but as the historic being *pro mundo*, which leads him with all his thinking – whereby thinking follows being (action) – into temporality, away from eternity towards the religionless man, to the godless man for whom the church must be present with God in Christ in order to be truly the church [*see below*, p. 128].

One can understand the amazement and the defensiveness of Barth when he read the remark. But one understands as well that there is a way branching in a different direction.

Bonhoeffer himself had the feeling of being on an unparalleled track. 'Sometimes I am shocked at the things I am saying,' he remarked in one of the very last letters (LPP, p. 131). It would not be easy to swallow the consequences, he said. Indeed it is not. But it is not all mystery, as Barth is suggesting. 'Even though our lives may be blown to bits by the pressure of events . . . yet we should still have a glimpse of the way in which the whole was planned and conceived, and at least it would still be possible to see what material we were building with or should have used had we lived' (LPP, p. 38). That glimpse is described most simply and concisely, and the material to be built with, in the short poem, 'Christians and Unbelievers' (verse 2):

> *Men go to God when he is sore bestead,*
> *find him poor and scorned, without shelter or bread,*
> *whelmed under weight of the wicked, the weak, the dead:*
> *Christians stand by God in his hour of grieving.*
>
> (LPP, p. 174)

This is the striking definition of what 'Christianity without religion' really is.

And now the *Encyclopaedia* entry: 'In his *Ethics* and *Letters and Papers from Prison*, Bonhoeffer outlines a highly individual interpretation of biblical concepts in a world that has come of age, in which neither metaphysical nor psychological categories are adequate. This posthumous work opens up possibilities for a revolution in the understanding of Christ's belief, not in a separate "religious" realm but in a dialectical

87

identity with this world and with Christ as one who is, in suffering, absolutely free "for this world".'

The aim of these lectures has been to demonstrate this in terms of three words: the message of Christ is *concrete* in itself; as such it is to be preserved *costly* and to be kept *worldly* from any escapism.

III

From a Letter of Karl Barth to Landessuperintendent P. W. Herrenbrück, 21 December 1952

... The letters, whatever one may make of their individual sentences (and I have let them work on me once again in their whole context since the beginning of your correspondence), are a particular thorn; to let them excite us can only do us all good – for, unlike 'demythologizing', this is unrest of a spiritual kind.

What an open and rich and at the same time deep and disturbed man stands before us – somehow shaming and comforting us at the same time. That is how I also personally remember him. An aristocratic Christian, one might say, who seemed to run on ahead in the most varied dimensions. That is why I always read his earlier writings, especially those which apparently or in reality said things which were not at once clear to me, with the thought that – when they were seen round some corner or other – he might be right. So too with these letters, parts of which of course astonish me too. One cannot read them without having the impression that there might be something in them. You are therefore certainly right to call your pastors' attention to them and to make some suggestions about their meaning.

But as always with Bonhoeffer one is faced by a peculiar difficulty. He was – how shall I put it? – an impulsive, visionary thinker who was suddenly seized by an idea to which he gave lively form, and then after a time he called a halt (one never knew whether it was final or temporary) with some provisional last point or other. Was this not the case with *The Cost of Discipleship*? Did he not also for a time have liturgical impulses — And how was it with the 'Mandates' of his *Ethics*, with which I tussled when I wrote [*Dogmatics*] III/4? Do we not always expect him to be clearer and more concise in some other context, either by withdrawing what he said, or by going even further? Now he has left us alone with the enigmatic utterances of his letters – at more than one point clearly showing that he sensed, without really knowing, how the story should continue – for example, what exactly he meant by the 'positivism of revelation' he found in me, and especially how the programme of an un-religious speech was to be realized.

As to the first, I have certainly been disturbed by the question of when and where I have asked anyone to 'take' or 'leave' the virgin birth, and by the question of what my neo-Calvinist well-wishers in Holland would think of me portrayed as a 'positivist of revelation'. But I am somewhat embarrassed by the thought that so sensible and well-meaning a man as Bonhoeffer somehow remembered my books (which he certainly did not have with him in his prison cell) in terms of this enigmatic expression. The hope remains that in heaven at least he has not reported about me to *all* the angels (including the church fathers, etc.) with just this expression. But perhaps I have indeed on occasion behaved and expressed myself 'positivistically', and if this is so then Bonhoeffer's recollections have brought it to light. Without being able to ask him personally, we shall have to make do with remaining behind, somewhat confused.

Similarly with the postulate of un-religious speech. I think that you have dealt rather too severely with him when (on your page 9) you tend to explain this in terms of existentialism, pre-understanding, etc. On the other hand you are right to indicate that he did not show any sign of putting the *kerygma* into 'other words', that is, doing what in practise Bultmann ends up with. Can he really have meant anything other than a warning against all unthought-out repetition of biblical and traditional images, phrases, and combinations of ideas, meaningless to the 'world' because the 'religious' speaker or writer does not think at all, or does not think properly, about what he is saying? But in the opinion that the stuff will somehow be God's Word he just lets fly – in much the same style as you will find happening about now – oh, I don't mean it in a bad sense, and how many of us really have the time and capacity to think things out in an orderly way? – under thousands of Christmas trees?

Certainly, Bonhoeffer has left us nothing tangible in this respect, and I almost think that it was not tangible to him either. What then remains for us but to take the best from him – in the way I have indicated or in some other way – without searching for a deeper meaning which he himself did not offer us, and perhaps had not even thought through himself? And what he says about sharing in the suffering of God, and so on, seems to me to be clearly a variation of the idea of *imitatio* which he rightly stressed. Why should one not allow oneself to be addressed like this by a man of whom it was asked and to whom it was also given that he not only thought it and said it, but also lived it? It has long been clear to me that I will have to devote a lot of room to this matter in the *Church Dogmatics*. Was it Bonhoeffer's view that the whole of theology must be put on this basis? It is possible that in his cell he did at times think this. But again he has left us no clues about details and about how he regarded the questions which touch upon his thesis. Well, you understand that I do not want to dismiss him when I ascribe to him, 'more or less', as one so nicely puts it, what I call 'the melancholy theology of the North German plain'. I am thankful enough that I myself lived there for fifteen years, and that I have absorbed a good deal of this Lutheran melancholy. That is how I understand Bultmann, too. But it is not yet clear, and neither Bultmann nor Bonhoeffer has been successful in making it clear, that we have to look for the last word in his direction.

None of this is meant as criticism of your concern with Bonhoeffer. All you have said has to be pondered. A lessening of the offence he has provided for us would be the last thing I should wish . . .

IV

Dietrich Bonhoeffer and Karl Barth's Positivism of Revelation

by Regin Prenter

In Dietrich Bonhoeffer's *Letters and Papers from Prison*, there are, as is well known, several instances where he discusses critically Karl Barth's so-called 'positivism of revelation'. This criticism and Bonhoeffer's often debated idea of the possibility of a religionless Christianity are very closely related in *Letters and Papers from Prison* (LPP, pp. 91*f.*, 95, 106–10), as is shown clearly in Ebeling's and Harbsmeier's analyses of that idea in *Die Mündige Welt* II (pp. 13, 185). But then, it does not seem to be immediately apparent what Bonhoeffer means by the positivism of revelation with which he charges Karl Barth. It is a known fact that Barth has himself expressed his uncertainty about that charge. On 21 December 1952, he wrote to Landessuperintendent P. W. Herrenbrück: 'Now he has left us alone with the enigmatic utterances of his letters – at more than one point clearly showing that he sensed, without really knowing, how the story should continue – for example, what exactly he meant by the "positivism of revelation" he found in me, and especially how the programme of an un-religious speech was to be realized' (page 90 above). Barth says that he may possibly have behaved and spoken like one who in fact holds a positivism of revelation. He goes on to say, however, that since we cannot ask Bonhoeffer, we must be content 'to remain behind, somewhat confused' (*ibid.*).

Must it remain there? Or should there not be a possibility of advancing a little in the clarification of that 'enigmatic' concept and its inherent criticism of Barth? The question has not only historical interest, for what is involved is the explanation of thoughts which are very important to both men. In any case Bonhoeffer was not concerned with secondary matters and we may ask whether Barth comes anywhere near Bonhoeffer's concern, as long as he admits merely to having behaved and spoken perhaps *occasionally* like one holding this particular positivism. It is quite certain that Bonhoeffer was not thinking of sporadic 'lapses' on Barth's part when he charges him with positivism of revelation. By using this term he undoubtedly wishes to describe a *constant* aspect of Barth's thought (LPP, pp. 91*f.*, 109*f.*).

It is the modest task of this address to point out those features of Barth's teaching on revelation which could have elicited Bonhoeffer's particular charge.

Let me point out, however, what I cannot and must not make my task in this paper. There is, for example, no intention of dealing in this address with the relation of Bonhoeffer to Barth in general. Something of that kind would involve a much longer and more involved study than is possible here; nor would it be possible to squeeze the results of such a study into the confines of a single address. We shall rather concentrate on one aspect only of Bonhoeffer's discussion with Barth, and we need yet another limitation of our topic. We shall not trace the origin of Bonhoeffer's criticism of Barth's so-called positivism of revelation historico-genetically. We shall neither attempt to find out which of Barth's writings especially led Bonhoeffer to make this charge nor look for its roots in Bonhoeffer's earlier writings. This is, as such, a very tempting piece of work because it is quite probable that Bonhoeffer's later criticism of Barth can be found, if not word for word, then at least in essence, in his earliest writings. But that would also be too much for a single address. My task is purely one of systematic theology. I shall first of all attempt to describe more or less clearly Bonhoeffer's concept of positivism of revelation in order to do away with its 'enigmatic' character, and then secondly analyse Barth's concept of revelation in the light of the question whether its basic tendency does in fact correspond to that of Bonhoeffer's concept. This is a very modest undertaking, a little bit of preliminary work for a thorough study of Bonhoeffer's relation to Barth's theology, something that has to be done eventually. But then even preliminary work is significant when it deals with essential questions, as it inevitably does here.

1. *The Concept of 'Positivism of Revelation' in the Letters and Papers from Prison*

Let us first of all turn to the much discussed places in the *Letters and Papers* where Bonhoeffer speaks of Barth's positivism of revelation (LPP, pp. 91*f.*, 95, 106–10).

Why does Bonhoeffer use the striking word 'positivism' in this connexion? We can see from the context in which this notion appears for the first time that Bonhoeffer uses the word positivism in order to show the unrelatedness of the statements of faith. Because they are unrelated, they are reduced to mere data (*posita*) and are to be accepted without any further elucidation. Here are those well-known, decisive sentences: 'Barth was the first theologian to begin the criticism of religion – and that remains his really great merit – but he set in its place the positivist doctrine of revelation which says in effect, "take it or leave it": virgin birth, trinity or anything else, everything which is an equally significant and necessary part of the whole, which has to be swallowed as a whole or not at all. That is not in accordance with the Bible . . . Positivism of revelation makes it too easy for itself, setting up, as in the ultimate analysis it does, a law of faith, and mutilating what is, by the incarnation of Christ, a gift for us. The place of religion is taken by the church – which in itself is good biblical teaching – but the world is made to depend upon itself and is left to its own devices, and that is all wrong' (LPP, p. 95: translation altered).

Decisive things are said here. We not only learn that, according to Bonhoeffer, 'positivism' in the doctrine of revelation means the establishment of a law of faith, so that the 'truths' of revelation must simply be accepted in the same unfounded fashion – no – we are also told under what conditions such positivism must arise. The unfounded, mere positivity of the truths of revelation results always from their unrelatedness to the *world*. Barth failed in the task of a religionless interpretation of the Gospel, which Bonhoeffer attributes to his positivism of revelation and to the harsh dualism of his doctrine of revelation. However, Bonhoeffer affirms such a dualism in the rudiments of that doctrine. Nowhere in his correspondence with Eberhard Bethge does Bonhoeffer criticize Barth's positivism of revelation without first of all praising him in glowing terms as the only one who has made a radical break with the 'religionizing' of the gospel and thereby has uncompromisingly rejected the secularization of the revelation of God in liberal theology. 'If religion is no more than the garment of Christianity – and even that garment has had different aspects at different periods – then what is a religionless Christianity? Barth, who is the only one to have started on this line of thought, has not proceeded to its logical conclusions, but has arrived at a positivism of revelation which has nevertheless remained essentially a restoration' (LPP, p. 91*f*.). Clearer still, 'Barth was the first to realize the mistake that all these efforts [he is thinking of Heim, Althaus, Tillich] (which were all unintentionally sailing in the channel of liberal theology) were making in having as their objective the clearing of a space for religion in the world against the world. He called the God of Jesus Christ into the lists against religion, *pneuma* against *sarx*. That was and is his greatest service (the second edition of his *Epistle to the Romans*, in spite of all its neo-Kantian shavings). Through his later *Dogmatics*, he enabled the church to effect this distinction in principle all along the line . . . However, he gave no concrete guidance, either in dogmatics or ethics, on the non-religious interpretation of theological concepts. There lies his limitation, and because of it his theology of revelation becomes positivist, a positivism of revelation, as I put it' (LPP, p. 109). What it means is this: Bonhoeffer's criticism of Barth's positivism of revelation rests completely on an unconditional recognition of his opposition to the monism of revelation of religionized Christianity. Liberal theologians and modern 'positivists' and generally all 'apologists' of Christianity sought to uphold Christianity against the world by the specific form of 'inwardness' labelled 'religion' by them. By their interpretation of Christianity as 'religion' (in *this* sense) they tried to create a place for it in or against the world. Through this – and that is what this means in the last resort – this world is given the right to ascribe to Christ his place in the world – a charge Bonhoeffer levels at liberal theology (LPP, p. 108). Barth has opposed this and by doing so he has done and is doing a great service. This dualism in the rudiments of the doctrine of revelation, through which we understand, firstly, that God in Christ stands over and against the world because he is the Lord of the world, and secondly, that God in Christ does not, as the object of some 'religion', become a part of the world by being placed in the sphere of inwardness, must not be extended into a consistent dualism, that is, into a doctrine of revelation that has no relation to the world. For God in Christ stands over and against the world as its Lord, as its creator and redeemer, not as its negation. In Bonhoeffer's opinion, Barth's positivism of revelation is characterized by just such an extension of the justifiable, dualistic rudiments in the doctrine of revelation into a conception of revelation which, in principle, has no relation to the world. For, as Bonhoeffer said, instead of

G   97

religion there is for Barth the church, which in itself accords with the biblical teaching; but, in a sense this puts the world on its own feet and leaves it to its own devices (something which for Bonhoeffer is not in accordance with that teaching). *This is where Barth's mistake lies.*

This mistake occurs when God *vis-à-vis* the world, constituted by him as creator and redeemer, is regarded as a negation of the world. If such were really the case, revelation, its content, its truth, has no relation to the world any more and will never have any. The consequence then must be a positivism of revelation. Then all the truths of revelation confront the whole worldly life of men without meaning. This unrelatedness of revelation to the world makes all individual features of revelation appear on the same level, whether it is the virgin birth, the trinity or something else.

The religionless interpretation[1] of theological concepts, which Bonhoeffer misses in Barth, would, on the contrary, regard the encounter of God with the world not as negation, but as Lordship. And the Lordship of God thoroughly excludes any unrelatedness between revelation and the world. On the other hand, it is quite clear that this very Lordship of God does not deny the coming of age of the world, to use Bonhoeffer's pregnant formula, but on the contrary it presupposes and confirms it. The religionless interpretation of the gospel which Bonhoeffer seeks is meant primarily to express the relation of *God's* revelation to the *world come of age.* Because we are all so deeply involved in the 'religious' interpretation of Christianity, this other interpretation is so difficult a thing to accomplish. For the religious interpretation of Christianity seeks precisely to salvage a place for Christianity in the modern world by refuting the adulthood of the world when it says that somehow the world in its

---

[1] We do not need to repeat here the profound analyses found in MW II. I shall deal with this complex of ideas only as much as an elucidation of the concept 'positivism of revelation' requires.

worldliness cannot do without God to complete its possibilities. In the religious interpretation of Christianity, God becomes, therefore, either a metaphysical hypothesis, a stopgap for our imperfect cognition (LPP, p. 106*f.*, 121*f.*, 164), or an existential makeshift in the boundary situations of human life (LPP, p. 92*f.*, 114*f.*, 122). This interpretation robs God of his Lordship (we may safely say of his creatorship). The world also is no longer taken seriously in its genuine worldliness, which is marked primarily not by the stress of the boundary situations, but on the contrary, by its adulthood (which we interpret: not only in its fallenness but in its createdness also). For the stop-gap of cognition or the *deus ex machina* of the despairing is not the lord and creator of which Christian faith speaks, nor is the world which one is able to relate to God only in its failures and breakdowns and not in its successes and triumphs, that world which is and remains God's creation – even after the fall! Thus, religionless interpretation must try to do exactly the opposite of religious interpretation: it must respect the world's coming of age and relate God to it. But how is that possible? Bonhoeffer searched through Barth in vain for the answer to this question. Instead he found unrelated truths of revelation, which were all on the same level, he found positivism of revelation. But how then is it done?

Up to now the discussion about Bonhoeffer's religionless interpretation of Christianity has shown how difficult it can be to grasp the meaning of his thoughts on this subject, as they are given tentative form in his *Letters and Papers*. And yet in their general silhouette they are clear enough. We must now recall them briefly in order to illuminate somewhat the background of his criticism of Barth's positivism of revelation. The formula by which Bonhoeffer usually expresses God's relationship to the world come of age is 'God's being for the world' (LPP, p. 95), which he often describes as God's suffering on account of the world (LPP, pp. 122, 174). The non-religious interpretation of revelation then consists in the

World Come of Age

fact that man's participation in God's revelation – faith – is more than specifically religious acts which belong to a sphere of inwardness, but finds expression in a suffering being for others in the life of the world. We recall the 'Outline for a Book', where we read: 'This concern of Jesus for others is the experience of transcendence. This freedom from self, maintained to the point of death, is the sole ground of his omnipotence, omniscience and ubiquity. Faith is participation in this Being of Jesus' (LPP, p. 165). And of the church it is said accordingly: 'The church is her true self only when she exists for others' (LPP, p. 166).

It would be completely erroneous to conclude from Bonhoeffer's 'religionless' concept of faith, that he had in mind a kind of secularization of the life of the church and that the religionless interpretation of faith would lead to a *substitution* for her worship in sermon and sacrament of merciful action in the world. For this would then mean that 'religionlessness' as such is identical with true Christianity, which Ebeling, in his excellent essay, rightly called a misinterpretation of Bonhoeffer (MW, II, p. 50f.). Bonhoeffer is concerned with 'interpretation', but it has to be remembered that he has something else in mind than Rudolf Bultmann's so-called 'existential interpretation'. By religionless interpretation of Christianity, Bonhoeffer means the relating of Christianity to the life of the world in its reality. It does not mean that Christianity, disguised as an existential relation by mythological (objectifying) conceptions, has to be stripped of this cloak and thus be made understandable and relevant to modern man. Religionless interpretation does not change Christianity, nor does it transfer it into a different categorical sphere (the understanding of existence) which Harbsmeier showed clearly in his comparison of Bultmann and Bonhoeffer and illustrated so well with the example of the resurrection (MW, II, pp. 82–5, 88–91). If the church is to interpret God's word to the (religionless) world today, this task must be done in a non-religious, decidedly worldly fashion, that is to say she must not connect this task and the religious attempt to create in or against this world a space for God. Quite on the contrary, she must relate it to the adult life of the world as such. If this is not done, a positivism of revelation will inevitably result, no matter how hard the struggle against 'religion'. God's word, proclaimed to the adult life of the world as such and brought into relation with it, does not then require some sort of 'translation' in order to be understood (not even an existential one). This is precisely what happens in the religious interpretation. Biblical concepts such as creation, fall, atonement, repentance, faith, the new life, the last things, already have a meaning – without translation – namely that of God's being for just that world (LPP, p. 165). In a positivism of revelation, such concepts lack the relation to the life of the world. Again, it is not the intention of Bonhoeffer that henceforth the church should no longer speak of God, Christ, reconciliation, baptism, communion, etc., but only of the world come of age. What he does want to say is that if the church today is unable to speak of God, Christ, reconciliation, baptism, communion, etc., *in such a way* that their meaning is immediately plain to the world, and to show that here is a witness to God's being for the world and not a call to man's salvation out of the world into a religious inwardness, then the church may be forced, for the sake of the Gospel, to be *silent* and witness to God's being for the world 'by example only'.

This introduces the important concept of 'secret discipline' (*Arkandisziplin*) which in my opinion is decisive for a proper interpretation of a non-religious interpretation but which has not as yet been given its due weight in the discussion of this matter. In the *Letters and Papers*, the concept of secret discipline is found in the most important sections. 'How do we speak (but perhaps we are no longer capable of speaking of such things as we used to) in secular fashion of God? In what way are we Christians in a religionless and secular sense; in what way are we the *ek-klesia*, "those who are called forth", not conceiving of ourselves religiously as specially favoured, but as wholly belonging to the world? Then Christ is no longer the object of religion, but something quite different, indeed, and in truth the Lord of the world. Yet what does that signify? What is the place of worship and prayer in an entire absence of religion? Does the secret discipline, or, as the case may be, the distinction between penultimate and ultimate (which you have met with me before) acquire fresh importance at this point?' (LPP, p. 92). These sentences follow immediately on the first critical remarks about Barth's positivism of revelation cited above. In the next letter where Bonhoeffer writes these words, 'take it or leave it, virgin birth, trinity or anything else', he continues: 'There are degrees of perception and degrees of significance, hence a secret discipline must be re-established whereby the *mysteries* of the Christian faith are preserved from profanation' (LPP, p. 95). Yes, this is what it says! And then comes the charge that positivism of revelation establishes a law of faith. I wonder why these emphatic remarks about the secret discipline have been given so little attention in the discussion so far about Bonhoeffer's non-religious interpretation of revelation. Surely this important concept is related to the significance for Bonhoeffer of the concrete example which is spoken of in his 'Outline'. ('The clergy should live solely on the free-will offerings of their congregations, or possibly engage in some secular calling.')

From the summary remarks about secret discipline and their relation in the *Letters and Papers* to the criticism of Barth's positivism of revelation we derive the following.

(1) For Bonhoeffer there is to be no interpretation in the sense of a reduction of the traditional content of faith. Wherever this interpretation cannot be made completely or in part, the content of faith in question is to be kept as it stands and must as mystery be *preserved from profanation*. What does profanation mean here? The content would lead us to think of the profanation which occurs in positivism of revelation,

which presents the mysteries of faith (e.g. trinity, virgin birth) to the world for mere acceptance, without showing clearly how they are related to the life of the world come of age. This only distorts 'religiously' the sense of the mysteries which consists in the being *for the world* on the part of God and the congregation. The profanation of the mysteries of revelation is just the distortion of their sense by a positivistic misjudging of their relations to the *secular life*, and from this they must be preserved by this temperate secret discipline.

(2) The religionless interpretation forces us to distinguish within the content of revelation between the mysteries which are to be preserved from profanation, and the truth of revelation which is interpretable in a secular fashion. Since, however, there is the possibility of the interpretation failing, it is necessary to guard the mysteries which this secret discipline upholds, in a way other than by a proclamation in terms of the secular interpretation. How? By cult and prayer, for example, in which the being for the world is not apparent, yet nevertheless very real – just think of the beautiful thoughts about intercession as the primary basis of congregational assembly and union (sc, p. 140*ff.*) – and by concrete example. This can only mean that an ascent through the stages of knowledge and significance, which Bonhoeffer cites as the reason why we need a secret discipline, is dependent on a non-cognitive upholding of the mystery by prayer and example. Any deepening of the comprehension of the mysteries of revelation, resulting for example from their non-religious interpretation, is possible only to the degree to which the church is in fact for the world by prayer and example. If a church spends her energy on carving herself a place by means of apologetics against the supposed threat of the world come of age, she will not make any progress in the comprehension of the mysteries of revelation. And if, as an act of repentance, the church today must admit that she was by and large for herself against the world instead of for the world against herself, then it is just part of this repentance

for her to draw Bonhoeffer's distinction between the stages of knowledge and significance in the establishment of a secret discipline. I find this interpretation of secret discipline as an act of the church's repentance in a section of those beautiful 'Thoughts on the Baptism of D.W.R.' (LPP, pp. 154–60). 'In the traditional rites and ceremonies we are groping after something new and revolutionary without being able to understand it or utter it yet. That is our own fault. During these years, the church has fought for self-preservation as though it were an end in itself, and has thereby lost its chance to speak a word of reconciliation to mankind and the world at large. So our traditional language must perforce become powerless and remain silent and our Christianity today will be confined to praying for and doing right by our fellow men. Christian thinking, speaking and organizing must be born anew out of this praying and this action' (*ibid.*, p. 160).

Only when one interprets secret discipline as an act of repentance on the part of the church, which was there for herself instead of for the world, is it possible to make sense of Bonhoeffer's apparently contradictory attitude to Karl Barth's orthodoxy. On the one hand Bonhoeffer supports Barth's return to the classical doctrines, to the great mysteries of the Christian faith. It is remarkable that Bonhoeffer does not only praise the second edition of Barth's *Commentary on the Epistle to the Romans* but goes on to say, as we cited earlier, that Barth's later *Dogmatics* enabled the church to effect all along the line this distinction between religion and Christianity, spirit and flesh. There is no doubt that Bonhoeffer thinks about the intention of the *Church Dogmatics* as positively as he does about the *Commentary on the Epistle to the Romans*. This also says something about Bonhoeffer's relation to Barth and Bultmann. By affirming unreservedly the intention of the *Church Dogmatics*, Bonhoeffer's attitude to classical doctrines is, like that of Barth, different in principle from that of Bultmann. Apparently, Bonhoeffer was never very interested in an existential interpretation which does not aim at eliminating, but at transforming the content of the classical tradition of dogmas. Bultmann is interested in making the contemporary proclamation of the Gospel understandable and relevant to contemporary man; not so Bonhoeffer. He seems never to have known the apologetic pathos which Bultmann shares with liberal theology in this aspect, although Bonhoeffer understood better than Barth the value of the liberal openness to culture as a sense for the relation of God's revelation to the world. This lack of apologetic pathos, coupled with a deep respect for classical dogmas, even where they are not immediately interpretable to us today, shows us a Bonhoeffer who is basically in accord with Barth's and not Bultmann's intentions. But this is only by the way.

We have now reached the point where we may proceed to Barth's doctrine of revelation. But let us recapitulate briefly the meaning and significance of positivism of revelation. It is that proclamation of God's revelation which presents its truths for mere acceptance without being able to show clearly how they are related to the life of the world come of age. For Bonhoeffer, the roots of positivism in Barth's doctrine of revelation are to be found in a certain consistent dualism, which depicts God's encounter with the world more as a negation of the world than as a genuine Lordship which upholds the world's being of age. The consequence of this is that there can be no doctrine of creation and of the creature. We shall see now whether there are in fact tendencies in Barth's doctrine of revelation which give some ground to the charge of positivism of revelation in Bonhoeffer's sense or whether he really misunderstood Barth's intentions here, a possibility at least to be reckoned with.

11. *Barth's Doctrine of Revelation*

Within the scope of a single address one must necessarily proceed summarily, for which reason I have decided to analyse Barth's concept of revelation as it appears in one of his earlier works, namely in the second edition of his *Commentary on the Epistle to the Romans*. Our presupposition is that the views expressed in that work about God's revelation are not opposed to those to be found in his later *Church Dogmatics*. Three features are characteristic of Barth's concept of revelation: (1) its actualism, (2) its analogism, and (3) its universalism.

Actualism in relation to revelation means that God is in the world of man only in each specific act of his self-revelation. In an actualistic concept of revelation there is no room for a *being* of the revealed or the revealer in the world. That which is revealed and the revealer are present only in the act of self-revelation on the part of him who reveals himself. This leads to a 'point by point' view of revelation. It has as such no extension in time, but occurs afresh each time (*je und je*). Before the act of revelation there is no reality of revelation in the temporal realm, there is only the expectation of revelation. After the act of revelation there is also no reality of revelation in the temporal realm, there is only the memory of the act of revelation, which is then a completed act. In the terminology of the *Commentary on the Epistle to the Romans*, revelation cannot be seen, it is forever removed from the sphere of the sensually perceptible. 'Jesus as the Christ is that wholly unknown plane, which intersects vertically from above the plane which we know. Within historical perceptibility, Jesus as the Christ can be perceived only as a problem, as a myth. As the Christ, Jesus brings to us the world of the father, of which we cannot and never will know anything within this plane of historical perceptibility.' These sentences are to be found in the exegesis of the very first verses of the Epistle (1. 4). The actualistic concept of revelation is defined similarly in many places, we may even say on every page of the book. These are just a few characteristic instances. 'Faith is . . . never perfect, never assured, never fully in our possession; from the psychological point of view, it is always and ever a leap into uncertainty, darkness, empty space, for flesh and blood cannot reveal *this* (i.e. God's righteousness) – see Matthew 16. 17 – no man can tell this to another man or even to himself. What I heard yesterday, I must hear anew today and again tomorrow and in each case it is Jesus' father in heaven who reveals and only he. Precisely because it is the revelation of God's righteousness, the revelation in Jesus is at the same time the most complete veiling and disguising of God. In Jesus, God becomes a true mystery, he becomes known as the unknown one, he speaks as the one who is eternally silent' (3. 22). 'Apart from the "instant" in which man stands naked before God and is clothed by him, apart from the moment when God moves man, all religions assume that there is a before and an after to that instant, and both these "periods" are invested with an honour and significance, equal or nearly equal to the instant, or at least not wholly incommensurable with or wholly incomparable to it. For this reason all religions afford the possibility of boasting of the things that man can do, have and be, as though they were divine . . . From the point of view of Jesus we must reckon otherwise: . . . what God is and does is and remains different from man's being and his actions. The here is separated unalterably from the there by the line which has been drawn between them – the line of death, which is also, of course, the line of life; it is the end, which is the beginning, the no which is the yes. *God* declares, *God* speaks, *God* redeems, *God's* goodwill elects and evaluates . . . Yes, the mortal must put on the immortal and the corruptible the incorruptible. Inasmuch, however, as this takes place through God's creative word, the mortal is taken out of mortality, the corruptible out of corruptibility, the world out of her temporality, materiality and humanity. But neither mortality and corruptibility nor *this* world are thereby in any way exalted, transfigured or affirmed. The "instant" is and remains unique, different and something foreign over and against all "periods" before or after, it does

not continue into the "after" nor find its roots in the "before",
it stands in no temporal, logical context, it is always and
everywhere the utterly new, always what God – who alone is
immortal – is, has and does. *Credo quia absurdum*' (3. 28). 'On
the one hand it is sure that Jesus' resurrection from the dead
is not an event of historical dimensions *next* to the other
events of his life and death, it is rather the "unhistorical"
(4. 17b, etc.) relation of his whole historical life to his origin
in God. It is just as certain on the other hand that my
"walking in newness of life", necessarily and really part of
my existence through the power of the resurrection, is not an
event *next* to other events in my past or present, nor will it
ever be one in my future. This "walking in newness of life"
which my ego, created anew by Christ, may, must, can and
wishes to do, as the affirmation of my citizenship in heaven
(Philippians 3. 20) and the vitality of my life hidden with
Christ in God (Colossians 3. 3) is my invisible point of view
and reference, the crisis which the finite in me undergoes
at the hand of the infinite. It is the threat and the promise
which, set beyond time and visibility, stand beyond *all* the
temporal and comprehensible events of "my" life, just
because the world is world, time is time and man is man. It is
that constant transcendence (*Futurum*) of my "walking in
newness of life", reaching with radical exclusiveness into my
continuing sinful life with the deadly and incommensurable
power of the resurrection. It is also the meaning and the
criticism of my temporal being, thinking and willing'
(Romans 6. 4–5). '*We reckon with the spirit*. Yes so we do, as if
he were an effective factor, a motive or a cause. And yet we
know that he is *none* of these, that he is rather *actus purus*, pure
actuality, pure *event* without beginning or end, without limits
or conditions, without space or time, that he is not one thing
besides others and thus also no cause for something else . . .'
(8. 1–2). There are hundreds of such statements in this
commentary. They represent the main tenet of the work. But
let us stop here, for what we have cited is enough to show us

the actualism of Barth's doctrine of revelation. Because of sinful man's rebellion against God, God's word cannot enter into this man's world. God's word is transformed there into something seen, something which man can manage on account of his sinful desire for mastery, which in his relationship to God takes the form of 'religion'. Consequently, God's word cannot have an extension in time, a history as such. It can only touch the world of sinful man in the form of a *futurum aeternum*, which breaks into man's existence each time anew, in the act of God's self-revelation.

All this does not mean, however, that Barth denies the temporal or spiritual reality of revelation. Quite the contrary! But sinful man immediately incarcerates revelation as a temporal and spiritual reality and transforms it into religion. In this sense there is never revelation without religion, since religion is the temporal realization of revelation, and revelation the eternal basis of the religion of temporal man. 'It is the truth of all religion that God speaks, but because of that it is never identical with the reality of religion' (3. 21). In the correlation of revelation and religion, revelation constitutes the divine, eternal aspect, and religion the human, temporal aspect of the eternal God's confrontation with temporal man. Revelation is God's eternal truth and when it becomes a reality in the temporal sphere, sinful man masters it and transforms it into religion. Thus Barth can translate the Pauline *Nomos* by 'religion' instead of law. For religion has on the one hand a divine origin, God's revelation on which its eternal foundation stands. On the other hand, however, it not only unveils sin but also increases sin, because it is revelation realized in time and as such it has been pulled into man's sinful rebellion.

But how is revelation related to religion? Can it be said without contradiction that on the one hand revelation is the truth of all religion and on the other that revelation is necessarily disfigured in religion? Barth touches on this problem of the relation between divine revelation and human religion in his exegesis of the opening verses of chapter 3. 'Precisely when we have learned that the materialization and humanization of the divine in some specific religious or redemptive history bear *no* relation to God, because God as God is abandoned thereby, we can also learn that whatever happens in the known world derives its meaning and significance from the unknown God. We may know that every impression of revelation refers to revelation itself, that all experiences bear in themselves an understanding by which they are judged and that time bears within it eternity as its own abrogation' (3. 2). These sentences are important for an understanding of Barth's actualism. Every impression of revelation – which for Barth means religion – constitutes a materialization and humanization of the divine, whereby God is abandoned as God. This is the negative aspect of the relation between revelation and religion. Revelation is always submerged in religion, for which reason God's revelation can never be appropriated in man's religion but must rather be given anew by God in each particular case. Every impression of revelation, being a temporal and spiritual reality of man, is no more than a trace of an earlier revelation, and not the continuation of the latter in time. And yet the negative aspect cannot be separated from the positive aspect of the relation between revelation and religion. For precisely in the negative the positive appears, in so far as religion, the trace left by an earlier revelation, no matter how utterly it disfigures revelation, always points to revelation, so that despite all its opposition to revelation it is also a service of some sort to it. In order to understand Barth's actualistic doctrine of revelation rightly, one must look at both the positive and the negative aspects of the relation between revelation and religion. Words such as the following are highly characteristic: 'All the rebellion against God throughout history cannot alter the fact, that *in* the course of that history there have always and everywhere been those peculiarities, those impressions of revelation, those *opportuni-*

ties and *open doors*, which from God's viewpoint, *could* call us
to our senses and lead us to an understanding' (3. 2–4). A
very clear expression of this dialectic, which undercuts any
one-sided negative criticism of Barth's views on revelation as
a judgement on religion, is to be found in his exegesis of
Romans 7. For example, 'The law has dominion over man –
this means that man is *completely* subject to *all* of the problematical aspects appearing within the possibilities of religion.
At every moment he cannot but be exalted and downcast, be
Moses *and* Aaron, Paul *and* Saul, open to God *and* hidden
from him, prophet *and* pharisee, priest *and* sacerdotalist, most
compelling demonstration of the positivity of the divine in
human realities *and* the peak of human negativity in relation
to the divine reality. Man is always both – the first by being
the second. Of all human possibilities it is precisely the
religious one which speaks most plainly about this dualism of
the here and the beyond, of presupposition and fact, of essence
and being, truth and reality, which inevitably dominate the
human' (7. 1). In his exegesis of the ninth chapter, Barth
speaks of the church and here this duality is clearly apparent.
The following quotations complement one another: 'In the
church, man knows and has all manner of divine things which
consequently he does not know and does not have. It is the
place somehow or other where he is taken out of the unknown beginning and end into the well-known centre, where
he does not have to number his days every instant in order to
have a heart of wisdom, but where he really *possesses* faith,
hope and love, where he really *is* God's child and really
waits and *works* for God's kingdom – as if they were things for
him to be, to have, to expect and to work for. The church is
the more or less comprehensive and forceful attempt to
humanize the divine, to bring it into the sphere of the world,
of time and of things and to make it into a practical object. . . .
The gospel is the downfall of this church, just as the church is
the dissolution of the gospel' (9. 1–5). 'If the church deliberately desired not to be Moses (which church would not

III

desire this?), then she would know and consider that she is
Pharaoh, the church of Esau, and then there would be room
for the absolute miracle, namely that because of this, because
of her humiliation before him (i.e. God) she could in fact be
Moses, the church of Jacob' (9. 17–18).

Let us recapitulate briefly the meaning of actualism in the
doctrine of revelation found in Barth's *Commentary on the
Epistle to the Romans*. God's revelation has no extension in
time, no worldly history, it is never seen, never an experience
or a possession. It is never 'being', but always an expected or
remembered 'act'. Actualism is the metaphysically formulated expression of the correlation of divine revelation and
human – therefore sinful – religion. God's revelation (as 'act')
is only possible and necessary when it is continually submerged (as being) in sinful man's religion. Even if the revelation of God could *become* human religion, a *being* in the world
of sinful man, it would only make itself irrelevant, because
then it would be a human possession, whereupon man, the
possessor, would no longer need to wait to receive God's
revelation. If God's revelation as act and the sinner's religion
as being are correlative, one can understand that revelation
and religion, God and man, are contingent. On the one hand,
religion as a reality in man's world is not more than an
'impression' of revelation. But on the other hand, only
religion as the trace of an actual revelation is capable of
calling man's attention to revelation, of preparing him for it
and pointing it out to him. Thus, man becomes God's child
and a sinner in the church, he is Pharaoh and Moses,
Esau and Jacob, the one who disfigures and the one who
receives revelation. The total crisis of everything human and
whatever pertains to it can become, as we saw, the opposite
by this dialectic, namely a high evaluation of man and
human existence. This reversal from the negative into the
positive, so characteristic of this work of Barth's, becomes even
plainer when we consider the analogism of Barth's thinking
on revelation in the *Commentary on the Epistle to the Romans*.

By analogism we mean the interpretation of human negativity as a witness or reference to God's positivity, for which reason it is encompassed and held by this positivity. It is remarkable how often and how strongly the *Commentary on Romans* emphasizes the positive in negativity and that which points to revelation or which parabolically reflects it in the world. It is something found not only in the man Jesus Christ, but also in other, yes, in all people. Here are only a few significant quotations: 'However ambiguous and questionable the position of men, searching and waiting for God, may be as a *human* position (2. 17–25), it performs, nevertheless, a distinct and necessary function as a symptom of *God's* will and action. . . . Compelled by their own experiences or those of others to become still in the face of the unknown, they demonstrate that this unknown as such *may* become the object of cognition. . . . The oracles of God, of which they are possessors and guardians, are the comprehensible signs of the incomprehensible truth that there is a redemption for this world, which is incapable of redemption. It is irrelevant whether they possess and are concerned with guarding Moses or John the Baptist, Plato or socialism or just that moral rationality which dwells in the ordinary everyday life, for in all of this possessing or guarding there is vocation, promise, parabolic possibility, an offer of or an open door to deepest perception' (3. 1–2). 'All that which is and occurs in and through man is brought into relation to God in Jesus. God then pronounces it valuable or worthless according to his judgement. Nothing can escape the action of this balance-wheel. Everything must subject itself to the test and be weighed. This critical viewpoint involves an understanding of the world, a comprehension of the human and an interpretation of history within their profane, relative and finally meaningless context but also within their parabolic and witnessing aspect, through which they witness to (3. 21) and are a reminder of the wholly other world, the wholly other man, the wholly other history – of God' (3. 27). 'Religion is man's ability to receive and retain an impression of God's revelation, it is his ability to reproduce and represent the transformation, the revolution and transition involved in the old man's new birth as the new man. Religion can put it into the comprehensible forms of man's mind and his creations. It enables him individually or as a group to assume and to reflect consciously or unconsciously a position which, corresponding to God's way with man, allows man to prepare himself for it, go along with it or follow after it' (5. 30). 'Speaking in temporal language or expressing it in comprehensible fashion, we may say that we are "related" to Christ in so far as our existence as an existence under tribulation, is (through no effort of our own) a likeness or analogue of his death. . . . This death, however, is that by which men are led to apprehend themselves in God: in their decline lies his increase, in their weakness his strength and in their death his life' (6. 5). 'Jesus Christ is shown forth and accredited as God's son, because in his sonship man's flesh, being under the dominion of sin, becomes a parable or likeness. Whatever is human, worldly, historical and natural appears in it what it is in fact: *only* a transparent thing, *only* an image, *only* a sign, *only* something relative in relation to God, the creator. . . . God sends his son into the midst of man's sin-ridden flesh in order to judge and crush there – and if not there, where else? – sin and man's rebellion against God. He is sent in order to remove the curse of death, the consequence of sin, where the flesh strives to be more than a parable and reaches for an absoluteness which is not only false but also man's own dissolution. This condemnation of sin, dwelling in man's flesh, this exposure of the true nature of the flesh as a parable only of the spirit takes place, as we have pointed out several times already . . . in the diminution of the life of Jesus, apparent plainly in his temptations, and, at its greatest depth, in Gethsemane and Calvary' (3. 3).

There are many similar statements in this particular work of Barth's, but these quotations suffice. They all show us a platonizing language which is found also in the whole of the *Church Dogmatics*, in which there is increasing reference to 'correspondence', analogy, likeness, image, etc. There is furthermore an especial, christologically orientated *'analogia fidei'*. The capacity of human life to be a parable of something higher despite its negativity becomes apparent only in Jesus Christ. In him, or rather in his death this capacity of man's flesh becomes visible or actualized, so to speak. What is actualized in him is, however, a potentiality of *us* all, the capacity of *our* flesh to point up to God, to correspond to him or to reflect him, all of which is, however, and we must not conceal it, an inverted correspondence in so far as our negativity corresponds to God's positivity. This analogism is the consequence of actualism. Because there can be no actual encounter between God and man *in* time, since God's revelation comes only in the act of self-revelation, in the moment of this act, there can be only analogies, likenesses, signs or images in those moments of time surrounding the moment of revelation. Using Barth's own illustration, there can be only the dust-cloud by which we notice the column of marching soldiers. However, there is *nothing* which cannot become an analogy in some sense – and this is the other aspect of the idea of analogy – precisely because God's revelation becomes temporal or a fact in analogies only. Hence the analogical interpretation of Christ's humanity and especially of his death – something that is carried over into the christology of the *Church Dogmatics*.[2]

Finally, let us turn to the universalism in Barth's concept of revelation. Universalism is the emphasis on the supra-temporal nature of revelation, which is apparent in actualism and analogism. Because of this nature, it is impossible either to make a decision in the temporal sphere concerning revelation or to separate conclusively those who respond to revelation

[2] See my article 'Karl Barths Umbildung der traditionellen Zwei-naturenlehre in lutherischer Beleuchtung', *Studia Theologica Scandinavica* IX, I, 1957 esp. pp. 30–43.

from those who do not. There are in fact such decisions and separations in the temporal sphere, but these are only analogies of God's eternal decision and presuppose the view that God's judgement and acquittal is directed equally to all and concerns everyone. Universalism is the necessary consequence of actualism or analogism or their given presupposition, if you like. If the reality of revelation is denied an extension in time and is bound to momentary acts of God's self-revealing, so that there can be only analogous references to the reality of revelation in the temporal sphere, then every human decision is also analogous, a reference to God's eternal decision, which itself is only apparent in the momentary act of God's revelation. Thus a universalistic idea of predestination seems to follow consistently from such a conception of revelation. This is already quite plain in the *Commentary on Romans* and even plainer in the *Church Dogmatics*. Commenting on 2. 16, Barth writes, 'From where comes the possibility of perceiving the ungodly in God? From where the possibility of erasing the vertical section by which men are separated according to the law, the religious from the irreligious, the moral from the immoral? From where the possibility of seeing that there is a horizontal section, which reveals *everywhere*, even to those most deeply submerged, that there is an access to God? The new day which dawned for men in the resurrection, the day of Jesus Christ, it is the day "according to my gospel" which brings in the transformation of all time into eternity and sheds the new light. . . . In the Christ an end has come, but also a beginning, a decline but also a renewal, and both are always for the *whole* world, for *all* men. . . . In Christ, the high and the low, the just and the unjust have the same access to the father after they have been commanded alike to halt before the unknown God. *All* flesh is grass and God desires that *all* men find salvation. For this reason God judges "the secrets of men's hearts". The condemnation, under which we stand, and the mercy, the power of forgiveness by which we are sustained and carried, concern us all, but are unobserv-

able and directed to the "secrets of men's hearts". There alone
they exist and are real. They are not real as long as the one
stands in the light, confronting the others in the shade. But
when both sides are covered in darkness at midnight, or
when both sides are bathed in light at noonday, this distinction between them is meaningless. Christ is both midnight
and noonday. Above all human distinctions God's compre-
hensiveness becomes visible. He himself poses the question of
God and answers it also, and places *all* men of *all* ranks and
all times under the *same* threat and promise.' This thought is
expressed more than once. 'At all times and places there *has
been* forgiveness of sins, at all times and places there has taken
place the miraculous outpouring on man of the abundance of
God's mercy, of his forbearance and long-suffering, at all
times and places men *have had* the sickness unto God and been
healed by him. Through Jesus however we have come to see
that this is so. . . . In Jesus is given a presupposition by which
we now see at all times and places not only . . . flesh and sin,
but beyond and behind them the judge, who by condemning
does in fact acquit wherever he finds in the "secrets of men's
hearts" a faithful acknowledgement of and commitment to
his faithfulness' (3. 27). In the exegesis of the ninth chapter,
Barth outlines a doctrine of predestination which is essentially
identical to that of his *Dogmatics*. 'We *are* – the absolute
miracle occurs – the church of Jacob, the community of the
elect. Who are "we"? Not this or that group of people who
can be quantitatively defined, no *numerus clausus*, no *numerus* at
all, no describable historical Israel as such. The imperceptive
suspension of all the overt divisions, which may and must
indeed take place among men, shows that it is God who loves,
elects and shows mercy. Only the church of Esau needs fences
which separate Israel from Edom, the Jews from the gentiles,
believers from the unbelievers. But when the eternal moment
comes and Jacob's church dawns in Christ those fences come
crashing down, and the gentile Esau enters into the service of
God and he and the host of outsiders participate in God's

promise' (9. 24–9). This universalistic doctrine of predestination is given a christological foundation in the interpretation
of 5. 12–18. 'It (i.e. the secret referred to in the rabbinical
saying: The secret of Adam that is of the Messiah) is the secret
of man, fallen irremediably from but also irrevocably bound
to God, which is veiled in the separation of Christ and Adam
but unveiled in their oneness. Both stand close to the line
between sin and righteousness, between life and death, but
the one gazes forwards, the other backwards. They are
utterly separated by the contrast apparent in them when
confronted, but inseparably united by the common origin of
those contrasts in the divine predestination to election or
rejection. They are thus united because the sin and death of
the one and the righteousness and life of the other span and
characterize all of human life and all dimensions of humanity,
and because the no of the one is always the yes of the other
and *vice versa*. The one is ectype, question, prophecy, the
other is archetype, answer, fulfilment, as surely as the movement which shows them moving to disunity is a genuine movement, as surely as righteousness and life in God stand in
absolute superiority, both initially and finally over and against
sin and death, as surely as the apparent polarity of the contrasts is abrogated when seen in the light of the critical
moment: *from* Adam *to* Christ this is God's way in and
among men.' The conclusion from this is drawn in the
commentary to 9. 13. 'It (i.e. predestination) does not
separate some men from others, but rather makes up their
deepest union. In its presence all stand in the same line,
Jacob is always Esau, Esau is Jacob in the eternal moment of
revelation. Jacob is the concealed Esau, Esau is Jacob in the
eternal moment of revelation. Jacob is the concealed Esau,
Esau the visible Jacob. The Reformers' teaching about predestination also speaks mythologically in this respect, in so far
as it applies election and rejection to the psychological unity
of the individual, to quantities called "the elect" and "the
rejected". Paul did not, could not have had this in mind,

since his concern was constantly *God's* interest in the individual and not the *individual's* interest in God. How could the temporal, eidetical, psychological individual ever be capable of eternal election or damnation, as he is merely the stage – and this is heavy enough for him to bear! – on which the election *and* rejection are accomplished in the hidden freedom of man, who rests in and is moved by God. We know the meaning of this duality in God. It is not an equilibrium but rather the victory of the former over the latter, the victory of grace over judgement, of love over hate, of life over death. But this victory is concealed from *us* at every moment of time. We cannot avoid this duality. For *us* the *visible* Jacob is Esau just as much as the *concealed* Esau can be only Jacob.'

To this concept of revelation, characterized by actualism, analogism and universalism, corresponds the so-called dialectical method of theology, which Barth outlined in his address: 'Das Wort Gottes als Aufgabe der Theologie' (reprinted as 'The Word of God and the Task of the Ministry' in the volume *The Word of God and the Word of Man*, Harper, N.Y., 1957, p. 186). 'As theologians we are to speak of God. But we are human beings and as such cannot speak of God. We are to acknowledge both our obligations and our inability and by that very acknowledgement give God the Glory.' In this address the dogmatic method of theology, which appropriated God's answer to man's question, and the critical method, which absolutized man's question and thereby muted God's answer, are set over against the dialectical method. It relates the yes, the positive of the dogmatic assertion to the no, the negative of the critical assertion, knowing full well that the middle between the yes and the no, between the positive and the negative, is the 'place' where God actually speaks and the truth is really to be found. Yet this middle is inaccessible to our speech, or to use the terminology of the *Commentary on Romans*, it is neither comprehensible nor eidetical.

When revelation is understood to be actualistic, analogistic and universalistic then such a dialectic is the only way to present God's revelation. When taken as a unity, those three characteristics express the supra-temporality of revelation. It is granted that God's revelation enters the sphere of time in the word become flesh, but it does not itself become temporal, it rather arrests temporal man before the eternal. For this reason time is always outside the sphere of eternity and *vice versa* in God's revelation. Time and eternity are interrelated in revelation, but the idea of analogy shows their separateness. This idea has a double meaning. Analogies are *only* references to eternity and as such are temporal, not eternal. But analogies are references to *eternity* and as such open to it, related to it. Actualism and analogism presuppose each other. When eternity touches the sphere of time in the act of revelation, time becomes transparent and the temporal reality becomes a reference to eternity. In this correlation of the divine act of revelation and the human analogical reference there is essentially the possibility of a twofold emphasis. One may on the one hand emphasize in revelation the distance between the divine and the human, between time and eternity, God and man. God's revelation as a pure act does not lodge in the temporal, the human is not made divine, it remains human, mortal, sinful, condemned. In the human sphere there are *only* analogies, *only* references, which as such are not divine, not eternal. On the other hand one may emphasize the relation of the human to the divine, of time to eternity, for time points *to* eternity, human distress and mortality reflect by their contrast God's might and mercy, so that it is possible 'now and then' to find 'open doors' for God's revelation within man's existence. Dialectics is the exercise of this change of emphasis in the full realization that God in his sovereign freedom decides anew in every instance whether or not revelation is a genuine encounter in time of the holy, eternal God with temporal, sinful man. *This* decision is not within the power of proclamation or theology. But Barth does not stop here, since it would mean that revelation were conceptualized merely formally. The possibility of a double emphasis is not one of many, nor is dialectics a logical game. There is a reflection involved, the reflection of the movement on the part of the temporal towards the eternal, a movement the origin and goal of which are found in God. The holy, eternal God is unconditionally superior to the mortal sinner; his freedom and grace want to conquer man's sin and death. Universalism is a *necessary* correlate to the dialectical movement which unites actualism and analogism. This movement presupposes constancy in God's eternal, universal redemptive will. This movement proceeds from that constancy and returns again to it. Barth's emphasis of God's formal freedom is not intended to make God's redemptive will problematical, it rather excludes man from the actual process of redemption and with him all the human uncertainty and relativity. Redemption is a certainty for God because it is his eternal, universal decision. Thus the basis and meaning of the dialectics of actualism and analogism are to be found in universalism. There is no doubt that Barth intends to express the unshakeable truth of the Gospel of Jesus Christ in his dynamic doctrine of revelation, the roots of which are in the Bible, in the history of redemption. He wants to testify to the miracle of revelation, to the fact that the eternal, holy God wishes and creates the communion with the lost sinner. But this interpretation moves the centre of gravity of redemptive history into eternity. In God's eternal decision, the actual basis of which is in his eternal love within the trinity, the man Jesus Christ is destined for communion with God. And *this* eternal election is the reality also of temporal man, indeed his only true reality. Whatever temporal entity challenges this reality is a lie, for falsehood is the essence of sin. By believing in Jesus Christ, temporal man accepts this, his only true, eternal reality. All temporality, all relativity and all sinful falsehood are put behind in faith. The comfort of the Gospel is the fact that man is *allowed* to do that. I think that one may cautiously summarize in this way the main tenet of the *Church Dogmatics*, especially its christology.[3] But then we have already found this to be the tenet of the *Commentary on Romans*.

Before returning to our principal question, what all this has to do with 'positivism of revelation', I would like to add a brief justification of the way in which I developed, in 1959, Barth's concept of revelation on the basis of his *Commentary on the Epistle to the Romans* of 1922. This work is rarely discussed today because it is assumed that the *Dogmatics* has outdated it. Nothing could be further removed from the truth! It is true that Barth has retracted formally a great deal of the contents of this book, but this does not amount to much materially. An example is the doctrine of predestination which we have just discussed. The *Commentary on Romans* clearly foreshadows the typical exposition of this doctrine in *Church Dogmatics* II. And the same is true for the doctrine of revelation. Everyone who knows the *Church Dogmatics* also knows that actualism, analogism and universalism constitute the basic structure of that gigantic work. The continuity of Barth's thought is really remarkable and worthy of admiration. But in his earlier work those features of the concept of revelation discussed here stand out more clearly and are more pronounced, for which reason I quoted from it rather than from the later work. But this was done in the conviction that nothing was said there which is not materially valid for the theology of the *Dogmatics* even if the terminology is not always identical. I cannot, of course, demonstrate this now. I may perhaps be permitted to refer again to my article on Barth's christology in vol. XI no. 1 of the journal *Studia Theologica Scandinavica*, where the fundamental significance of actualism, analogism and universalism in Barth's thought is documented by citations from the *Dogmatics*.

[3] See my article referred to in note 2, esp. pp. 66–88.

Bonhoeffer and Barth's Positivism of Revelation

III. Positivism of Revelation?

Are we now justified in seeking some indications in this conception of revelation which support Bonhoeffer's contention that it expresses a positivism of revelation?

When we analysed Bonhoeffer's meaning of positivism of revelation we attempted to show that the main characteristic of this positivism was the absence of a relation between revelation and man's life in the world come of age. I indicated then that according to Bonhoeffer the unrelatedness in Barth's conception resulted from a consistent dualism maintained in this conception. On account of this unrelatedness God's confrontation of the world becomes its negation, whereas it should be a confrontation in which God's Lordship over the world becomes apparent. Does Barth really interpret God's confrontation of the world as its negation? Does he really present the truths of revelation for mere acceptance without showing their relation to the world? In my opinion, it is unquestionably false to attribute *such* a positivism of revelation to Barth. Barth is certainly no gnostic. As a theologian of the church he wishes to proclaim the world as God's good creation and man as God's partner in the covenant. It is not necessary at all to go deeply into his *Church Dogmatics* in order to see that.

It is equally false to think that Barth is not vitally interested in establishing the relation between revelation and the secular life of man. Remember the sections on ethics in the *Church Dogmatics*. But then the charge of positivism of revelation is not *meant* to be so crude. We have seen that Bonhoeffer always gave his unconditional approval to the basic intention of Barth's theology. His criticism arises only in the shadow of this approval. All we must do then is to show where the point of difference lies at which the ways of these two thinkers part so that we may explain, from Bonhoeffer's point of view, why Barth's way might look to be one of positivism of revelation.

In his *Act and Being* Bonhoeffer raised several critical

questions in regard to the actualism of Barth's concept of revelation, questions which are of greatest importance for us now. He thinks for example that behind the dissolution of the God-man relation into pure acts is a purely formal understanding of God's freedom. 'In revelation it is a question less of God's freedom on the far side from us, i.e. his external isolation and aseity, than of his forth-proceeding, his *given* Word, his bond in which he had bound himself, of his freedom as it is most strongly attested in his having freely bound himself to historical man, having placed himself at man's disposal. God is not free *of* man but *for* man. Christ is the Word of his freedom. God is there, which is to say: not in eternal non-objectivity but (looking ahead for the moment) "haveable", graspable in his Word within the Church' (AB, pp. 90–1). This trend of thought is characteristic for Bonhoeffer. In an actualistic understanding of revelation, which shows God to be non-objective, he misses the possibility of a God who shows in his suffering that he is for man in the world.

For Bonhoeffer it is a fatal mistake of Barth to substitute for the concept of creator and Lord the concept of subject. He has maintained that elsewhere. By this substitution God becomes the subject also of my own new existence, my theological thinking, instead of the creator and Lord of both. But as a non-objective God he cannot confront me, a person, in the sphere of time.

Bonhoeffer sets against this the being of God revealed in Christ in the church. 'The object of faith is the person of Christ, which is preached in the congregation. This is an object which resists inclusion in a transcendental I, or any non-objectification: it stands as person over against man as a person. The person is a unity which overrides the bifurcation of "entity" and non-entity; it is objective, i.e. knowable, yet by virtue of its genuine *ob*jectivity, its freedom from the knower, freedom *not* to be, it never falls into the power of the knowing I. It gives itself through the Word to the I in the act of faith, which for its part acknowledges the freedom of the self-giving person and testifies thus to his absolute extrinsicality' (AB, p. 138*f.*). There again is a typically Bonhoefferian thought; the existence of revelation as the being of Christ in the congregation, 'Christ existing as congregation'.

Both of these criticisms are surely justified. But is there a straight line from them to the criticism of Barth's positivism of revelation? Yes – there is. Again I must proceed in a summary fashion; may I therefore refer you again to an article of mine: 'Glauben und Erkennen bei Karl Barth' in *Kerygma und Dogma*, II, No. 3, July 1956.

Let me try to show briefly how I see this straight line from Bonhoeffer's critical question in *Act and Being* to his criticism of Barth's positivism of revelation. In *Act and Being* we perceive Bonhoeffer's suspicion that behind Barth's actualistic conception of revelation there hides a transcendentalism. For him this means that the question of God is now placed in a sphere in which cognition is placed above being. God exists in so far as he is comprehended by faith as God. This places the main emphasis in one's understanding of both revelation and faith on cognition at the expense of being. God exists in so far as he unveils himself to man. And man exists before God in so far as he comprehends God in faith and thus also himself. In this transcendentalist thought-form there can be no room for God's being for man in the historical Jesus Christ and the real being of man in Jesus Christ in the church.

There now is the point where the two ways part and proceed in opposite directions. For Barth, the dialectics of the theology of revelation must increasingly search for that constant point in universalism, in God's eternal decision, because for him cognition is above being. This way leads from the *Commentary on Romans* to his book on Anselm, that very important work, which is given far too little attention, and from there right into the *Dogmatics*. Dialectics necessarily becomes scholasticism – and please do not take it ill that I use this word; it is really not a derogatory term in my vocabulary! If revelation is really God's giving himself to man's cognition and if faith is the obedient acceptance of this revelation of God, then the theologian must dare – in faith, yes – but really *dare* to understand God in his revelation. *Fides quaerens intellectum!* The point of reference for this *intellectus*, seeking the unity of the scriptural witness, is Jesus Christ, as the word of God. He is the one in whom from eternity all men are elected by God to condemnation *and* acquittal, to death *and* through death to life eternal. Thus cognition will necessarily dare to enter God's supralapsarian eternity in order to search his unity. Thus all theological inquiry will seek to comprehend his inner-trinitarian love and his supralapsarian predestination, just because the historical Jesus – or redemption through him – is the focal point of the understanding of faith. The supralapsarian speculation, which is developed in the *Church Dogmatics* and which in its own way is splendid, is however *quite* far removed from the passion for this world, which became so significant for Bonhoeffer, especially in the last years of his life. Can one not understand then that Bonhoeffer wishes to oppose this powerful, speculative trend in Barth with a secret discipline in order to preserve the mysteries of God from profanation? Is it so hard to understand that for Bonhoeffer this trend looked like an attempt at restoration – that is, like a positivism of revelation? There the movement turns away from the world towards eternity. It is not a crude, gnostic negation of the world, of course not. There is an ethics for *secular* life in this *summa* also. But everything is seen here from the point of view of man's eternal reality, and that means a new temptation to regard the world as not having come of age.

In order to see *that*, it is necessary to look at the other side of this scholastic or speculative or supralapsarian trend of the *Church Dogmatics*, namely the bitter struggle against every natural theology, which for Barth seeks to have an understanding of God apart from revelation, from the Gospel. The derivation of the commandments from the Gospel (cf. *Evangelium und Gesetz*) is part of this uncompromising struggle against natural cognition of God and follows consistently from it. According to Barth, man's true being is seen only in Jesus Christ, and its reality is in fact identical with its comprehension as the truth. Hence every possibility of a true understanding of God and man apart from the Gospel must be denied. This does not mean that such an understanding is barbarian as if, so to speak, there were no genuine understanding of man apart from theology. It would even be ridiculous to attribute such a view to a humanist of Barth's stature (consider only his outstanding knowledge of Mozart!). What Barth seems to say is that such an understanding needs a final interpretation and confirmation from the Gospel in order to be true. This is applicable also to Mozart! This leads to the kind of literary theocracy found for example in such writings as *Rechtfertigung und Recht* and *Christengemeinde und Bürgergemeinde*, in which Barth attempts to establish a christological foundation for worldly authorities. One may ask whether Bonhoeffer would have gone along with Barth here, had he been able to read those works, or whether he would have regarded them as attempts to give a new 'religious' interpretation of secular life, in which God is again to be the 'stop-gap' in our insufficient knowledge and the church again denies the world its status of adulthood. Behind Barth's struggle against every form of natural consciousness of God is unquestionably a different ethos than the one behind Bonhoeffer's chapter on ultimate and penultimate things in his *Ethics*, a chapter which Bonhoeffer related to his thoughts of secret discipline. Could such a struggle against 'all natural theology', accompanied by a strong trend of supralapsarian speculation in an evangelical universalism of redemption, appear as a positivism of revelation, which would only leave the world to itself, in the eyes of someone who like Bonhoeffer knew the first two volumes of the *Dogmatics* only? In these volumes this universalism is *very* prevalent. Would someone who, like Bonhoeffer, takes the penultimate very seriously for the sake of the ultimate and who wishes to impose on himself and the church a secret discipline because of this, find here a positivism of revelation? In this connexion one of Bonhoeffer's side-remarks merits attention: 'Barth and the Confessing Church have led us to entrench ourselves again and again behind the "faith of the church" and to evade the honest question and the honest answer as to what we really believe. For that reason there is a lack of fresh air even in the Confessing Church' (LPP, p. 165). Thus I wonder whether it is in fact possible to deny as completely and as rigidly the possibility of any natural consciousness of God as do Barth and especially his students – for example my Danish colleague, Dr. N. H. Søe – without moving in the direction of positivism of revelation.

Barth's and Bonhoeffer's ways have in fact parted and moved in opposite directions at that point of difference to which we referred. We might label it conveniently act (i.e. cognition) versus being (i.e. action).

With Barth everything points to eternity – undoubtedly in the service of the gospel – in order to anchor man's salvation solidly and unshakeably in God's eternal decree, even in God's eternal being as self-love. Bonhoeffer moved in another direction. He too wants to guard the mystery of God; as one of Barth's school, so to speak, he too wants to free the gospel from the chains of religion. But he sees the mystery of God and his love, not as the eternal Aseity in its inner-trinitarian relations, but as the historic being *pro mundo*, which leads him with all his thinking – whereby thinking follows being (action) – into temporality, away from eternity towards the religionless man, to the godless man for whom the church must be present with God in Christ in order to be truly the church.

The main line of Barth's thought leads to a cognitive interpretation of the entire history of revelation. It is a history in which we come to *know* who God is and what we are in his eternal decision. This same interpretation forces Barth to interpret baptism cognitively, for which reason he refutes infant baptism. Nothing is more typical of Barth's thought than his criticism of infant baptism. For Bonhoeffer, on the other hand, the main line of his intentions leads to an ontic interpretation of the history of revelation, as it is found in his first work, *Sanctorum Communio*. 'Being in Christ, being for the world' is not identical with cognition (especially not with scientific-theological cognition). This being rather precedes cognition. Christ existing as congregation precedes our being and the cognition which is embraced by this being, for which reason our being in him goes beyond our comprehension of this being. Thus it needs to have a non-epistemological expression.

> *Men go to God when he is sore bestead,*
> *find him poor and scorned, without shelter or bread,*
> *whelmed under weight of the wicked, the weak, the dead:*
> *Christians stand by God in his hour of grieving.* (LPP, p. 174).

There a being is spoken of which encompasses all comprehension. Hence Bonhoeffer's different interpretation of infant baptism. *Act and Being* concludes with some thoughts on infant baptism and the faith of children as *actus directus*. Baptism is man's call into childhood and can be understood only eschatologically (AB, p. 182). These same thoughts are expressed again in his *Letters and Papers*, where in a letter dated 27 July 1944 he relates them to the religionless interpretation. 'The problem of "natural religion" is also that of "unconscious Christianity", a subject with which I am more and more concerned. Lutheran dogmatics distinguishes between *fides directa* and *fides reflexa*, especially in connexion with infant baptism. I should not be at all surprised if we have put our finger on a very far-reaching problem here' (LPP, p. 126). It is easy to see that being is again placed above cognition, whereas in Barth's rejection of infant baptism cognition, consistently with his whole way of thinking, is placed above being, so that baptism can have a cognitive significance only, which of course rules out infant baptism.

If we pay attention to these different lines of thought, which proceed from a common basis in the ideas and concerns of these two men, we can understand that Barth's cognitive interpretation of the history of revelation, allied with the speculative trend of his exegesis of scripture and the struggle against natural theology, *could* easily look like a positivism of revelation to Bonhoeffer. One can also understand that a necessary defence of Barth against a crude and vulgar version of this charge – something that *never* occurred to Bonhoeffer – does not mean that Bonhoeffer's criticism of Barth has thereby been refuted. It seems to me that if we see this criticism against the background of the point at which, as we showed, the difference arises, there do appear questions about Barth's whole theology which have not been conclusively answered and thus still stand with their full weight.

V

'The Letters are a particular thorn'

Some Themes in Bonhoeffer's Prison Writings

by William Hamilton

... The letters, whatever one may make of their individual sentences ... are a particular thorn; to let them excite us can only do us all good – for, unlike 'demythologizing', this is unrest of a spiritual kind.

What an open and rich and at the same time deep and disturbed man stands before us – somehow shaming and comforting us at the same time. That is how I also personally remember him. An aristocratic Christian, one might say, who seemed to run on ahead in the most varied dimensions. That is why I always read his earlier writings, especially those which apparently or in reality said things which were not at once clear to me, with the thought that – when they were seen round some corner or other – he might be right. So too with these letters, parts of which of course astonish me too. One cannot read them without having the impression that there might be something in them
(Karl Barth to P. W. Herrenbrück, see p. 89 above).

In a recent book, the English critic John Bayley remarks: 'Like all great works of art, *Othello* deprives us of the confident sense of ourselves *vis-à-vis* the rest of the world' (*The Characters of Love*, p. 149). If this is true of art, we have perhaps found a reason why Protestant theology is so strangely drawn to the arts today, as strangely drawn, in its way, as theology in the past has been drawn to philosophy. The reason may be that we feel a good theology ought to deprive us of our confidence about our relation to the world. Is this why we are reading Bonhoeffer today, almost without knowing why? Nearly every other Protestant possibility is a confident one: Schleiermacher facing the Romantic movement; Ritschl's bourgeois man at home in culture, commerce, or family; Tillich and Bultmann knowing that one must take modern man seriously; Barth knowing that one must never take him so. Instead of all these, we read: 'Man is challenged to participate in the sufferings of God at the hands of a godless world' (LPP, p. 122).

It will be some time before too much will have been spoken and written about Bonhoeffer, and there is plenty of work to be done on him. In this study I am concerned only with the prison writings, and only with a few themes there. I will quote extensively so that the relevant material may be before us, and make only a few proposals for its ordering and interpretation.

1. *The First Formulation of the Idea of Worldliness*

There are several extracts from the letters that can be seen as a kind of preliminary skirmish with the issues Bonhoeffer later formulated more carefully in his demand for a non-religious interpretation of Christianity and his description of the coming of age of the world. In these early passages, the relation between this-worldliness and other-worldliness is set down in more traditional terms. The first is dated 18 December 1943 (pp. 56–7), the second 23 January 1944 (p. 64).

And on the Christian aspect of the matter, there are some lines which say:

> . . . *that we remember, what we would fain forget,*
> *That this poor earth is not our home*

– a very important sentiment, though one which can only come right at the end; for I am sure we ought to love God in our *lives* and in all the blessings he sends us. We should trust him in our lives, so that when our time comes, but not before, we may go to him in love and trust and joy. But, speaking frankly, to long for the transcendent when you are in your wife's arms is, to put it mildly, a lack of taste, and it is certainly not what God expects of us. We ought to find God and love him in the blessings he sends us. If he pleases to grant us some overwhelming earthly bliss, we ought not to try and be more religious than God himself. For then we should spoil that bliss by our presumption and arrogance; we should be letting our religious fantasies run riot and refusing to be satisfied with what he gives. Once a man has found God in his earthly bliss and has thanked him for it, there will be plenty of opportunities for him to remind himself that these earthly pleasures are only transitory, and that it is good for him to accustom himself to the idea of eternity. . . .

I am sure we honour God more if we gratefully accept the life he gives us with all its blessings, loving it and drinking it to the full, grieving deeply and sincerely when we have belittled or thrown away any of the precious things of life (some people grumble at such behaviour and say it is bourgeois to be so weak and sensitive), than we do if we are insensitive towards the blessings of life, and therefore equally insensitive towards pain.

In these passages, Bonhoeffer suggests that there is a time for this-worldliness and a time for other-worldliness. Both are necessary, but this-worldliness receives a special defence.

A little later, Bonhoeffer returns to this idea, but now there is less tension between this- and other-worldliness. Instead of there being a time for each, he suggests here that both need to be in play, always and at the same time. He draws on the musical analogy that meant so much to him. (He once suggested that the polyphonic form has special relevance for the Protestant precisely because of the analogical light it can throw on this problem.) This is from 20 May 1944 (pp. 99–100).

What I mean is that God requires that we should love him eternally with our whole hearts, yet not so as to compromise or diminish our earthly affections, but as a kind of *cantus firmus* to which the other melodies of life provide the counterpoint. Earthly affection is one of these contrapuntal themes, a theme which enjoys an autonomy of its own.

We are on the way to the non-religious interpretation, but not quite there yet. And, I suspect, we are even further away from 'participating in the sufferings of God at the hands of a godless world'. This-worldliness is the penultimate, other-worldliness or love of God with the whole heart is the ultimate. The first is the way to the second, the second is present but concealed in the first. There is no christological reflection springing from this formulation of the problem, and this is perhaps significant. Bonhoeffer largely draws from the Old Testament's hearty worldliness, and during this time we often hear him state that it is dangerous to want to rush to the New Testament too readily or too heedlessly. His reflections on 'our theme' (as he often refers to this subject in his letters to Bethge) will become more complex and more christological.

11. *The Non-Religious Interpretation*

We should not be too confident about our ability to discover exact stages in the development of this theme. Indeed, the decisive exposition of what I am calling the second phase, the call for a non-religious interpretation of Christianity, comes in point of time nearly a month before the last passage quoted above. But in spite of this overlapping, there are some new things here that we have not yet met, and we need to have before us the whole of this remarkable passage. The date is 30 April 1944 (pp. 91–3).

The thing that keeps coming back to me is, what *is* Christianity, and indeed who *is* Christ for us today? The time when men could be told everything by means of words, whether theological or simply pious, is over, and so is the time of inwardness and conscience, which is to say the time of religion as such. We are proceeding towards a time of no religion at all: men as they are now simply cannot be religious any more. Even those who honestly describe themselves as 'religious' do not in the least act up to it, and so when they say 'religious' they evidently mean something quite different. Our whole nineteen-hundred-year-old Christian preaching and theology rests upon the 'religious premise' of man. What we call Christianity has always been a pattern – perhaps a true pattern – of religion. But if one day it becomes apparent that this *a priori* 'premise' simply does not exist, but was an historical and temporary form of human self-expression, i.e. if we reach the stage of being radically without religion – and I think this is more or less the case already, else how is it, for instance, that this war, unlike any of those before it, is not calling forth any 'religious' reaction? – what does that mean for 'Christianity'?

It means that the linchpin is removed from the whole structure of our Christianity to date, and the only people left for us to light on in the way of 'religion' are a few 'last survivals of the age of chivalry', or else one or two who are intellectually dishonest. Would they be the chosen few? Is it on this dubious group and none other that we are to pounce, in fervour, pique, or indignation, in order to sell them the goods we have to offer? Are we to fall upon one or two unhappy people in their weakest moment and force upon them a sort of religious coercion?

If we do not want to do this, if we had finally to put down the western pattern of Christianity as a mere preliminary stage to doing without religion altogether, what situation would result for us, for the church? How can Christ become the Lord even of those with no religion? If religion is no more than the garment of Christianity – and even that garment has had very different aspects at different periods – then what is a religionless Christianity? Barth, who is the only one to have started on this line of thought, has still not proceeded to its logical conclusion, but has arrived at a positivism of revelation which has nevertheless remained essentially a restoration. For the religionless working man, or indeed, man generally, nothing that makes any real difference is gained by that. The questions needing answers would surely be: what is the significance of a church (church, parish, preaching, Christian life) in a religionless world? How do we speak of God without religion, i.e. without the temporally-influenced presuppositions of metaphysics, inwardness, and so on? How do we speak (but perhaps we are no longer capable of speaking of such things as we used to) in secular fashion of God? In what way are we in a religionless and secular sense Christians, in what way are we the *Ek-klesia*, 'those who are called forth', not conceiving of ourselves religiously as specially favoured, but as wholly belonging to the world? Then Christ is no longer an object of religion, but something quite different, indeed and in truth the Lord of the world. Yet what does that signify? What is the place of worship and prayer in an entire absence of religion? Does the secret discipline, or, as the case may be, the distinction (which you have met with me before) between penultimate and ultimate, at this point acquire fresh importance? . . . The Pauline question whether circumcision is a condition of justification is today, I consider, the question whether religion is a condition of salvation. Freedom from circumcision is at the same time freedom from religion. I often ask myself why a

Christian instinct frequently draws me more to the religionless than to the religious, by which I mean not with any intention of evangelizing them, but rather, I might almost say, in 'brotherhood'. While I often shrink with religious people from speaking of God by name – because that name somehow seems to me here not to ring true, and I strike myself as rather dishonest (it is especially bad when others start talking in religious jargon: then I dry up almost completely and feel somehow oppressed and ill at ease) – with people who have no religion I am able on occasion to speak of God quite openly and as it were naturally. Religious people speak of God when human perception is (often just from laziness) at an end, or human resources fail: it is in fact always the *deus ex machina* they call to their aid, either for the so-called solving of insoluble problems or as support in human failure – always, that is to say, helping out human weakness or on the borders of human existence. Of necessity, that can only go on until men can, by their own strength, push those borders a little further, so that God becomes superfluous as a *deus ex machina*. I have come to be doubtful even about talking of 'borders of human existence'. Is even death today, since men are scarcely afraid of it any more, and sin, which they scarcely understand any more, still a genuine border-line? It always seems to me that in talking thus we are only seeking frantically to make room for God. I should like to speak of God not on the borders of life but at its centre, not in weakness but in strength, not, therefore, in man's suffering and death but in his life and prosperity. On the borders it seems to me better to hold our peace and leave the problem unsolved. Belief in the resurrection is not the solution of the problem of death. The 'beyond' of God is not the beyond of our perceptive faculties. Epistemological theory has nothing to do with the transcendence of God. God is the 'beyond' in the midst of our life. The church stands not where human powers give out, on the borders, but in the centre of the village. That is the way it is in the Old Testament and in this sense we still read the New Testament far too little on the basis of the Old. The outward aspect of this religionless Christianity, the form it takes, is something to which I am giving much thought . . .

Let us list some of the themes in this passage.

(1) Longing for the eternal, which formed a part of the Christian attitude in the previous stage, now seems to be part of what is meant by 'religion', and is thus more decisively rejected than before. We belong wholly to this world. Two means are used to protect this from distortion: one is the penultimate-ultimate distinction that he had already dealt with in *Ethics*. We do not live in two worlds, we live in one

world, this one, the world without God. We live in the penultimate, and must not try to live anywhere else, though we believe in the ultimate. The other device is the 'secret discipline', which is a way of witnessing to the ultimate without attempting to call attention to it or to give it structure. Both faith and church are thus utterly hidden, secret, unnoticed.[1]

(2) We see a decisive rejection of the religious *a priori*, and the affirmation that men can live, do live, and perhaps should live without the God who is the answer to their problems. This is both a descriptive statement about the life of the world as Bonhoeffer saw it, and an attack on the theological position of his own professor of theology, Reinhold Seeberg.

What does *religious a priori* mean? It is the unspoken presupposition, carried through the centuries, that man needs the idea of God in order to develop himself, to solve his problems, and to understand the world. On this presupposition preaching was formed and texts were interpreted religiously in accordance with it.[2]

We will find him returning to this, particularly in the extract to follow. A question might be raised at this point, however. It is not clear just who it is that is radically without religion. Is it all men, is it 'modern man', or is it a small group of men? Is this a theological affirmation about all men

[1] If the hiddenness of faith in the life of the world is a relatively new idea in Bonhoeffer (*The Cost of Discipleship* being necessarily concerned with visibility), the idea of the hiddenness of the church is one he has used before. This passage is from the 1933 Christology lectures at the University of Berlin: 'The Church goes on its own way of lowliness with this Lowly One. It cannot strive for a visible confirmation of its way while it renounces itself at every step. But as the lowly church, it may not look at itself in vain conceit, as though its lowliness were visible proof that Christ was present there. Lowliness is no proof, at least it is not a proof that one can refer to. There is no law or principle here which the church has to follow; this is a fact, in short, God's way with the church' (c, p. 117; cf. 'Outline for a Book', LPP, pp. 163–6).

[2] Albrecht Schoenherr, 'Bonhoeffer's Thought on the Church and its Preaching in the World which has come of Age', MW, I, p. 77.

or a piece of apologetic strategy? There may be a wavering back and forth between these two positions. But if it is a theological statement, it suggests a very interesting and very odd type of theology – one that tries to do its work without a special doctrine of God.

(3) Another theme, started here, and picked up later, is this. We can no longer begin with man in his weakness, in his despair, man who is going to die. Theology has no special interest in boundary-situations. We should speak to man in his life and prosperity, not in his weakness. We are not interested in 'the kind of faith that issues from despair'. Death and the fear of death have no power to move man any closer to God. This is partly an attack on Luther's use of the law-gospel distinction and partly an attack on existentialism, perhaps especially on Heidegger and his influence. Was it Heidegger's politics that made Bonhoeffer reject the theological usefulness of his philosophical analysis? Again we should ask, is this apologetic strategy or the way to a specific theological stand? If it is the latter, it is an interesting theological position – one that tries to do its work without an eschatology. We can also note that one of the consequences of his attack on existentialism and psychotherapy as preparations for the gospel is a rejection of religion as inwardness. He will develop this in the passage, quoted below, from the letter of 8 July 1944.

These three themes in the 30 April letter are really one theme, and I think it can be claimed that what we have is the earlier problem of worldliness put now in a slightly different way. Because of the necessary worldliness of the Christian, he is driven to a search for a non-religious understanding of Christianity.

He turns, in the letter of 25 May 1944 (p. 104), to his attack on theologies of correlation, on Christianity as the answer to otherwise unanswerable human problems.

We should find God in what we do know, not in what we don't; not in outstanding problems, but in those we have already solved. This is true not only for the relation between Christianity and science, but also for wider human problems such as guilt, suffering and death. It is possible nowadays to find answers to these problems which leave God right out of the picture. It just isn't true to say that Christianity alone has the answers. In fact the Christian answers are no more conclusive or compelling than any of the others. Once more, God cannot be used as a stop-gap. We must not wait until we are at the end of our tether: he must be found in the centre of life: in life, and not only in death; in health and vigour, and not only in suffering; in activity, and not only in sin.

Nowhere in his thought does Bonhoeffer approach Barth more closely than here. And nowhere in Bonhoeffer's work are we more closely questioned and challenged: Is it really possible to make a thorough rejection of Christianity as a need-fulfilling, problem-solving, answer-giving structure? Yet there is a sense in which Bonhoeffer is also to be seen as returning to a concern of liberal theology. Bonhoeffer himself sees this, and the following passage from the letter of 8 June 1944 (p. 110) describes what he takes his relation to the other theological currents to be. It cannot be claimed that this passage is either accurate or clear, though it is an important part of the evidence we are assembling.

Bultmann would seem to have felt Barth's limitations in some way, but he misconstrues them in the light of liberal theology, and hence goes off into the typical liberal process (the 'mythological' elements of Christianity are dropped, and Christianity is reduced to its 'essence'). I am of the view that the full content, including the mythological concepts, must be maintained. The New Testament is not a mythological garbing of the universal truth: this mythology (resurrection and so on) is the thing itself – but the concepts must be interpreted in such a way as not to make religion a pre-condition of faith (cf. circumcision in St. Paul). Not until that is achieved will, in my opinion, liberal theology be overcome (and even Barth is still dominated by it, though negatively) and, at the same time, the question it raises be genuinely taken up and answered – which is not the case in the positivism of revelation maintained by the Confessing Church.

The world's coming of age is then no longer an occasion for polemics and apologetics, but it is really better understood than it understands itself, namely on the basis of the gospel, and in the light of Christ.

What we have noted as the first and the third themes in the letter of 30 April 1944 return in a passage from 27 June 1944 (p. 112).

Salvation means salvation from cares and need, from fears and longing, from sin and death into a better world beyond the grave. But is this really the distinctive feature of Christianity as proclaimed in the Gospels and St. Paul? I am sure it is not. The difference between the Christian hope of resurrection and a mythological hope is that the Christian hope sends a man back to his life on earth in a wholly new way which is even more sharply defined than it is in the Old Testament.

The Christian, unlike the devotees of the salvation myths, does not need a last refuge in the eternal from earthly tasks and difficulties.

There is surely something of Bultmann here, and the familiar rejection of Christianity as solutions to problems. Note especially the 'refuge in the eternal' phrase. This is certainly somewhat different from the idea of the eternal as the *cantus firmus* having its proper and appropriate place, that we saw in the letters of 18 December 1943 and 20 May 1944. This is also an important passage for anyone who wishes to maintain that Bonhoeffer's final theological vision is non-eschatological. But because of its importance, the adequacy of the implied exegesis should certainly be questioned. It is doubtful whether he has done full justice to 'Christianity as proclaimed in the Gospel and St. Paul'. One wonders whether it is possible, wise, or necessary, to search for this kind of biblical documentation for his position. As we shall shortly see, Bonhoeffer is on firmer ground when he gives up this kind of exegetical defence and returns to a more broadly christological one.

One final passage needs to be recorded in this section devoted to the non-religious interpretation. In the 8 July 1944 letter (pp. 116–18), he returns to his attack on inwardness, and to his rejection of existentialism and psychotherapy.

When God was driven out of the world, and from the public side of human life, an attempt was made to retain him at least in the sphere of the 'personal', the 'inner life', the private life. And since every man still has a private sphere, it was thought that he was most vulnerable at this point. . . .

From the theological point of view the error is twofold. First, it is thought that a man can be addressed as a sinner only after his weaknesses and meannesses have been spied out. Second, it is thought that man's essential nature consists of his inmost and most intimate background, and that is defined as his 'interior life'; and it is in these secret places that God is now to have his domain!

On the first point it must be said that man is certainly a sinner, but by no means mean or common. To put the matter in the most banal way, are Goethe or Napoleon sinners because they were not always faithful husbands? It is not the sins of weakness, but the sins of strength, which matter here. It is not in the least necessary to spy out things. The Bible never does so.

On the second point it must be said that the Bible does not recognize our distinction of outer and inner. And why should it? It is always concerned with *anthropos teleios*, the *whole* man, even where, as in the Sermon on the Mount, the decalogue is pressed home to refer to inward disposition. It is quite unbiblical to suppose that a 'good intention' is enough. What matters is the whole good. The discovery of inwardness, so-called, derives from the Renaissance, from Petrarch perhaps. The 'heart' in the biblical sense is not the inward life, but the whole man in relation to God. The view that man lives just as much from outwards to inwards as from inwards to outwards is poles apart from the view that his essential nature is to be understood from his intimate background.

That is why I am so anxious that God should not be relegated to some last secret place, but that we should frankly recognize that the world and men have come of age, that we should not speak ill of man in his worldliness, but confront him with God at his strongest point, that we should give up all our clerical subterfuges and our regarding of psychotherapy and existentialism as precursors of God. The opportunity of these people is far too unaristocratic for the Word of God to ally itself with them. The Word of God is far removed from this revolt of mistrust, this revolt from below.

Here is the 'aristocratic' Bonhoeffer to whom Barth referred, with his deep respect for the inviolability of the inner life of another man. We have already noted the possibility of Bonhoeffer's hostility to Heidegger's politics. Would it be irrelevant to add the reminder that Bonhoeffer's father was the professor of psychiatry at the University of Berlin, that he was apparently an agnostic?

We are nearly finished with our collection of the relevant material for this second stage, the stage of the non-religious interpretation. One further question remains to be asked. Just what is the theological foundation for this radical proposal? We have already observed that the foundation for the first stage, his general defence of Christian worldliness, is, more often than not, the Old Testament rather than the New. And we have also observed that where Bonhoeffer suggests specific exegetical grounds for the non-religious interpretation he is neither clear nor convincing. I think it can be claimed that he desired to found this general plea on christological grounds. Some of the evidence for this should be noted. Here is a continuation of the passage from 25 May 1944, already cited above (p. 104).

> The ground for this lies in the revelation of God in Christ. Christ is the centre of life, and in no sense did he come to answer our unsolved problems. From the centre of life certain questions are seen to be wholly irrelevant, and so are the answers commonly given to them – I am thinking for example of the judgement pronounced on the friends of Job.

It is not clear just what 'Christ' means in this context, and this rather generalized reference to Christ can also be seen in the last sentence of the 8 June 1944 passage, and in the passage on Christ's Lordship over the world from the 30 April 1944 letter, both quoted above.

But the lines of this christological foundation sharpen, and two quite different directions shortly emerge. In the letter of 27 June 1944 (pp. 112–13) he writes:

> The Christian, unlike the devotees of the salvation myths, does not need a last refuge in the eternal from earthly tasks and difficulties. But like Christ himself ('My God, my God, why hast thou forsaken me?') he must drink the earthly cup to the lees, and only in his doing that is the crucified and risen Lord with him, and he crucified and risen with Christ. This world must not be prematurely written off. In this the Old and New Testaments are at one. Myths of salvation arise from human experiences of the boundary situation. Christ takes hold of a man in the centre of his life.

Here we find that it is the suffering, the dereliction, and the cross that are the signs of the full acceptance of Jesus of the world. This passage reminds us of many passages in the much earlier 1933 christology lectures, delivered at the University of Berlin, where the humiliation-christology of Luther was very much to the fore. Note, for example, the very Lutheran statement on the atonement from these lectures.

But everything depends on the fact that it is *he* who took the flesh with its liability to temptation and self-will. *He* did this and that, which seem to the onlooker to be sin and failure, and must be evaluated as such. Because it is *he*, these statements, of course, appear in a different light. It is really human flesh that he bore – but because *he* bears it, this flesh is robbed of its rights. He pronounces the verdict on his action. He has anguish as we do; it is his anguish. He is tempted as we are; it is his temptation. He is condemned as we are, but because *he* is condemned, we are saved through him. In the light of this 'He' the harshest and most scandalous expressions about this humiliated God-man must be ventured and tolerated. He was really made sin for us, and crucified as the *peccator pessimus*. Luther says that he is himself robber, murderer and adulterer as we are, for he bears our sin, and in so doing describes the ultimate foundation of all christological statements. As the one who bears our sin, and no one else, he is sinless, holy, eternal, the Lord, the Son of the Father (c, pp. 112–13).

But the cross is not the only element in the event of Jesus Christ that Bonhoeffer has in mind in defending the non-religious interpretation. Jesus as a man, as a teacher, is a man in the centre of life, and not at all one who gives answers to ultimate questions arising on the boundary of existence. Alongside the emphasis on the cross and suffering, then, we find at this stage an even stronger emphasis on the life of Jesus and his way with men. Here is an important portion of his 30 June 1944 letter (pp. 114–15) that shows this clearly.

Let me carry on a bit with the theological reflections I started a little while ago. I began by saying that God is being increasingly edged out of the world, now that it has come of age. Knowledge and life are thought to be perfectly possible without him. Ever since Kant, he has been relegated to the realm beyond experience.

Theology has endeavoured to produce an apologetic to meet this development, engaging in futile rear-guard actions against Darwinism. At other times it has accommodated itself to this development by restricting God to the so-called last questions as a kind of *deus ex machina*. God thus became the answer to life's problems, the solution of its distresses and conflicts. As a result, if anyone had no such difficulties, if he refused to identify himself in sympathy with those who had, it was no good trying to win him for God. The only way of getting at him was to show that he had all these problems, needs and conflicts without being aware of the fact or owning up to it. Existentialist philosophy and psychotherapy have both been pretty clever at this sort of thing. It is then possible to talk to a man about God, and methodism can celebrate its triumph. If, however, it does not come off, if a man won't see that his happiness is really damnation, his health sickness, his vigour and vitality despair; if he won't call them what they really are, the theologian is at his wit's end. He must be a hardened sinner of a particularly vicious type. If not, he is a case of bourgeois complacency, and the one is as far from salvation as the other.

You see, this is the attitude I am contending against. When Jesus blessed sinners, they were real sinners, but Jesus did not make every man a sinner first. He called them out of their sin, not into their sin. Of course, encounter with Jesus meant the reversal of all human values. So it was in the conversion of St. Paul, though in his case the knowledge of sin preceded his encounter with Jesus. Of course Jesus took to himself the dregs of human society, harlots, and publicans, but never them alone, for he sought to take to himself man as such. Never did Jesus throw any doubt on a man's health, vigour or fortune, regarded in themselves, or look upon them as evil fruits. Else why did he heal the sick and restore strength to the weak? Jesus claims for himself and the kingdom of God the whole of human life in all its manifestations.

This theme can be discovered in Bonhoeffer's earlier writing. *The Cost of Discipleship*, first published in German in 1937, contained an attack on certain elements in traditional Lutheran theology, and Bonhoeffer himself was aware of the christological shift that it represented, when compared to the 1933 Christology lectures. In 1935 Bonhoeffer had written to his brother about a theological change he found himself compelled to make, and it can be assumed that the shift of emphasis from the cross to the life of Jesus is part of that change.

When I began with theology, it looked to me like something else – perhaps a more academic affair. It has now become something else entirely. But I believe myself to be finally on the right track – for the first time in my life. And that pleases me very much. I am only worried that I, out of great anxiety over the opinions of men, will go no further, but remain stuck. I believe that I first became really inwardly clear and really candid when I just began by taking the Sermon on the Mount seriously (GS, III, p. 25).

We can assume that he felt that some of the christological themes from the 1933 lectures needed to be altered, and that the criticism of Luther needed to be carried through at the centre, on the point of Christology.

Thus, in searching for a genuine christological basis for the non-religious interpretation, Bonhoeffer in the letters draws on both his traditional Lutheran humiliation-christology, and on the new perspectives to which he had come in *The Cost of Discipleship*. These two themes of the cross and the life are not, at this point, fully reconciled. It will be interesting to see whether this reconciliation takes place in the prison material to follow.

III. *The Coming of Age of the World*

Bonhoeffer seems to move on only one front at a time. In this third section, we will find no substantial clarification of the problem of the christological foundation, but we can, I think, discern a new way of stating the demand for a non-religious interpretation. I refer to a phrase that we have already seen in the 8 June 1944 extract, a phrase now become synonymous with Bonhoeffer's name: 'the coming of age of the world', 'the adulthood of the world' (*die mündige Welt*). If the non-religious interpretation is a demand based on a particular reading of the relation of God to the world, 'coming of age' is Bonhoeffer's unique description of that relation. We must have before us the fragments in which Bonhoeffer tries to say what he means. The extracts which follow are from the 8 June (p. 106) and 16 July 1944 (pp. 120–2) letters respectively.

The movement beginning about the thirteenth century (I am not going to get involved in any arguments about the exact date) towards the autonomy of man (under which head I place the discovery of the laws by which the world lives and manages in science, social and political affairs, art, ethics and religion) has in our time reached a certain completion. Man has learned to cope with all questions of importance without recourse to God as a working hypothesis. In questions concerning science, art, and even ethics, this has become an understood thing which one scarcely dares to tilt at any more. But for the last hundred years or so it has been increasingly true of religious questions also: it is becoming evident that everything gets along without 'God', and just as well as before. As in the scientific field, so in human affairs generally, what we call 'God' is being more and more edged out of life, losing more and more ground.

Catholic and Protestant historians are agreed that it is in this development that the great defection from God, from Christ, is to be discerned, and the more they bring in and make use of God and Christ, in opposition to this trend, the more the trend itself considers itself to be anti-Christian. The world which has attained to a realization of itself and of the laws which govern its existence is so sure of itself that we become frightened. False starts and failures do not make the world deviate from the path and development it is following; they are accepted with fortitude and detachment as part of the bargain, and even an event like the present war is no exception. Christian apologetic has taken the most varying forms of opposition to this self-assurance. Efforts are made to prove to a world thus come of age that it cannot live without the tutelage of 'God'. Even though there has been surrender on all secular problems, there still remain the so-called ultimate questions – death, guilt – on which only 'God' can furnish an answer, and which are the reason why God and the Church and the pastor are needed. Thus we live, to some extent, by these ultimate questions of humanity. But what if one day they no longer exist as such, if they too can be answered without 'God'? We have of course the secularized off-shoots of Christian theology, the existentialist philosophers and the psychotherapists, who demonstrate to secure, contented, happy mankind that it is really unhappy and desperate, and merely unwilling to realize that it is in severe straits it knows nothing at all about, from which only they can rescue it. Wherever there is health, strength, security, simplicity, they spy luscious fruit to gnaw at or to lay their pernicious eggs in. They make it their object first of all to drive men to inward despair, and then it is all theirs. That is secularized methodism. And whom does it touch? A small number of intellectuals, of degenerates, of people who regard themselves as the most important thing in the world and hence like occupying themselves with themselves. The ordinary man who spends his everyday life at work, and with his family, and of course with all kinds of hobbies and other interests too, is not affected. He has neither time nor inclination for thinking about his intellectual despair and regarding his modest share of happiness as a trial, a trouble or a disaster.

The attack by Christian apologetic upon the adulthood of the world I consider to be in the first place pointless, in the second ignoble, and in the third un-Christian. Pointless, because it looks to me like an attempt to put a grown-up man back into adolescence, i.e. to make him dependent on things on which he is not in fact dependent any more, thrusting him back into the midst of problems which are in fact no problems for him any more. Ignoble, because this amounts to an effort to exploit the weakness of man for purposes alien to him and not freely subscribed to by him. Un-Christian, because for Christ himself is being substituted one particular stage in the religiousness of man, i.e. a human law. Of this more later.

But first a word or two on the historical situation. The question is, Christ and the newly matured world. It was the weak point of liberal theology that it allowed the world the right to assign Christ his place in that world: in the dispute between Christ and the world it accepted the comparatively clement peace dictated by the world. It was its strong point that it did not seek to put back the clock, and genuinely accepted the battle (Troeltsch), even though this came to an end with its overthrow.

Overthrow was succeeded by capitulation and an attempt at a completely fresh start based on consideration of the Bible and Reformation fundamentals of the faith. Heim sought, along pietist and methodist lines, to convince individual man that he was faced with the alternative 'either despair or Jesus'. He gained 'hearts'. Althaus, carrying forward the modern and positive line with a strong confessional emphasis, endeavoured to wring from the world a place for Lutheran teaching (ministry) and Lutheran worship, and otherwise left the world to its own devices. Tillich set out to interpret the evolution of the world itself – against its will – in a religious sense, to give it its whole shape through religion. That was very courageous of him, but the world unseated him and went on by itself: he too sought to understand the world better than it understood itself, but it felt entirely misunderstood, and rejected the imputation. (Of course the world does need to be understood better than it understands itself, but not 'religiously', as the religious socialists desired.) Barth was the first to realize the mistake that all these efforts (which were all unintentionally sailing in the channel of liberal theology) were making in having as their objective the clearing of a space for religion in the world or against the world.

He called the God of Jesus Christ into the lists against religion,

147

'*pneuma* against *sarx*'. That was and is his greatest service (the second edition of his *Epistle to the Romans*, in spite of all its neo-Kantian shavings). Through his later dogmatics, he enabled the Church to effect this distinction in principle all along the line. It was not that he subsequently, as is often claimed, failed in ethics, for his ethical observations – so far as he has made any – are just as significant as his dogmatic ones; it was that he gave no concrete guidance, either in dogmatics or in ethics, on the non-religious interpretation of theological concepts. There lies his limitation and because of it his theology of revelation becomes positivist, a 'positivism of revelation', as I put it.

In theology it is first discernible in Lord Herbert of Cherbury, with his assertion that reason is the sufficient instrument of religious knowledge. In ethics it first appears in Montaigne and Bodin with their substitution of moral principles for the ten commandments. In politics, Machiavelli, who emancipates politics from the tutelage of morality, and founds the doctrine of 'reasons of state'. Later, and very differently, though like Machiavelli tending towards the autonomy of human society, comes Grotius, with his international law as the law of nature, a law which would still be valid, *etsi deus non daretur*. The process is completed in philosophy. On the one hand we have the deism of Descartes, who holds that the world is a mechanism which runs on its own without any intervention of God. On the other hand there is the pantheism of Spinoza, with its identification of God with nature. In the last resort Kant is a deist, Fichte and Hegel pantheists. All along the line there is a growing tendency to assert the autonomy of man and the world.

In natural science the process seems to start with Nicolas of Cusa and Giordano Bruno with their 'heretical' doctrine of the infinity of space. The classical cosmos was finite, like the created world of the Middle Ages. An infinite universe, however it be conceived, is self-subsisting *etsi deus non daretur*. It is true that modern physics is not so sure as it was about the infinity of the universe, but it has not returned to the earlier conceptions of its finitude.

There is no longer any need for God as a working hypothesis, whether in morals, politics or science. Nor is there any need for such a God in religion or philosophy (Feuerbach). In the name of intellectual honesty these working hypotheses should be dropped or dispensed with as far as possible. A scientist or physician who seeks to provide edification is a hybrid.

At this point nervous souls start asking what room there is left for God now. And being ignorant of the answer they condemn the whole development which has brought them to this pass. As I said in an earlier letter, various emergency exits have been devised to deal with the situation. To them must be added the *salto mortale* back to the middle ages, the fundamental principle of which, however, is heteronomy in the form of clericalism. But that is a counsel of despair, which can be purchased only at the cost of intellectual sincerity. It reminds one of the song:

> *It's a long way back to the land of childhood,*
> *But if only I knew the way!*

There isn't any such way, at any rate not at the cost of deliberately abandoning our intellectual sincerity. The only way is that of Matthew 18. 3, i.e. through repentance, through *ultimate* honesty. And the only way to be honest is to recognize that we have to live in the world *etsi deus non daretur*. And this is just what we do see – before God. So our coming of age forces us to a true recognition of our situation *vis-à-vis* God God is teaching us that we must live as men who can get along very well without him. The God who is with us is the God who forsakes us (Mark 15. 34). The God who makes us live in this world without using him as a working hypothesis is the God before whom we are ever standing. Before God and with him we live without God. God allows himself to be edged out of the world and on to the cross. God is weak and powerless in the world, and that is exactly the way, the only way, in which he can be with us and help us. Matthew 8. 17 makes it crystal clear that it is not by his omnipotence that Christ helps us, but by his weakness and suffering.

This is the decisive difference between Christianity and all religions. Man's religiosity makes him look in his distress to the power of God in the world; he uses God as a *deus ex machina*. The Bible, however, directs him to the powerlessness and suffering of God; only a suffering God can help. To this extent we may say that the process we have described by which the world came of age was an abandonment of a false conception of God, and a clearing of the decks for the God of the Bible, who conquers power and space in the world by his weakness. This must be the starting-point for our 'worldly' interpretation.

We find in these two decisive passages some themes with which we are already familiar. There is the recurring rejection of Christianity as the answer to ultimate questions, and there are further reflections by Bonhoeffer on what he takes to be his relationship to other theologians working in the same area.[3]

[3] Some notice should be taken of Barth's present attitude to Bonhoeffer. The rather measured openness of the letter, quoted at the beginning of this essay, is not present in his more formal writings, and

World Come of Age

One important clue here for our understanding of the world's coming of age is the historical interpretation. Bonhoeffer gives a particular reading of the intellectual history of the West since the middle ages that has rarely been characteristic of Christian theologians. The process of secularization has generally been treated as a calamity, or at least as a serious deviation that ought to be arrested. But in this historical survey Bonhoeffer really tries to reclaim the

---

Bethge is almost bitter in his remarks about Barth's delayed and ambiguous words of praise for Bonhoeffer's work. Barth was apparently stung by Bonhoeffer's 'revelation-positivism' remark. Incidentally, Prenter's analysis of this accusation (p. 93 f. above) is an admirable one. In KD, IV, 3, first half, pp. 18–38, there is an implied rejection of Bonhoeffer's final views, and the following extract from Barth's *The Humanity of God* suggests, in spite of the debt Bonhoeffer owed to Barth, the great distance there is between the work of the two men:

'The question of *language*, about which one must speak in reference to the so-called 'outsiders', is not so burning today as is asserted in various quarters. This is true in the first place because, again thinking in terms of the humanity of God, we cannot at all reckon in a serious way with *real* 'outsiders', with a 'world come of age', but only with a world which *regards* itself as of age (and proves daily that it is precisely not that). Thus the so-called 'outsiders' are really only 'insiders' who have not yet understood and apprehended themselves as such. On the other hand, even the most persuaded Christian, in the final analysis, must and will recognize himself ever and again as an 'outsider'. So there must then be no particular language for insiders and outsiders. Both are contemporary men-of-the-world – all of us are.

A little 'non-religious' language from the street, the newspaper, literature, and, if one is ambitious, from the philosopher may thus, for the sake of communication, occasionally be in order. However, we should not become particularly concerned about this. A little of the language of Canaan, a little 'revelation-positivism', can also be a good thing in addressing us all and, according to my experience, in which I am certainly not alone, will often, though not always, be still better understood even by the oddest strangers, (pp. 58–9).

This is excellent polemic, though one feels it tells us a good deal more about Barth than he intended it should. The decisive role his doctrine of election plays in this remark is important. It is this that makes it impossible for him to have any fundamental interest in the kind of thing that concerned Bonhoeffer at the end of his life.

heritage of the Renaissance and the Enlightenment as good, desirable and necessary to the Christian. The process of secularizing is affirmed, not reluctantly, sadly, or for the sake of realism or relevance. The coming of age of the world means the secularization of all life, even the religious life of man, and thus the non-religious interpretation is not just a possible apologetic strategy, it is demanded by intellectual honesty.

The church will have to recognize the coming of age of modern man as his fundamental way of understanding himself. It must unshakeably affirm it, in spite of the great self-security in which modern man goes his way.[4]

Do we still have enough passion or imagination or strength or horror in us to feel this monstrous thing which can only be expressed in this paradox: secularization and godlessness are the historically necessary outcome of Christianity, perhaps even the necessary consequence of the gospel?[5]

The meaning of this coming of age is underlined in these extracts by the use of a phrase that we find with increasing frequency from this point on: *etsi deus non daretur*, as if God were not given. Modern men, Christians, indeed all men must learn to live as if God were not given. The sharpest formulation of this idea that Bonhoeffer ever achieved is in the 16 July extract quoted above, and the relevant sentences should again be set down:

So our coming of age forces us to a true recognition of our situation *vis-à-vis* God. God is teaching us that we must live as men who can get along very well without him. The God who is with us is the God who forsakes us (Mark 15. 34). The God who makes us live in this world without using him as a working hypothesis is the God before whom we are ever standing. Before God and with him we live without God. God allows himself to be edged out of the world and on to the cross. God is weak and powerless in the world, and that is exactly the way, the only way, in which he can be with us.

[4] Schoenherr, *op. cit.*, pp. 79–80.
[5] Oskar Hammelsbeck, 'Concerning Bonhoeffer's Idea of the World Come of Age', *ibid.*, pp. 50–1.

Here is both the clearest statement of the meaning of the world's coming of age, and a suggestion of how Bonhoeffer will work out the problem of the christological foundation. Regin Prenter is quite right to sum up the situation thus:

> The religionless interpretation of theological concepts, which Bonhoeffer misses in Barth, would . . . regard the encounter of God with the world not as negation, but as Lordship. And the Lordship of God thoroughly excludes any unrelatedness between revelation and the world. On the other hand, it is quite clear that this very Lordship of God does not deny the coming of age of the world (to use Bonhoeffer's pregnant formula) but on the contrary it presupposes and confirms it (p. 98 above).

The meaning of 'the Lordship of God' is partly hinted at in the lines from the 16 July letter cited just above, but it will be even more clearly indicated in the final stage of Bonhoeffer's thinking on these matters. Thus the new thing in Bonhoeffer's thought is neither the open acknowledgement of the inevitability of secularization, nor the particular christology, but the combination of these two factors. This combination gives Bonhoeffer both his uniqueness and his distinctness from the other theologians of our day, and partly explains his fascination for us all.

Of course, secularization had been greeted before Bonhoeffer by many other sons of Christendom, but by none with this christology as a background or by doing it in the name of Christ. The new discovery seems to be the full and positive value given to modern secularization accepted as our peculiar Christian heritage, not in spite of, but because of, our faith. Secularization is to be understood not just as defection and guilt but as the necessary business of Christianity. Its promise lies in throwing out all idolatries. Secularization might frighten the present churches, because they have made it a terrible demon or devil. Yet with Bonhoeffer it is no longer the menacing giant but the necessary and positive counterpoint in God's symphony (Bethge, p. 77 above).

IV. *Participation in the Sufferings of God*

This is not quite all we have on these matters from Bonhoeffer's pen. We must conclude by setting down the decisive passages from the letters of 18 and 21 July 1944

'The Letters are a particular Thorn'

(pp. 122–4 and 125–7). These dates are significant, for the first letter was written just before the 20 July plot against Hitler's life, in which many of his comrades were involved, and the second was written after he had heard of the failure of that plot, and when, presumably, he knew that his own execution was all but assured.

Man is challenged to participate in the sufferings of God at the hands of a godless world.

He must therefore plunge himself into the life of a godless world, without attempting to gloss over its ungodliness with a veneer of religion or trying to transfigure it. He must live a 'worldly' life and so participate in the suffering of God. He *may* live a worldly life as one emancipated from all false religions and obligations. To be a Christian does not mean to be religious in a particular way, to cultivate some particular form of asceticism (as a sinner, a penitent or a saint), but to be a man. It is not some religious act which makes a Christian what he is, but participation in the suffering of God in the life of the world.

This is *metanoia*. It is not in the first instance bothering about one's own needs, problems, sins, and fears, but allowing oneself to be caught up in the way of Christ, into the Messianic event, and thus fulfilling Isaiah 53. Therefore, 'believe in the gospel', or in the words of St. John the Baptist, 'Behold the lamb of God that taketh away the sins of the world'. (By the way, Jeremias has recently suggested that in Aramaic the word for 'lamb' could also mean 'servant' – very appropriate, in view of Isaiah 53). This being caught up into the Messianic suffering of God in Jesus Christ takes a variety of forms in the New Testament. It appears in the call to discipleship, in Jesus' table fellowship with sinners, in conversions in the narrower sense of the word (e.g. Zacchaeus), in the act of the woman who was a sinner (Luke 7), an act which she performed without any specific confession of sin, in the healing of the sick (Matthew 8. 17, see above), in Jesus' acceptance of the children. The shepherds, like the wise men from the east, stand at the crib, not as converted sinners, but because they were drawn to the crib by the star just as they were. The centurion of Capernaum (who does not make any confession of sin) is held up by Jesus as a model of faith (cf. Jairus). Jesus loves the rich young man. The eunuch (Acts 8), Cornelius (Acts 10) are anything but 'existences over the abyss'. Nathanael is an Israelite without guile (John 1. 47). Finally, Joseph of Arimathaea and the women at the tomb. All that is common between them is their participation in the suffering of God in Christ. That is their faith. There is nothing of religious method here. The religious act is always something partial, faith is always something whole, an act involving the whole life. Jesus does not call men to a new religion, but to life. What is the nature of that life, that participation in the powerlessness of God in the world? More about that next time, I hope.

Just one more point for today. When we speak of God in a non-religious way, we must not gloss over the ungodliness of the world, but expose it in a new light. Now that it has come of age, the world is more godless, and perhaps it is for that very reason nearer to God than ever before.

Later I discovered and am still discovering up to this moment that it is only by living completely in this world that one learns to believe. One must abandon every attempt to make something of oneself, whether it be a saint, a converted sinner, a churchman (the priestly type, so-called!) a righteous man or an unrighteous one, a sick man or a healthy man. This is what I mean by worldliness – taking life in one's stride, with all its duties and problems, its successes and failures, its experiences and helplessness. It is in such a life that we throw ourselves utterly into the arms of God and participate in his sufferings in the world and watch with Christ in Gethsemane. That is faith, that is *metanoia*, and that is what makes a man and a Christian (cf. Jeremiah 45). How can success make us arrogant or failure lead us astray, when we participate in the sufferings of God by living in the world?

These two pieces of material bring to an end the evidence we have at hand for estimating the significance of Bonhoeffer's final vision of the relation of God, Christ, man and the world. We can read here many of the old and familiar themes, but there are some fresh and original turnings in the argument.

The distinction between the ultimate and the penultimate is gone, and instead we have 'participating in the sufferings of God at the hands of a godless world'. We seem not to be asked to live *etsi deus non daretur*, but in the sufferings of the God who is very much given and at hand. The world come of age seems somewhat pushed aside, and in its place is the world in which God suffers. The curious last sentence in the 18 July extract points in this direction: 'Now that it has come of age, the world is more godless, and perhaps it is for that very reason nearer to God than ever before.'

Secularization seems not, after all, to be such a good way

to describe the God-world relation. God may have withdrawn from the world, but he has not withdrawn from us.
As Bonhoeffer had said earlier, and which we are now prepared to understand, 'God allows himself to be edged out of
the world and on to the cross.' (16 July 1944). The world
come of age is now seen as the world in which God suffers.
The world come of age, which before had seemed to demand
a non-religious interpretation, receives as 'religious' an
interpretation as one can conceive. Do these July letters
permit us to say that Bonhoeffer has set aside the demand
for a non-religious interpretation? In one sense, at any rate,
the poem 'Christians and Unbelievers' (p. 174) stands as
his final interpretation of God and the world. Can we say,
even in his definition of the terms, that it is a non-religious
one?

> *Men go to God when they are sore bestead,*
> *Pray to him for succour, for his peace, for bread,*
> *For mercy for them sick, sinning or dead:*
> *All men do so, Christian and unbelieving.*
>
> *Men go to God when he is sore bestead,*
> *Find him poor and scorned, without shelter or bread,*
> *Whelmed under weight of the wicked, the weak, the dead:*
> *Christians stand by God in his hour of grieving.*
>
> *God goeth to every man when sore bestead,*
> *Feedeth body and spirit with his bread,*
> *For Christians, heathens alike he hangeth dead:*
> *And both alike forgiving.*

We have already noted Prenter's remark that the God-
world relation is conceived by Bonhoeffer not as a negation
but as a Lordship. We are now in a position to see just what
this Lordship involves. It is a particular interpretation of the
Lordship of Jesus. Earlier in his writings, in the *Ethics*,
Bonhoeffer had made some proposals for a theology of the
secular based on a view of Jesus' Lordship (E, pp. 63, 64, 70).
Here he had protested against thinking in two realms,

secular-sacred, church-world, revelation-rational. This was based, however, on a somewhat different view of the Lordship of Jesus from what we find in the last letters. In *Ethics*, Jesus was seen as the triumphant Lord, in whom the whole reality of the world, secular and religious, was drawn together. This united world is now wholly in Jesus' hands. But now, at the end of his life, Bonhoeffer returns to the idea of Lordship, but it is no longer a Lordship of triumph and completion, but of suffering and humiliation. If Bonhoeffer was aware of moving away from the humiliation-christology of his 1933 Berlin lectures in *The Cost of Discipleship* and in what we know as the early pages of the *Ethics*, these final letters from prison seem to return to that same 'theology of incarnation and humiliation, the fullness of God to be found in that limited, weak, and humiliated man Jesus, who took the risk of utter human concreteness'.[6]

This Lutheran theology of humiliation has never found a more fitting setting. Some words from those early University lectures fit exactly the situation ten years later.

Jesus Christ is not God in a divine *ousia*; he is not God in a demonstrable and describable way; he is God in faith. There is no such thing as this divine essence. If Jesus Christ is to be described as God, then we may not speak of this divine essence, of his omnipotence and his omniscience, but we must speak of this weak man among sinners, of his cradle and his cross. When we consider the Godhead of Jesus, then above all we must speak of his weakness (c, p. 108).

[6] Thus Bethge describes the christology of the Berlin lectures, and it can precisely describe the christology of these late letters. Cf. 'The Challenge of Dietrich Bonhoeffer's Life and Theology', p. 38 above. There is an interesting passage from the *Ethics*, apparently written before imprisonment, that anticipates this final position: 'The cross of atonement is the setting free for life before God in the midst of the godless world; it is the setting free for life in genuine worldliness' (E, pp. 262–3).

'The Letters are a particular Thorn'

Bonhoeffer may have rejected the law-gospel distinction of Lutheran theology, but at the end this christological vision, so much like the early Luther, becomes the final theological foundation for his understanding of the world. And it is important that the tension we noted earlier between the life of Jesus and the cross of Christ has disappeared, and in place of this tension is the single vision of Jesus, the man for others. Two passages from Bethge point this out.

There was, all the time, Bonhoeffer's Lutheran *Kondeszens*-christology, which separated him from the early Barth and was widened and deepened to the *Christokrator* whose omnipotence is his humanly suffering and being for others – this strikingly simple formula, 'the man for others', not as a simplification but as the reminiscence and the result of a long struggle with christology and its history: deity not in monstrous almightiness but in weakness and repudiation.

But who is Jesus? How is he real for us? Bonhoeffer wants to re-check the doctrinal shape of the churches in order to prove that Christ is precisely . . . the man for others against individualistic inwardness. He is lonely and forsaken without transcendent escape. He worships not in provinciality but in the midst of real life. He, though longing for him, does not experience the *deus ex machina*. Thus the time for religion might have gone, but not the time for Jesus, or if you like, for the *theologia crucis* (pp. 76 and 80f. above).

The tension between the life and the cross is overcome in the formula, God's being for the world.[7] Cross and discipleship become a single vision of the same truth. A passage from the outline for a book included in the volume of prison letters and papers (pp. 163–6) indicates the coming together of incarnation and crucifixion, cross and Jesus' life among men.

[7] As Prenter, p. 99f. above, rightly points out: 'The formula by which Bonhoeffer usually expresses God's relationship to the world come of age is "God's being for the world" (*das Fürsein Gottes für die Welt*), which he often describes as God's suffering on account of the world. The non-religious interpretation of revelation then consists in the fact that man's participation in God's revelation – faith – is more than specifically religious acts which belong to a sphere of inwardness, but finds expression in a suffering being for others in the life of the world.'

Encounter with Jesus Christ, implying a complete orientation of human being in the experience of Jesus as one whose only concern is for others. This concern of Jesus for others is the experience of transcendence. This freedom from self, maintained to the point of death, the sole ground of his omnipotence, omniscience and ubiquity. Faith is participation in this Being of Jesus (incarnation, cross and resurrection). Our relation to God is not a religious relationship to a supreme Being, absolute in power and goodness, which is a spurious conception of transcendence, but a new life for others, through participation in the Being of God. The transcendence consists not in tasks beyond our scope and power, but in the nearest Thou to hand. God in human form, not, as in other religions, in animal form — the monstrous, chaotic, remote and terrifying — nor yet in abstract form — the absolute, metaphysical, infinite, etc. — nor yet in the Greek divine-human of autonomous man, but man existing for others, and hence the Crucified.

Thus, Karl Barth is quite right when he describes the theology of these July letters as a theology of *imitatio Christi*. He rightly describes it so, but he obviously doesn't like it.

And what he says about sharing in the suffering of God, and so on, seems to me to be clearly a variation of the idea of *imitatio* which he rightly stressed . . . It has long been clear to me that I will have to devote a lot of room to this matter in the *Church Dogmatics*. Was it Bonhoeffer's view that the whole of theology must be put on this basis? It is possible that in his cell he did at times think this (p. 91 above).

We have set down, in this study, nearly all of the relevant theological material from the published prison letters and papers of Bonhoeffer. We have tried to put it in order. In so doing, we have traced two different themes through four stages. The first theme might be called the problem of the world. We saw Bonhoeffer begin with a plea for worldliness, move to a demand for a non-religious interpretation of Christianity, move on to a description of the world come of age, and conclude with a description of the life of the Christian today as a participation in the sufferings of God at the hands of a godless world. The second theme concerns the theological justification for the several views of the Christian in the world. We saw Bonhoeffer begin with an essentially Old Testament definition of worldliness. We moved forward and saw two distinct christological themes weaving in and out of the argument: the life of Jesus and the cross of Christ. For a while these themes were not wholly resolved. But at the end, in the final conception of the suffering Lordship of Jesus, seen in both his life with men and his suffering and death the two merged into a single vision, both acting as signs of God's being for the world. How sharply these 'themes' and these 'stages' ought to be distinguished is difficult to say. The purpose of this study is more to set down the relevant material than to claim as correct any special interpretation.

When we have looked over this material, just what is it that we have before us? To use our theological jargon, I suppose one could say that we have here a proposal for a specific theology of culture, or more exactly, a theology of secular culture. It includes both a description of man in the world today and a christology to illumine that description.

The christological background gives the courage to let everything be what it is. Bonhoeffer liberates the Christians so that they can listen to Feuerbach and Nietzsche and give them their honest share for their contribution . . . It had not been heard before with this emphasis that Christ's Lordship corresponds to secularity, discipleship to participating in this-worldliness. The natural, the profane, the reasonable, the human, the polyphony of real life gets its share not against, but in, Christ (Bethge, p. 78 above).

It is a theology of secular culture that is in some opposition to the alternative available in our time. In the modern world as interpreted existentially by a Tillich or a Bultmann, men are seen, in their acts and in their despair, unconsciously longing for God, and in their negations of God unconsciously witnessing to him. Our work in this kind of world is to enter into a theological criticism and interpretation of the world. In the modern world as interpreted by the religious liberal, the work of man still remains a work of ethical transformation. In the world of Barth, the distinction between the man with God and the man without God is radically relativized, and our work is to point such men, insiders or outsiders, to the holy scriptures where all men may perceive that a decision for them has already been taken by the gracious election of grace given men in Jesus Christ. In Bonhoeffer we can find a fairly clear alternative theology of culture to these. The modern world is come of age; it is a godless world and man's work is to participate in God's sufferings in the world, to watch with Christ in Gethsemane. If this incomplete vision of Bonhoeffer should prove to be the best one for us, at least for a while, what would this mean? How would it alter the way we look at our theological tasks? Is this theological vision, as I have suggested, really a vision of a theology without a doctrine of God, a doctrine of the church, an eschatology? Is such a thing possible? What would our beloved professors say? What would the ecumenical movement say? And finally, if this vision should prove to be the best one for us for a while, how would it alter the way we look at the godless (if so it be) world? How would it change the way we go about our work of conversation with literature, art, science, psychotherapy? What new clarity could this vision bring to the vexing problems of race and peace? These are just a few of the questions that this unnerving material raises for us today. I don't see how we can disagree with Karl Barth when he remarked that 'the letters are a particular thorn; to let them excite us can only do us all good – for, unlike "demythologizing", this is unrest of a spiritual kind'.

VI

Bonhoeffer and the Young Luther

by Regin Prenter

To what extent the theologian Dietrich Bonhoeffer drew from the ideas of the young Luther is a historical question which shall not concern us here. When Bonhoeffer and the young Luther meet in the title of my paper, it is their essential kinship I think of, not the historical dependence of Bonhoeffer upon Luther.

The point of comparison between them is the way they have correlated the theology of the cross with the theology of the Word.

The young Luther, the author of the early lectures on the Psalms, the *Epistle to the Romans*, the *Epistle to the Galatians* and the *Epistle to the Hebrews* (1513–18), had already, in the so-called 'tower experience', made the rediscovery of the gospel.[1] He had already become a 'theologian of the Word'. In 1519 he wrote, in the *Short Commentary on the Galatians*: 'The Word, I say, and the Word alone, is the vehicle of the grace of God' (*Weimarer Ausgabe*, II, 509, 14). In 1519 this was no new insight for him, for in his first lectures on the Psalms he had said:

The words are namely the vehicle and the feet through which the truth comes into us and upon us, *and* for who has never cried so anxiously

[1] Cf. my article, 'Der barmherzige Richter: Iustitia dei passiva in Luthers Dictata super Psalterium 1513–1515'. *Acta Jutlandica* XXXIII, 2, Aarhus 1961, especially pp. 9–23 and 121–4.

for the words? But because the invisible things are hidden in the words through faith, when one has the words one has everything, through faith, though in a hidden way. And so it is clear that this verse in its literal sense does not aim at the future church or its goods, but at the present church and its goods: which are none other than the gospel of grace, which is the sign and Word not for invisible things but for things to be hoped for (WA, IV, 376, 14).

But this theology of the Word appears in the young Luther in the form of a theology of the cross, which is to be regarded as the necessary correlate of his theology of the Word.

All goods are hidden in and under the cross. Hence they are neither to be sought nor understood except under the cross. So, wretched one that I am, I find in the scriptures nothing but 'Jesus Christ and him crucified'. Jesus Christ is indeed all good that is given to the righteous in scripture, he is joy, hope, glory, power, wisdom. But he is the crucified one, so they do not 'rejoice' in him unless they 'hope' and 'love' him, and despair of themselves and hate their own name.[2]

Luther writes thus in an exposition of Psalm 5. 12, which Vogelsang in his edition regards as a fragment from the second series of lectures on the Psalms in 1518, but which is perhaps even earlier.[3]

In Bonhoeffer's *The Cost of Discipleship* we find a similar union of a theology of the Word with a theology of the cross, which is directed polemically against the representatives of a pseudo-Lutheranism who were advocating an allegedly Reformation theology of the word without the necessary correlate of a theology of the cross, and who thus became pseudo-prophets of cheap grace.

In this union of a theology of the cross with a theology of the Word I see the connexion between Bonhoeffer and the young Luther, though this union is certainly not without its problems.

We come upon the concept of the 'theology of the cross',

[2] *Unbekannte Fragmente aus Luthers zweiter Psalmenvorlesung, 1518,* edited by Erich Vogelsang, Berlin, 1940, p. 88, 28.

[3] See H. Beintker, 'Zur Datierung und Einordnung eines neuen Luther-Fragmentes', in *Wissenschaftliche Zeitschrift der Universität Greifswald,* I, 1951–2. Sprachwissenschaftliche Reihe Nr 2–3, p, 70*ff.*

theologia crucis, in the young Luther not only in the famous 21st Heidelberg Thesis, but also in the *Lectures on the Epistle to the Hebrews*, in the gloss on chapter 12. 11:

These are the two opposites that often occur in scripture: judgement and justification, wrath and grace, death and life, evil and good. And these are the mighty works of the Lord: 'his work which is alien to him, that he may thus do his own work'. In a wonderful way he makes the conscience glad, as in Psalm 4, 'In distress hast thou comforted me', that is, 'thou hast given me room'. And of the infusion of grace we read in Romans 5 'And experience produces hope, and hope does not disappoint us'. This is the theology of the cross, or as the Apostle says, 'The Word of the cross is a scandal to the Jews, and folly to the gentiles, because it is hidden from their eyes' (Hirsch-Rückert, p. 85, 17).

The theology of the cross is thus not just some particular area of theology, such as the theology of the passion of Christ, but it is theology, that is, exposition of scripture, in its entirety in so far as it is able to perceive the hidden unity in all the visible contradictions of the revelatory act of God in Jesus Christ; that is, so far as it is able to hold fast to God's justification in his judgement, to his grace in his wrath, to his gift of life in death, to the good to come in the midst of evil, or as we read in the comment on Isaiah 28. 21 (in an expression often used by Luther), so far as it can grasp God's own work, his *opus proprium*, in and through his alien work, his *opus alienum*. In the 21st Heidelberg Thesis Luther contrasts the theology of glory with this theology of the cross:

The theologian of glory calls evil good and good evil. The theologian of the cross says how things really are. This is clear, because so long as he does not know Christ he does not know the God who is hidden in sufferings. So he prefers works to sufferings, and glory to the cross, and power to weakness, and wisdom to folly, and, in general, good to evil. Those are the ones whom the Apostle calls enemies of the cross of Christ. Because they hate the cross and sufferings, they in truth love works and their glory. So they call the good of the cross evil, and the evil of works good. But I have already said that God can only be found in sufferings and the cross. So the friends of the cross say that the cross is good and works are evil, because through the cross works are destroyed and Adam, who is still more built up by works, is crucified. For it is impossible for a man not to be proud of his good works, unless he has been humbled and destroyed by sufferings and evils, till he knows that he himself is nothing, and his works are not his but God's (WA, I, 362, 21).

In such words we have the whole Luther, not just the young Luther in his closeness to medieval monkish piety. This can be shown without difficulty by a quotation, for example, from the *de servo arbitrio*:

God has assuredly promised his grace to the humbled, that is, to those who have surrendered themselves and are in despair. No man, indeed, can be humbled until he knows that his salvation lies entirely beyond his own powers, designs, endeavours, will, works, and entirely depends upon the discretion, designs, will and work of another, namely, upon God alone. For so long as man is convinced that he can accomplish even a small portion of his salvation, he relies upon himself and does not basically despair of himself. So he does not humble himself before God, but seeks, or hopes, or at least desires a place, a time, and a work by which he may at last attain to salvation. But he who does not doubt that everything depends on God's will despairs entirely of himself, he chooses nothing, but awaits the God who works there. He is nearest to grace that he may be saved. Therefore these things are preached for the sake of the elect, that, humbled and reduced to nothing in this way, they may be saved. The others resist this humiliation, they even condemn the teaching of this despair in themselves, they want something, however slight, to be left to them, which they can manage themselves. They remain secretly proud, and adversaries of the grace of God (WA, XVIII, 632, 29).

Therefore that there may be room for faith everything that is believed must be hidden. It is most thoroughly hidden when it is directly opposed to appearance, to the sense, and to experience. Thus when God makes alive, he does it by slaying. When he justifies, he does it by making us guilty. When he leads us to heaven, he does it by leading us to hell, as it is written, 'The Lord kills and brings to life; he brings down to Sheol and raises up' (I Samuel 2. 6) (WA, XVIII, 633, 7).

The God of the gospel is thus, according to Luther, the God who reveals himself in the cross of Jesus Christ, the God hidden in suffering. Only that man is justified before this God who himself carries the cross and whose works under this cross have become nothing. The cross which destroys our works and ruins us, however, is not a 'self-chosen' cross, as in so many forms of medieval mysticism of the cross. It is not the symbol of a way of life which we by some form of *imitatio Christi* can realize by ourselves. No, the cross which kills us and our works is the cross which comes upon us in the real sufferings and temptations of our own life, and is identical, in a mysterious way, with the cross which the Reconciler Jesus Christ bore for the sake of our sin.

This is the novelty and peculiarity of the young Luther's theology of the cross in comparison with medieval imitative piety. In the *imitatio Christi* Christ's cross was not simply identical with our cross. For his cross was the ideal upon which ours was to be modelled. But for the young Luther the cross of Christ is not primarily the pattern of humility, which has been given to us to be imitated, but it is the true punishment for our sin, which he endured in our place. So in the young Luther's theology of the cross the words, 'God has revealed himself in the cross of Jesus Christ', have a twofold meaning. First they mean, 'God's love for sinners can be recognized by them only in the love with which the Son of God bore punishment in their place on the cross.' In this sense the young Luther often describes Christ himself as the justification given to us by God in the gospel, through which we, in faith in him, are justified before God. 'For just as Christ is the mercy and truth of God for us, so he is also the justification and the peace of God for us' (WA, IV, 13, 36). In this interpretation of the words the young Luther is a true Reformation theologian of the Word.

But secondly the words mean, 'This love of God which we recognize only in the cross of Jesus Christ is accepted by us only so far as we willingly take up our own cross. For because Christ on his cross truly bore our punishment, and because his cross is thus ultimately identical with our cross, when we hate our own cross we hate his cross as well, and when we love his cross we love our own cross.' In this sense the young Luther often identifies faith with humility, *fides Christi* with *humilitas* as *condemnatio sui*.[4] In this second interpretation of the

4 Cf. R. Prenter, Der Barmherziger Richter, pp. 132–40.

words Luther is a theologian of the cross. And it seems as if he thereby materially modifies his theology of the Word. For the Word which speaks from the cross of Christ here seems to become ominously dependent upon the humility and readiness of the hearer to take up his own cross. But there can be no doubt that the young Luther could not relinquish this second interpretation of the words, 'God reveals himself in the cross of Jesus Christ.'

This problematic interpretation of the theology of the Word by means of the theology of the cross we find in Bonhoeffer as well. In *The Cost of Discipleship* the thesis is presented that 'only the believer is obedient, and only he who is obedient believes.' Corresponding to this thesis are the two apparently contradictory sentences from the young Luther's first lecture on the Psalms: 'On the basis of faith I now recognize that I was just nothing and wretched' (WA, IV, 272, 36), and 'No one is justified by faith unless he has already confessed himself through humility to be unjust. This is humility' (WA, IV, 345, 29). In Bonhoeffer's words this is, 'Only the believer is humble, and only the humble man believes.' The first half of this sentence would certainly still be regarded as good Reformation theology, and it expresses very well the usual theology of the Word. But the second half of the sentence could only be accepted as Reformation theology with certain reservations, for here faith is made dependent on human conditions. A concealed synergism may be glimpsed.

But the thought of the second half of the sentence ('only the humble man believes') is not only to be found in the young pre-Reformation Luther. We heard exactly the same thing in the *de servo arbitrio*: 'Therefore these things are preached for the sake of the elect, that, humbled and reduced to nothing in this way, they may be saved. The others resist this humiliation, they even condemn the teaching of this despair in themselves . . . they remain secretly proud, and adversaries of the grace of God' (WA, XVIII, 632, 29).

The young Luther and Bonhoeffer thus both recognize that the ability to believe is joined to a condition about the desire to believe. But this has nothing to do with synergism. The believer does not make it possible for Christ to come to him by the fulfilment of a condition, but Christ makes it possible for the believer to come to him through the fulfilment of that condition by the believer. Luther expresses this in his interpretation of a word-pair which often occurs in the Psalter: *iustitia-iudicium dei*. Christ is the justification which has been given to us from God. But he is this as the Crucified One, as the one who bears our judgement in our place. So he is our justification (*iustitia*) and our judgement (*iudicium*) in one. If the faith by which we are justified before God, the *fides Christi*, is a fleeing to the crucified one who bears our curse, this faith is impossible if we are unwilling to acknowledge the judgement which is passed upon us in him. For our being judged cannot be separated from him as the Son of God who has become flesh and has been crucified. To want to escape this judgement is to want to escape the crucified one, and is thus a desire not to believe in him. In this sense it is true that the Word of Christ, in order to find faith in us, is made dependent on a condition within us. But this is so because the Word proclaims the Christ who has become flesh and was crucified, that is, the Christ who assumed our flesh and bore our curse, and not a 'Christ in himself'.

If we do not fulfil that condition which we must fulfil in order to be able to believe, we have already denied the content of the Word; we have denied the incarnation and the reconciliation: we have deprived the substitution of Jesus Christ of reality. When one disputes the necessity of fulfilling this condition in order to believe (say, in 'Reformed' orthodoxy) one denies in the last resort that the Son of God has become flesh. Then the cross of Christ ceases to be the true cross, which is identical with my cross, my rejection and my curse. The cross becomes instead a 'principle', for example the principle of cheap grace (the orthodox Lutheran perversion of the cross) or the principle of the *imitatio Christi*, of self-chosen suffering, of a readiness for death which I myself have accepted and affirmed (the medieval, and the modern liberal or modern existentialist perversion of the cross).

In Luther as well as in Bonhoeffer the theology of the cross as a correlate of the theology of the Word, the condition for the ability to believe which rests in obedience and humility, is understandable only on the basis of this christological centre. Every theology of the Word which does not require a theology of the cross as correlate is docetic. It transforms Christ, the content of the Word, into a principle of grace, and thus transforms faith into an intellectual acceptance of this principle. This is a *theologia verbi* as a *theologia gloriae*. Both the young Luther and Bonhoeffer combat such a theology of the Word with their *theologia crucis*. In the name of the authentic faith in the Word of the crucified one they must affirm that there is no faith without humility, that is, without obedient discipleship.

Only on this basis does it seem to me that we can fully understand those thoughts of the later Bonhoeffer on the non-religious interpretation of the gospel in a world come of age which have been discussed with such liveliness at our earlier meetings.

The clearest passage is in a letter of 16 July 1944 (LPP, p. 121*ff.* Translation altered and missing sentence added).

And the only way to be honest is to recognize that we have to live in the world *etsi deus non daretur*. And this is just what we do recognize – before God! God himself compels us to recognize this. So our coming of age leads us to a true recognition of our situation before God. God teaches us that we must live as men who manage to deal with life without God. The God who is with us is the God who forsakes us (Mark 15. 34). The God who lets us live in the world without the working hypothesis of God is the God before whom we are ever standing. Before God and with God we live without God. God allows himself to be driven out of the world on to the cross. God is powerless and weak in the world, and that is exactly the way, the only way, he is with us and helps us. Matthew 8. 17 says quite clearly that Christ does not help by his omnipotence, but by his weakness, his suffering! Here is the critical difference from all religions. Man's religiosity sends him in his need to the power of God in the world, God is the *deus ex machina*. The Bible sends man to the powerlessness and suffering of God; only the suffering God can help. To this extent we may say that the process we have described by which the world came of age was an abandonment of a false conception of God and a freeing of one's look for the God of the Bible, who wins power and space in the world by his powerlessness. This must surely be the starting-point for the 'worldly interpretation'.

It is clear that the idea of the world come of age and of non-religious interpretation is a *theologia crucis* (directed against the *theologia gloriae* of religiosity), which is, moreover, closely connected to the young Luther's *theologia crucis*. The religious interpretation of Christianity operates with a false idea of God, in which God is conjured up as the *deus ex machina* for the solution of otherwise insoluble human problems. This God ('the working hypothesis of God') who is supposed to have power in the world, that is, a power over the world which is put into our hands, is God as a principle, not the God who has become flesh. When he appears in the garb of Christ – as in the religious interpretation of Christianity – Christ himself is interpreted as a principle, as the author of some 'Christ-like quality' which we wish to press upon the world, by means of which we try simultaneously to deprive the world of its maturity and Christ of his incarnation in the fallen world. The true God does not allow himself to be transformed into a principle for the christianizing of the world. For he has indeed become flesh: he hangs on the cross, the tree of life, which stands in the centre of the world, and he does not turn up, like the god of the stop-gaps, only in the so called boundary situations. With and before this true God we live without God, that is, without the false God, without God as a principle, without God as a power over the world which is put into our hands. One cannot live *with* the false God of the religious interpretation of Christianity, and one cannot stand *before* him. For as a principle God exists merely in the minds of men. The true God, the incarnate Son of God on the cross, must leave us, forsake us, in order to approach us and meet us as a person. He leaves us alone, without any divine help for our lives. He lets us come of age in order to be able to help us. He does not help us as a power within our own sphere of power. He helps us through his worldly weakness, in which he is close to us as the loving person of God.

It is indisputable that Bonhoeffer is saying here that the powerless God really does help us, that through his power-lessness in the world he really does win power and space. This is also said in the well-known poem, 'Christians and Unbelievers': (LPP, p. 174).

> *Men go to God when they are sore bestead*
> *Pray to him for succour, for his peace, for bread,*
> *For mercy for them sick, sinning, or dead:*
> *All men do so, Christian and unbelieving.*

So Bonhoeffer does not say that one can escape religious idolatry by no longer coming to God in one's need, or by trying to replace religious idolatry by an irreligious atheism, say in the form of a Christianity without the cultus, a this-worldly, merely ethical Christianity. This kind of thing would not be a *theologia crucis* at all, but an irreligious, atheistic theology of glory. No: 'all men do so, Christian and unbelieving'. They all go to God – to some God or other – in their need and pray to him for succour. They do it because they are men.

But the true God, who is not an idol, confronts the Christians among these men. The true God, God in his need, the crucified God:

> *Men go to God when he is sore bestead,*
> *Find him poor and scorned, without shelter or bread,*
> *Whelmed under weight of the wicked, the weak, the dead:*
> *Christians stand by God in his hour of grieving.*

Here again we find Bonhoeffer speaking of standing by God, living with and before God, as we heard in the letter of 16 July 1944. This true God, unlike an idol, is not to be found at the boundaries of human existence, where human power changes into powerlessness. Like the tree of life in paradise he stands in the centre of the world. There he stands in his suffering.

There, he is the help which all men seek. There, where religious people did not seek him, who knew him only in the boundary situations of their life as the powerful completion of their own powerlessness, he comes to them and helps them – in the centre of their 'normal' life, where men are healthy and are leading a successful life in their world come of age.

> *God goeth to every man when sore bestead,*
> *Feedeth body and spirit with his bread,*
> *For Christians, heathens alike he hangeth dead:*
> *And both alike forgiving.*

Certainly God's help is a help for men. But it is not a help which appears only as a completion of human powerlessness, in order to be transformed into human power. God's help is the daily bread for body and soul, and it is forgiveness. Thus it is quite clear that forgiveness, as well as bread, is to be understood 'non-religiously'. It is not a psycho-therapeutic cure for especially guilt-laden neurotics, but like bread it is a necessity of life for all men. It is what permits men to live, and liberates them from just 'having to live'.

I mentioned the cross as the tree of life in the centre of paradise. This image is found in the last chapter of the short work, *Creation and Fall*, surely the loveliest and most profound of all Bonhoeffer's writings.

Christ on the cross, the murdered Son of God, is the end of the history of Cain, and thus the end of history as a whole. This is the last desperate assault on the gateway to paradise. And under the beating sword, under the cross, mankind dies. But Christ lives. The stem of the cross becomes the staff of life, and life is now established anew on that accursed field, in the midst of the world. In the centre of the world, on the wood of the cross there wells up the source of life, and all who thirst for life are called to this water, and he who has eaten of the wood of this life will never more hunger or thirst. A strange paradise is this mount of Calvary, this cross, this blood, this broken body, a strange tree of life, this stem on which God himself had to suffer and die – but it is the very kingdom of life, which God in grace has given again, kingdom of resurrection, it is the opened door of imperishable hope, of expectation, and of patience. Tree of life, cross of Christ, centre of the fallen and preserved world of God, it is the end of the story of paradise for us.

> *Today he opens again the door*
> *Of paradise the fair,*
> *But the angel is no longer there.*
> *To God be glory praise and honour* (cf. CF, p. 95*f.*)

What Bonhoeffer means by the centre of the world can be seen in his exposition of Genesis 2. 8–17. 'It is peculiar to man that his life circles always round its own centre, but he never takes possession of it' (cf. *ibid.*, p. 50). This centre from which his life flows to him is therefore also his boundary. *'Man's boundary is in the centre of his life,* not at its edge. The boundary which is sought on the edge of man's life is the boundary of his created state, of his techniques, of his possibility. The boundary which is in the centre is the boundary of his reality, simply the boundary of his life' (cf. *ibid.*, p. 51). Through the fall man has transgressed his boundary and become his own creator (cf. *ibid.*, p. 73). 'Man is *sicut deus.* Now he lives from his own powers, now he creates his life himself, he is his own creator, he no longer needs the creator, he has himself become the creator, in so far as he creates his own life. So his creatureliness is settled and destroyed' (cf. *ibid.*, p. 73). He has fallen into the power of death. For '. . . to be dead . . . means to have life not as a gift but as a command . . . To be dead means having to live . . . In life as a command something is demanded of me that I am not in a position to fulfil. I am to live from myself, out of my own powers, and I cannot' (cf. *ibid.*, p. 54*f.*).

So life after the fall is a constant dying, 'having to live' without being able to live, because the presupposition for being able to live, the tree of life in the centre, God himself as the giver of reality to my life, is denied. In order to see the relation between this theology of creation and fall and the ideas of the world come of age and the non-religious interpretation of Christianity, it is important to see that it is precisely the religious interpretation of belief in God that is peculiar to fallen man. Because fallen man exists in death, that is, in having to live from his own powers, yet without being able to live in this world, he tries to get God into his power, so that through him – not as the centre, not as the giver of life, but as the *deus ex machina* of the boundary situations – he may take possession of the power of living from himself.

But on Golgotha the tree of life once more stands in the centre of the world. That is to say, here again life is seen as a gift of the Creator and at the same time as the boundary. One is tempted to express the meaning of this new tree of life by an antithesis to Bonhoeffer's definition of being dead. Being dead is to have life as a command. To be alive, on the other hand, would be to receive death as a gift. To be dead means to *have* to live. To be alive would mean to be permitted to die.[5]

There is no doubt of the relation between these thoughts about Christ as the centre of the world and the letter of 25 May 1944, where the theme of non-religious interpretation is mentioned:

As far as the idea of 'solutions' is concerned, the Christian answers are no less and no more compelling than other possible solutions. Here too God is not a stop-gap. God wishes to be recognized not just at the boundary of our possibilities, but in the centre of life; in life, and not only in death, in health and vigour, and not only in suffering, in activity and not only in sin. The basis for this lies in the revelation of God in Jesus Christ. He is the centre of life, and he did not come in order to answer our unsolved questions (cf. LPP, p. 104 – translation altered).

And similarly in the letter of 30 April 1944:

Religious people speak of God when human perception (often just because they are too lazy to think) is at an end, or when human resources fail: it is in fact always the *deus ex machina* whom they bring

[5] Cf. *Christology*, 1933, the section on 'The Place of Christ', c, pp. 61–6.

marching in, either for the pseudo-solving of insoluble problems or as the strength for when human resources fail – always, that is to say, in the exploitation of human weakness or on the boundaries of human existence. Of necessity this goes on only until men in their own strength push back the boundaries a little further, and God becomes super-fluous as a *deus ex machina*. Talk of human boundaries at all seems to me now to be a questionable matter. Is even death today, since men scarcely fear it any more, and sin, which they scarcely understand any more, still a genuine boundary? It always seems to me that in these ways we were only anxious to make room for God. I should like to speak of God not at the boundaries, but in the centre, not in weak-nesses, but in strength, not therefore in death and guilt, but in man's life and good. On the boundaries it seems to me better to be silent and to leave unsolved what is insoluble. Resurrection faith is not the solution of the problem of death. The 'beyond' of God is not the beyond of our power to know. The transcendence of epistemological theory has nothing to do with the transcendence of God. God is the beyond in the midst of our life. The church does not stand where human powers fail, on the boundaries, but in the midst of the village. So it is in the Old Testament, and by this token we still read the New Testament far too little on the basis of the Old (*ibid.*, p. 93 – translation altered).

In order to avoid attributing any pseudo-christian vitalism to such remarks, we must keep in mind the centre to which they are referring. It is the centre of the tree of life. And the church which stands and speaks in this centre is the church under the cross. The moving anti-religious affirmation of life which is to be found in such passages in the letters comes from the cross. One can and may affirm natural life, health, work, indeed everything this-worldly, because the tree of life of the cross of Jesus stands at the centre, and because from this centre there flows the permission to die in place of having to live. And it is the permission to die which alone contains a genuine ability to live in this world, where having to live destroys this ability. As in the religious interpretation of Christianity God and Christ are transformed into a principle and thus misunderstood as a power which is in man's hands, a power which in real life is powerless, so on the other hand in the non-religious interpretation of the gospel God in his

174

powerlessness, the crucified one, is a real power in the centre of human ability.

The theology of the cross is concerned with a genuine encounter between the church under the cross and the world come of age. Put precisely, the world is only of age when it is faced with the church of the cross, and the church is only the church of the cross when it is faced with the world come of age.

The world which faces the church today is the modern secularized civilized world. The world has finally outgrown all earlier attempts at christianization and has come of age in its relationship to the church. The church which respects and affirms the fact that the world has now come of age is solely the church under the cross. Since the church no longer wishes to rule the world, it lives for the world in the crucified one.

This 'being for the world' on the part of the church does not in the least mean that the church has taken on the form of the world. On the contrary, the church was in the form of the world when it wanted to christianize it by means of the 'religious' interpretation of Christianity. Thus in Bonhoeffer's ideas concerning the non-religious interpretation of the gospel in the world come of age, nothing is retracted from what he said in *The Cost of Discipleship* about the need for Christians to break with immediacies and about their salvation as separation from the world, or about their frontal attack on the world, or about the visibility of the church. Nor is anything retracted of what he said in *Life Together* about 'Christian brotherhood'. All this is an indispensable presupposition of the non-religious interpretation.

For how does the crucified one stand in the centre of the world if he is there for the world? Certainly not as the principle for the christianization of the world. He is there as the preached Christ, but that is not the whole story. A principle, too, can be 'preached', when preaching is understood as the presentation of a doctrine. But the fact that the living Christ, the crucified and risen Christ, is preached, means that he is proclaimed as the one who is present in person.[6] That is why, as Bonhoeffer makes clear in his 1933 Christology lectures, and in the second part of *The Cost of Discipleship*, the sacraments and the congregation itself belong with the proclaimed Word to the form of the present Christ. 'As Christ is present as the Word and in the Word, as the sacrament and in the sacrament, so too he is present as community and in the community', we read in the Christology lectures (c, p. 59). And he adds: 'The presence in Word and sacrament is related to his presence in the community as reality to figure. Christ is the community by virtue of his being *pro me*. His form, indeed his only form, is the community between the ascension and the second coming.' This is in exact accordance with *The Cost of Discipleship*, where we read: 'The earthly body of Jesus underwent crucifixion and death. In that death the new humanity undergoes crucifixion and death. Christ had taken upon him not a man, but the human form, sinful flesh, human "nature", so that all whom he bore suffer and die with him. It is all our infirmities and all our sin that he bears to the cross. It is *we* who are crucified with him, and we who die with him. True, his earthly body undergoes death, but only to rise again as an incorruptible, glorious body. It is the same body – the tomb was empty – and yet it is a new body. And so as he dies, Jesus bears the human race, and carries it onward to resurrection. Thus, too, he bears for ever in his glorified body the humanity which he had taken upon him on earth' (cd, p. 214).

Here one may even speak of an embodiment of the gospel. The reconciliation proclaimed in the gospel by the substitution of Jesus Christ for sinners is not a quasi-legal fiction. It is not proclaimed of him that he was dying *as if* he had committed our sins. It is said that he is dying *because* he had committed our sins. For he had assumed our sinful flesh.

[6] Cf. the important parallel in *Christology*, 'The present Christ', c, pp. 43–67.

The forgiveness of sins which the gospel promises us in him is thus no general idea, which can be lectured about, but it is bodily fellowship with him. 'How then do we come to participate in the body of Christ, who did all this for us?' asks Bonhoeffer, and he replies: 'We participate in the body of Christ through the two sacraments of his body, baptism and the Lord's Supper . . . The sacraments begin and end in the body of Christ, and it is only the presence of that body which makes them what they are . . . The word of preaching does not make us members of Christ's body; the sacrament . . . must be added. Baptism incorporates us into the unity of the body of Christ, and the Lord's Supper fosters and sustains our fellowship and communion (*koinonia*) in that Body' (CD, p. 215). Through this bodily participation in the body of Christ the congregation itself becomes the body of Christ in this world. Through those who are made part of his body in this way, the crucified and risen Christ lives in the centre of the world. He exists through the Holy Spirit as the church (*ibid.*, p. 215).

The gospel, the preaching of the crucified and risen one, is only the true preaching of the gospel when there is this embodiment.

So this embodiment of the Word in the sacrament and in the visible community in Bonhoeffer's *The Cost of Discipleship* is a genuine expression of his theology of the cross in correlation with his theology of the Word.

In *The Cost of Discipleship* this embodiment of the Word acquires great hermeneutical significance. For by its means Bonhoeffer is able to actualize in the community of the risen one the theology of discipleship which he unfolds in the first half of the book on the basis of the Synoptic Gospels. 'If we would hear his call to follow, we must listen where he is to be found, that is, in the church through the ministry of Word and sacrament. The preaching of the church and the administration of the sacraments is the place where Jesus Christ is present. If you would hear the call of Jesus you need no personal revelation: all you have to do is to hear the sermon and receive the sacrament, that is, to hear the gospel of Christ crucified and risen. Here he is, the same Christ whom the disciples encountered, the same Christ whole and entire. Yes, here he is already, the glorified, victorious and living Lord. Only he himself can call us to follow him' (CD, p. 201*f.*).

If we eliminate this side of his theology of the cross in the interpretation of Bonhoeffer's ideas about the non-religious interpretation of the gospel in a world come of age, then we are bound to understand his suggestions as a kind of secularization of the gospel. For in that case the living, crucified and risen Christ, existing as the church, no longer stands at the place of the tree of life in the middle of the world. For then he has again been replaced by a principle, by an ideological camouflaging of the gospel, a new accommodation of the gospel to one of the many world views of the time. If we understand his views about the non-religious interpretation of the gospel in this way, then Bonhoeffer has basically said nothing new. But he has laid the foundation upon which syncretist theologians can construct a 'Christianity suited to the time and to the style', similar to the attempts of the 'German Christians' in the Third Reich. I therefore believe that it is very important, in interpreting Bonhoeffer's theology, not to separate his thoughts about discipleship and about a non-religious interpretation as two parts of an historical development. But they must be held together, as I have tried to do here, and interpreted in the context of one and the same theology of the cross.

In this connexion it is not unimportant to note that we find a parallel to this aspect of Bonhoeffer's theology of the cross in the young Luther. For the theology of the cross was of extreme hermeneutical importance to the young Luther as well. This is especially clear in the first *Lectures on the Psalms*, in the radical transformation of the so-called *quadriga*, the doctrine of the four-fold meaning of scripture. I cannot go into details here, but must give my view summarily.[7] In the so-called 'literal prophetical' exposition of the Psalms Luther interprets the 'I' of the Psalms of lament as Christ. So the humiliation of the incarnate Son of God is emphasized with unprecedented radicality. In these Psalms Christ is always surrounded by enemies who mock and persecute him. In the tropological exposition everything that is said 'literally' of Christ and his enemies is expounded in terms of the new man, the believer, or of his flesh, the old man. The combination of the literal-prophetic (we say, the *heilsgeschichtlich*-christological) and the tropological (we say, the anthropological-soterio-logical) exposition is effected by the proclamation and faith. The tropological exposition is related to Christ's second, spiritual coming, and the literal-prophetic to his first coming in the flesh. I quote a few lines from the *scholia* on Psalm 85:

The tropology of the Psalm will be easily apparent, I think, from what has been repeatedly said. For what is said about the first coming in the flesh has also to be said at the same time about the spiritual coming. In fact the coming in the flesh is ordered and takes place on account of this spiritual coming. Otherwise it would be of no benefit. Hence we may use these words 'mercy and truth' of Christ only on account of the second coming. That is the whole intention of the first coming. For what would have been the use of God becoming man if we were not saved through faith in him? Thus Christ is called justice, peace, mercy and our salvation, in his person, because of his effective-ness upon us. But it is by faith in Christ that we are justified and through which he reigns in us (WA, IV, 19, 31).

When Christ enters a man spiritually through the Word and faith, his struggle with his enemies is repeated. These are now present in the man himself. Luther says this very plainly in his *scholia* to Psalm 31:

Certainly this is the rule for the tropological exposition: whatever Christ laments in the Psalms, and whatever he prays in bodily pain, in the literal sense of the words, is lamented and prayed in the same words by every believing soul who is born in Christ and taught by him, and

[7] I have established the detail for the following Luther interpretation in the work mentioned above, notes 1 and 4.

179

who knows that he is tempted by sin or fallen into sin. Because Christ is to this day spat upon, slain, tortured and crucified in ourselves. So in every way, and without cessation, Christ is waylaid by the flesh with its senses, the world with its pleasures, and the devil with his insinuations and temptations, just as the Jews waylaid him in the body (WA, III, 167, 20).

This means that for Luther, too, faith is a real bodily participation in the living Christ which engages the believer in a real struggle with the enemies of Christ. This struggle between the spirit and the flesh, between the new and the old man, is, according to the tropological exposition, inseparable from faith. Faith means to be crucified in and with Christ. Faith *is* discipleship.

The sacrament and the church began to matter as subjects for the young Luther only after the controversy about absolution. So one cannot trace in him precisely the same line from the bodiliness of discipleship to the sacrament and to the visible church as we can see in Bonhoeffer. This is the limit of the analogy. None the less the emphasis that is already noticeable in Luther's first writings on the sacrament on the bodiliness of the sacraments is not unrelated to his theology of the cross. I quote a few sentences from his sermon on the Lord's Supper of 1519:

He has not only instituted simply these two sacraments over everything, but he has given his truly natural body in the bread and his truly natural blood in the wine, that he may give a perfect sacrament or sign. Then at the same time as the bread is transformed into his true natural body and the wine into his true natural blood, we too become true in the spiritual body, that is, we become drawn into and transformed in the communion of Christ and all the saints, and through this sacrament we are placed in all the virtue and grace of Christ and his saints (WA, II, 749, 7).

Both in word and content this comes very close to what we quoted earlier from the second part of *The Cost of Discipleship*. For the young Luther, too, there is no faith that does not involve bodily discipleship, that is, a real community with Christ and his saints. That is especially clear in the sacrament of fellowship. The struggle of the older Luther against the enemies of the sacrament is already intimated in the young Luther.

Both in the young Luther and in Dietrich Bonhoeffer the theology of the cross is to be regarded as a correlate of their theology of the Word. In this they are related. In Luther's time, as today, there is an alleged 'Reformed' theology of the Word without that correlate. The older Luther fought it in the Antinomians, and Bonhoeffer fought it in the pseudo-Lutheranism of the time of the church struggle. There was and there is also a theology of the cross without a theology of the Word as its correlate. The young Luther encountered it in the form of the *imitatio* of medieval mysticism of the cross; and perhaps if Bonhoeffer's *The Cost of Discipleship* is interpreted in isolation in a too pietistic fashion he could be regarded as being nearer to these medieval mystics than to the young Luther. But that, I think, would be a mistake. Like the young Luther Bonhoeffer wanted a theology of the Word which was at the same time a theology of the cross.

The contemporary theological climate is not favourable to such a union of a theology of the Word with a theology of the cross. This is especially true of the hyper-nationalist church in Denmark, where there is not even the legacy of a church struggle. It is certainly not always easy to harmonize a theology of the Word and a theology of the cross in either the young Luther or Bonhoeffer. But it is here that I see the advantage of their theology over all modern, slick and unproblematic repristinations of an allegedly 'pure' Reformed theology of the Word. I cannot regard it as a sign of theological health to settle with the young Luther's theology of the cross as 'merely' pre-reformed, and with Bonhoeffer's theology of the cross in *The Cost of Discipleship* as suspiciously non-reformed.

VII

Concerning the Reception and Interpretation of Dietrich Bonhoeffer

by Hanfried Müller[1]

Anyone who has anything to do with Dietrich Bonhoeffer today realizes again and again the amazing extent to which he provides answers to questions that only now, some twenty years later, begin to raise their heads. He anticipated solutions for problems we are only now beginning to recognize as our problems. When I speak here of 'us' and 'we', I mean those among us who see the necessity of thinking in the light of the revolutionary upheaval of our time, during the course of which central Europe has seen the socialization of society. A Protestant church which still bases its thinking on a Christendom which it regards as the definitive ideology for the Western world simply does not know what it is doing. In the midst of these uncertainties, one discovers Dietrich Bonhoeffer.

Our reception and interpretation of Bonhoeffer cannot be independent of the position that we ourselves take; for only from our own position do the questions and problems arise whose solutions we find in a critical acceptance of his heritage.

[1] The content of this lecture, delivered at the Bonhoeffer-Tagung in Berlin on 3 August 1961, is based on a paper given in November 1956 at the central candidates' seminar for theological faculties in the DDR in Leipzig (published in part in the *Neue Zeit* of 3 and 12 December 1956). It also concerns paragraph 18 of my book *Von der Kirche zur Welt*, Leipzig and Hamburg, 1961.

Reception and Interpretation of Bonhoeffer

We can interpret Bonhoeffer only if we use his heritage as a *living* heritage, and that means only if we continue to suffer, struggle and hope where he has suffered, struggled and hoped – certainly not by formal imitation, but with the same ends in mind, and no doubt under altered historical conditions, yet looking in the same direction. His heritage would be neither understandable nor fruitful were we to try to preserve it in some neutral, indifferent and apparently objective manner, detached from all controversy with and within the church and the world. If we do not wish to continue Bonhoeffer's struggle, then we will not be able to follow his thinking, or take up his theology and carry it forward. Otherwise we would slide into a Bonhoeffer orthodoxy, an ultimately sterile imitation which tries in vain, by reconstructing and systematizing, to make a dead man speak. Any heritage treated in such a fashion cannot but remain mute.

I believe that the right way to follow Bonhoeffer is to take up his development, his path, his intention and the tendency of his work: to follow him rather than stifle his vigour and vitality with a system. I think that understanding of the *whole* Bonhoeffer will come about not by systematizing everything he thought as though it were all on the same level, and thus relativizing it, but rather by taking up the *movement* of his thought in its entirety as the thing which can lead us further. Then the question arises (especially for those who were and are close to Bonhoeffer) which direction he would have taken had he been allowed to live to see the liberation in 1945. What is at stake is really the question (no doubt unhistorical, but which none the less cannot be waved aside as naïve by any historico-methodological sophistry): where would Bonhoeffer stand today? And here, just because the question seems so insoluble (and formulated in this way really is insoluble), and because it seems so irreverent and base to use Bonhoeffer's heritage to further one's own ends, to claim and exploit it for one's own purposes, one is inclined to restrict oneself to the very historical understanding of Bonhoeffer which will drain the life-blood from his heritage.

If the question: Where would Bonhoeffer stand today? cannot be answered on this basis, it can certainly be answered in the form: Who may legitimately take up Bonhoeffer? In this form the question is not left to the contingent and subjective decision of the individual, but is directed towards the historical and objective significance of a development which is already concluded.

The lively interest in Bonhoeffer today stems from the fact that Bonhoeffer's thoughts are not dead, but are full of anticipations of our time. For during the last period of his life, Bonhoeffer thought deliberately in terms of the future. The ultimate responsible question became for him 'how the coming generation is to live' and he knew that 'only out of this historically responsible question' could 'fruitful, if also, for the time being, humiliating solutions arise' (LPP, pp. 138–9).

By Bonhoeffer's last period I mean (and most scholars would concur) the period of the second world war, during which time he did not publish anything of his own (as a result of his political activity in the 20 July Resistance Movement: an activity at first limited, but increasing until his arrest). He left behind only fragments, sketches, notes and letters, many of which have been assembled in the *Ethics* and the *Letters and Papers from Prison* as evidence for his development at that time. In these two collections we see that, unlike the second and first periods, Bonhoeffer is no longer dealing primarily and almost exclusively with the church but much more with responsibility for the whole of society; because in this period Bonhoeffer acted and suffered in responsibility for society.[2] In the same way, this is a period of looking to the

---

[2] Certainly Bonhoeffer's final theological utterances have to do with 'performing a service for the church of the future' (LPP, p. 166). But this service really involves directing the church to the 'this-worldliness of Christianity', i.e. not towards clericalism but towards historical responsibility.

future, in which ideas are expressed for the expected event, namely, the break-up of Nazism. At times he thinks of society ecclesiastically, at other times anti-clerically; on the one hand he envisages an inner victory over Nazism on the basis of the old social structure of Europe and of political circumstances brought about by Fascism itself; on the other hand he is thinking of a social upheaval and the break-down of the old bourgeois order.

If, then, this wartime period is to be seen as a unity as far as its social responsibility and social outlook are concerned, then it should be seen as the unity of an immense *development* (objectively conditioned, no doubt, by the change in the character of the war during its course). Indeed, this was a process of rethinking that was intellectually revolutionary – and here as with the whole of Bonhoeffer's heritage the unity and wholeness is not that of a system, but rather that of a process which cannot legitimately be understood metaphysically, but only dialectically.

Here let me raise the question of the legitimate reception of Bonhoeffer and deal with it in the light of this wartime period, dominated as it is by the sharpest contradictions – and thus by what is qualitatively the most significant development – that may be found anywhere in Bonhoeffer's works. We obscure this development and these contradictions if we diminish either the overall value of the letters or the objectivity and general validity of their message for the future development of theology. We may do this by agreeing with Barth's scepticism concerning these 'enigmatic utterances', or by attempting to do in our interpretation what Moltmann does: interpret the letters by means of the *Ethics*, then this in turn by means of the preceding period, so that the final thoughts are seen simply as a turning towards a new theme or as a broadening of the horizon. We may also, however, speak with Hammelsbeck and others of an *ersatz* religion, or of a religion as *ersatz*, where Bonhoeffer speaks of religionlessness, and we may, lastly, relativize the problems of the letters as 'open questions', or subjectivize and individualize them by pointing to the frontier situation in which they arose.

Actually, all these tendencies to undermine the general validity of the new thoughts in the letters only demonstrate the contradiction which is sensed within this last period, only to be abolished through a systematic harmonizing rather than a dialectical interpretation – whether they devalue these thoughts by methodically holding them alongside the earlier writings (even the *Ethics*) as their source, or by working them back into the *Ethics* and explaining them in such a way that they find a place for themselves there.

Now, this contradiction is undoubtedly there. Let me single out just two examples. The Bonhoeffer of the *Ethics* can speak of *ersatz* religion in examining the phenomenon of the coming religionlessness – indeed, he can speak of the 'religion of Bolshevism' and depict Western godlessness in its entirety as religious (E, p. 39). But only the *Letters and Papers from Prison* speak seriously of religionlessness. Actually, Western secularization appears to Bonhoeffer in the *Ethics* as something threatening: 'the people found that they had come of age' (E, p. 37) is connected with the description of the great apostasy and degeneration of the Western heritage. But in the *Letters and Papers from Prison* the world come of age forms the centre of an optimistic way of thinking – not as endangered and threatened, but in its legitimate autonomy – and the description of apostasy and degeneration seems an illegitimate apologetic (LPP, p. 107: 8 June 1944). But even this contradiction is not like a clean cut between the *Ethics* and the letters; its lively force pushes ahead and impels one forward. It is far less schematic, a contradiction within the fragments of the *Ethics* and the letters which characterizes the development of the entire period, but in such a way that it becomes clearly visible at the end that the solution of this contradiction is found, that it is resolved, even though Bonhoeffer lacked the time to eliminate the things he had overcome.

This contradiction is merely the reflection of the contradiction which characterized the historical period out of which
these documents emerged. It is the period of the second world
war. It extends from the initial German victories in the
struggle for a new, imperialistic partitioning of the world; to
the turning-point of the war in the attack on the Soviet
Union, the struggle for liberation among those people
oppressed by Germany, and the Battle of Stalingrad; and
beyond, to the landing of the Western allies in Cherbourg
and the military defeat of Germany. Within this area
determined primarily by the war, the inner political development was completed.

The original goal of Bonhoeffer, as with the political powers
with which he identified himself at this time, was the rescue
of the grand heritage of the Christian West in the face of
Nazism. Here one overlooks, as Bonhoeffer did at the
beginning, the fact that Fascism is itself the last stage of
decay, the putrefaction of the superannuated bourgeois
society in Germany, and cannot be countered by a restoration
of this society – for this would be at the same time the restoration of the source of Fascism. And yet Visser't Hooft certainly
describes Bonhoeffer's view in 1939 and 1940 correctly when
he says: 'The victory of Nazism would mean the end of the
Christian West, but defeat in the war the end of Germany.
For him (Bonhoeffer) there was no question on which side he
stood.'[3]

Accordingly, Bonhoeffer attempted at this time to mobilize
all potential forces on behalf of the Christian West. He
joined the 20th July circle. This movement did not fail
accidentally and only outwardly; it failed necessarily and
inwardly, for it is impossible to overcome Fascism, the final,
decadent phase of Imperialism, on the basis of a humanistic,
bourgeois-conservative heritage bound to a social order
which cannot, because of its very nature, destroy the seed-
bed of Fascism. The wheel of history will not be turned

[3] *Das Zeugnis eines Boten*, Geneva, 1945, p. 6.

backwards. The 20th July movement must be divided into two groups. There were those who, recognizing the inhuman character of Nazism, saw Fascism for what it was and rejected it. These people made an initial and at first formal move to reject Nazism as totalitarianism, then took the step towards actually overcoming it within the social order. But there were also those who rejected Nazism for the sake of preserving Fascism – which Nazism had hopelessly compromised – and who therefore denied only the form and not the content of Fascism.

This period saw the clarification of Bonhoeffer's intellectual ideas, which is what makes the fragments and letters so interesting. They reflected Bonhoeffer's intellectual and theological development, and it was in them that the battle between old and new took place – and the new, for which the soil had been prepared from an early date by many thoughts and encounters, won the day.

Therefore (and here I want to show briefly how the development within the fragments is to be understood), one must not overlook that basic feature of the *Ethics* which is characterized by the projected title, 'The Foundation and Structure of a United West'. It is the same basic feature as the one which is expressed most significantly in the section 'Inheritance and Decay' – although, as already noted, this is only *one* basic feature, traversed and contradicted by many others.[4]

Here I shall sketch the change in Dietrich Bonhoeffer's historical understanding during the second world war, by comparing this line of thought in the *Ethics* to the thoughts of the *Letters and Papers from Prison* – limiting myself considerably by leaving out of consideration not only the theological (in the narrower sense) concepts of the *Ethics*, but also those parts of the *Ethics* which oppose the basic feature we are considering. From this standpoint it may easily be understood how the

[4] Cf. E, p. 25*ff*. The projected title is mentioned in the introduction, p. x.

specifically theological thoughts of Bonhoeffer in the *Ethics* and letters are related to his intellectual struggle; how they sometimes even serve a dual function – being conditioned on the one hand by his aim to legitimize and coordinate the conservative resistance theologically, and playing an active part on the other hand, in coordinating and legitimizing his resistance, thus reflecting as well as accelerating the process.

In any event, one can neither understand what is attractive and important in Bonhoeffer's rich life and thought, nor begin fully to comprehend the real value of his final ideas as a conquest of tradition, as a position won only at the cost of a painful denial, if one overlooks the 'conservative' Bonhoeffer who reveals himself in that view of the *Ethics* which is directed towards a restoration of the heritage of the Christian West.

For how is one to give due respect to the revolutionary thoughts of the letters (measured against Bonhoeffer's social station and his intellectual tradition) if one overlooks the full extent of his journey? Above all, how could this journey convince us if we did not realize the care and passion with which his heritage has been examined piece by piece – to find out whether and how far it is still capable of bearing the future of mankind, before being overcome and replaced by new ideas?

Bonhoeffer found freedom for the future in his heritage. For him, the present was filled with an experienced and beloved past and, at the same time, with openness for the vigour and goodness of the future. For this reason, he was never one of those nihilistic anarchists who thoughtlessly cut themselves off from any continuity with the heritage of history, never a counter-revolutionary who deemed himself free from responsibility for the future.

Both the nihilist and the heroic versions of Fascist ideology were repellent to him. During those war years he moved from a position which grew out of remembering the best traditions of bourgeois culture, out of an obligation towards the 'No' spoken against Nazism by his and Germany's humanist heritage, into that new 'No' spoken against Fascism for the sake of coming generations and with a view towards a new, coming order – the step from conservative opposition to Hitler into that anti-Fascism which discovered its freedom no longer in a restoration of the past but in boldly grasping what was to come, taking leave of the cherished past for the sake of the possibility of the life of the future.

'By the time you are grown up,' he wrote at the baptism of his grand-nephew, 'the old country parsonage and the old town villa will belong to a vanished world.' He foresees the 'revolutionary times ahead', suspects something of the coming elimination of the difference between city and country, and thinks, not without a perceptible air of resignation:

We shall have to keep our lives going rather than shape them, to hope more than plan, to endure, rather than forge ahead. But we do want to preserve the souls of you young people, the new generation, so that out of these resources you may plan, build, and give form to a new and better life . . . For you, thought and action will have a new relationship. You will think only where you have to be responsible by acting. For us, thinking was much more the luxury of the onlooker; with you it will be entirely subordinate to service in action . . .

And then the conclusion of this view, so open to the future:

It should not be difficult for us to forfeit our privileges, recognizing the justice of history. We may have to face events and changes which run counter to our rights and wishes. But if so, we shall not give way to bitterness and fruitless pride, but consciously submit to divine judgement, and in generous and selfless participation in the whole of life, and in the sufferings of our fellow men, prove our vitality (LPP, pp. 155, 157-8, 159: translation altered).

But there were many contradictions and resolutions in Bonhoeffer's far-ranging journey up to this fresh look into a future determined neither by Nazism nor by the beloved past (which Nazism eventually annihilated and left incapable of restoration), but rather by some new society. It was the serpentine path of a man who, because he was such a typical representative of the German bourgeoisie and his church, shows in an exemplary way how, with genuine repentance, the church subjects herself to the criticism of the gospel and is thus freed to serve the future, instead of opposing it in 'fruitless pride'.

The heritage of Dietrich Bonhoeffer was stratified, as was the heritage of both classes which were linked together in the rule of Germany and in which he was rooted: the aristocracy and the bourgeoisie. His opposition to Nazism was determined by this heritage – and the more his opposition became directly political, the more clearly this heritage claimed its due. The dual nature of this heritage – so typical for capitalistic Germany as distinguished from those European states stamped by completed bourgeois revolutions – harboured many contradictions, and it was this that determined Bonhoeffer's attitude during the first part of the war.

His view of history expresses itself in the *Ethics* most significantly in the sections entitled 'Ethics as Formation', 'Inheritance and Decay', and 'Guilt, Justification, and Renewal'. It was conceived in the hope that Nazism could be overcome from within the past, i.e. carried through as a bourgeois-conservative, wholly anti-revolutionary self-liberation of the bourgeois German state – not the German people – from Nazism. So it is an attempt to disregard all the contradictions in the Western politico-cultural heritage, above all to disregard the contradiction between this highly differentiated heritage and the possibilities of the future, in order to conjure up once more the *fata morgana* of the unity of this heritage as a political goal and fight a battle against its own decay, Fascism.

At this time, Bonhoeffer indeed seemed the last honest Christian Westerner. To him the Christian West did not represent the cheap propaganda line of the reactionary, nor the demagogue's ideology of unity which masks imperialist goals, but rather the painstakingly preserved claim to the heritage of the fathers. Bonhoeffer knew there could be no enduring future growth without roots in the past; he knew the dangers of a nihilist romanticism as well as a nihilist heroism:

In the face of the peril of the void there is no longer any meaning in the question of the historical inheritance which requires of those who shall receive it that they shall both develop it in the present and hand it on to the future. There is no future and there is no past. There is only the moment which has been rescued from the void, and the desire to snatch from the void the next moment as well. Already what belongs to yesterday is consigned to oblivion, and the affairs of tomorrow are still too far off to impose any obligation today. The burden of yesterday is shaken off by glorifying the misty past, and tomorrow's task is evaded by speaking rather of the coming millennium (E, p. 106).

And so, resolutely, he turned to his heritage and tested it according to its capacity to bear the future.

In the *Ethics*, Bonhoeffer attempts to find in the form of Christ the unity of all forces which could be mobilized against Fascism, by looking at what he thought possible, namely, the restoration of liberty in Germany through the heritage of the West.

In our historical identity, therefore, we stand already in the midst of Christ's taking form, in a section of human history which he himself has chosen. It is consequently in this sense that we regard the West as the region for which we wish to speak and must speak, the world of the peoples of Europe and America in so far as it is already united through the form of Jesus Christ (E, p. 87.)

Thus we have here the problem of reality seen as realization: the problem of 'realizing the revelational reality of God in Jesus Christ among his creatures' – to indicate the framework in which this basic idea of the *Ethics* is expressed. This concept of reality is characterized by making concrete and manifesting the Lord of Faith not in his humility and powerlessness, but in the visibility and tangibility of his historical power. Certainly, this is very carefully broken through dialectically and is finally dissolved by reality itself, with its demand for realism and relevance. The impossibility of this theology of history, which is utopian as well as aiming at a *theologia gloriae*, can thus be understood and reflected upon.

Here we shall say no more of this later contradiction between the real content of Christian faith and its history, and its interpretation in terms of the heritage of its integration with feudalism. The deep contradiction within this heritage which has been understood as essentially Christian threatens to break apart the whole conception.

First a conflict becomes evident within the understanding of what is Christian as a power of history. Bonhoeffer thinks that the Western world, supported by the Roman heritage, has always seen the unity of nature and grace, God's 'Yes' to his creatures, as expressed in the incarnation of God. But Germany (not by chance the land of the Reformation) has more often drawn from the Greek heritage the diastasis between nature and grace, the 'No' of the creature of God, as expressed in the cross of Christ. In his varied formulations in the *Ethics*, Bonhoeffer says again and again how improper it is 'to establish a separate theology of the incarnation, a theology of the cross, or a theology of the resurrection, each in opposition to the others, by a misconceived absolutizing of one of these parts' (E, p. 131). We should not overlook the historical motive behind this dogmatically correct sentence: the struggle for the unity of Christian thought against Nazism means the reunification of the 'Western' and the 'German' heritage.

Here something which was not strange to Bonhoeffer is left behind. We recognize that in our world the hallmark of all theology indeed remains the humiliation of the incarnate one, whether it is a theology of the cross, resurrection, or incarnation. We are called to discipleship, as witnesses to the exalted one in the existence of the church and in our own baseness to bear witness in and through ourselves to the scandal which the *ensarkos* gave in his humiliation. This line of thought, of the *theologia crucis* developed by Bonhoeffer in his *Christology* and given an extraordinarily concrete form in *The Cost of Discipleship*, remains the explosive element of the historico-theological system which he preserves in the *Ethics*, and is carried through on a higher level in the *Letters and Papers from Prison*. Thus, in the prison letters, much of what was recognized historically in the *Ethics* is legitimately secularized.

But the problem of the Reformation weighs more heavily than the problem of the difference between the Western heritage determined by Rome and that determined by Greece:

The unity of the West is not an idea but an historical reality, of which the sole foundation is Christ . . . The Reformation broke asunder the *corpus christianum*, the historical order of the Christian West, which was ruled and held together by Emperor and Pope in the name of Jesus Christ . . . The *corpus christianum* is resolved into its true constituents, the *corpus Christi* and the world . . . (E, p. 93*ff.*).

Bonhoeffer completely overlooks the fact that the *corpus christianum* itself was nothing less than the consequences of the feudalization of Christianity – the price paid for the christianizing of feudal Europe. Western unity became Christian because Christianity had become the ideology of feudalism, an ideology not of the lords alone, but of the whole social system – so that even the social battles of the time were fought between the great church and the sects within the embracing Christian order. Thus he was not able, at that moment, to see how final was the disappearance of this reality of the *corpus christianum*. He therefore underestimates the depth of the break brought about in church history by the Reformation, when he speaks of the *corpus Christi*, the church, as 'the true unity of the West' (E, p. 31).

It is true that with his hypothesis he sees the new problem: this unity is shattered along with the unity of the church. But

the guilt and the distress which this inheritance entails are shared in common by the whole of Western Christendom; they cannot be removed by human endeavour. At the same time, however, the fact that they are recognized for what they are marks the beginning of a new awareness of Western unity which persists despite and even through this separation (E, p. 96).

Bonhoeffer seems to be successful in maintaining the unity of the West as an all-embracing intellectual-cultural, political and historical heritage despite the opposition between Rome and Wittenberg, between Germany and the Mediterranean countries. But an ideology which unifies all opponents of Nazism in order to annihilate it, but which preserves its social *basis* (the late-bourgeois social order), is only qualified to appeal to feudalistic-conservative forces. The heritage of bourgeois liberalism has not yet been taken into account. The resolution of this contradiction will clearly be accomplished in an attempt to understand the heritage of the bourgeois revolution.

Here the contradictions become especially thorny. If one calls up forces against Hitler's *counter-revolution* which, at the same time, is misunderstood as a revolution on the basis of its social demagogy; if therefore a restoration is called for which is, so to speak, a self-cancelling counter-revolution, then only the bourgeois and not the revolutionary, the liberal and not the democratic heritage of the French Revolution can be included. In this, the estimate of the French Revolution will necessarily be self-contradictory. But instead of recognizing this contradiction objectively and historically (as the replacement of one parasitic society which hindered progress by another parasitic society which, at the time, furthered progress) Bonhoeffer, though continually running up against this contradiction, separates the intellectual achievements of the revolution, which he affirms, from the social achievements which he denies (in both their bourgeois and, even more, their revolutionary character). This shows once more how a man in the field nearest to his interests – as Bonhoeffer in that of intellectual emancipation – acts and judges more progressively than in any other. In a singular fashion two elements are mingled in Bonhoeffer's outlook on history, which reflect the real contradictions within the bourgeois revolution. First, there is a subjective contradiction resulting from his bondage to the feudal heritage, over against the social and political revolution in general; secondly, there is his subjective reception of revolution, in so far as he could understand it – in accordance with his social position as an intellectual – as a revolutionary liberation of his intellect from the heteronomy of the middle ages.

His fundamental judgement of the bourgeois revolution is devastating: 'The new unity which the French Revolution brought to Europe . . . is therefore Western godlessness' (E, p. 102). This is (unlike a promising godlessness which Bonhoeffer also knows, and apart from the theoretical godlessness of a few atheistic thinkers in Western history), a godlessness which is itself 'a religion, a religion of hostility to God'. 'It cannot break loose from its past. It cannot but be religious in essence. That is why to the human eye it is so hopelessly godless. Western godlessness ranges from the religion of Bolshevism to the midst of the Christian churches!' (E, p. 102). Simply as an aside, one should note that this thought is frequently the starting-point today for interpreting the *Letters and Papers from Prison* in terms of the *Ethics*. Here, Bonhoeffer concludes his discussion: 'By the loss of the unity which is possessed through the form of Jesus Christ, the Western world is brought to the brink of the void . . .' 'What the West is doing is refusing to accept its historical inheritance for what it is. The West is becoming hostile towards Christ. This is the peculiar situation of our time, and it is genuine decay' (E, pp. 105, 108).

But the effect of the French Revolution is not only negative. Here, too, some bridge-building is necessary. One cannot renounce the whole of its heritage if it is to be useful in mobilizing the entire heritage of the Christian West – including the bourgeois and conservative heritage – for the battle against its decay. On the one hand the French Revolution is, as a revolution and in its revolutionary heritage, a threat to the desired new order. On the other hand it is the source of the modern bourgeois society which is to be liberated from its Fascist barbarism and thus restored. The all-embracing renewal of the West cannot come about through medieval feudalism, through the Christian West alone. No, in the renewal of the inheritance which Bonhoeffer has in mind, the modern world must simultaneously come into her own.

In this part of the *Ethics* America does not appear by accident as the great example of a society which is bourgeois but nevertheless Christian:

The American Revolution was almost contemporary with the French one, and politically the two were not unconnected; yet they were profoundly different in character. The American democracy is not founded upon the emancipation of man but, quite the contrary, upon the kingdom of God and the limitation of all earthly powers by the sovereignty of God.

But here too, where democracy is based upon Christianity, where indeed 'democracy alone is regarded as the Christian form of the state' (E, pp. 104, 105), there occurs, though in a more concealed way, the process of secularization. Thus a look at the American version of the bourgeois revolution does not rescue Bonhoeffer from the contradictions inherent in all bourgeois revolutions, namely, that the bourgeois revolution must be accepted as a bourgeois inheritance, and rejected as a revolutionary inheritance.

The French Revolution was the laying bare of emancipated man in his tremendous power and his most terrible perversity. Emancipated man meant here emancipated reason, an emancipated class and an emancipated people (E, p. 97).

But at the same time:

Emancipated reason rose to unsuspected heights. The free exercise of reason created an atmosphere of truthfulness, light and clarity . . . Intellectual honesty in all things, including questions of belief, was the great achievement of emancipated reason and it has ever since been one of the indispensable moral requirements of Western man. Contempt for the age of nationalism is a suspicious sign of failure to feel the need for truthfulness . . . We cannot now go back to the days before Lessing and Lichtenberg (E, p. 97*f.*).

And again, on the other hand:

Behind the bourgeoisie, there loomed the dark menace of the masses, the fourth estate. All it stood for was simply the masses and their misery (E, p. 100).

197

The bourgeois revolution is the father of the socialist revolution, not because it is bourgeois, but because it is revolutionary. Therefore:

The masses have equal contempt for the laws of blood and for the laws of reason. They make their own law, the law of misery. It is a violent law, and short-lived. We today are standing at the culmination and crisis of this uprising (E, p. 100).

It is not only the masses which threaten:

Nation was a revolutionary concept. It sided with the people against the government, with becoming against being, and with the organic against the institutional. It was thought from below, in opposition to thought from above. . . . Prussia had a sound instinctive sense of the revolutionary implications of the notion of nationhood, and refused to accept them. . . . Nationalism evokes the counter-movement of internationalism. The two are equally revolutionary. To both of these movements Prussia opposed the state. Prussia wished to be neither nationalistic nor international. In this respect its thought was more Western than was that of the Revolution (E, p. 101*f.*).

Because of space limitations, I must end this list of quotations. In so far as one views this ethical fragment of Dietrich Bonhoeffer's in its historical perspective, it is clear that he is seeking a weapon against Nazism – which he did not recognize as a counter-revolution but understood naïvely as a revolution. In a battle with a counter-revolution mistaken for revolution, the revolutionary must present himself ideologically as a counter-revolutionary, although he may be working as a revolutionary. The contradictions within this point of view are obvious. How can the feudal heritage of the medieval *Reich* walk hand in hand with the heritage of its gravediggers, humanism and the Reformation? How can the Prussian conception of the state, a patriarchal and enlightened absolutism, be reconciled with the concept of the nation, the creation of the bourgeois movement towards autonomy? How is Bonhoeffer, who has gone through the school of a reformed theology of diastasis, to find his way back to that humanistic-humanitarian Christianity which is to be a refuge in the midst of barbarism for all bourgeois virtues, justice, decency and reason?

More difficult and more pressing is the question of the historical durability or practicability of this standpoint at the time it originated. Historically false and impractical views can of course claim an historical validity for their time – no one can doubt the historical justification for utopian views. Were Bonhoeffer's historical theology and historical philosophy justified in this sense? Or does that which is decaying fight its own consequences? Is this battle anything more than a ruling class turning disgustedly away from its own old age, its decay? Is this a turning away which, given the best intentions, is ultimately unfruitful because it is not a turning towards what is new and is to come?

It is clear that these conceptions, after they had failed to fulfil their original goal (that of serving a bourgeois self-liberation of the German people from Nazism), may provide a foundation for a highly dangerous historical anachronism. After the bourgeois liberation from Nazism had foundered, and Nazism itself was irredeemably discredited after the collapse of 1945, people were tempted to discard as Nazi the national and social demagogy which had deceived and swindled the masses of their own interests. At the same time a Christian and democratic demagogy arose which served to reorganize Fascism on the basis of its apparent anti-Fascism.

There is today an illegitimate desire to look upon the ideology of the Christian West, which once wanted to unite the opponents of Fascism on a bourgeois basis, as favouring Fascism. The unity of the West, the community of Europe, the negation of nationalism and internationalism, the welding of medieval conceptions of order and institution (as also of the Prussian idea of the state) into the restoration of bourgeois society, the overcoming of the differences between Protestant and Catholic, the German and Mediterranean peoples, dependence upon the one country which carried through a bourgeois revolution in a Christian democratic direction, America – all this is combined with a rejection of Communism and a refusal to examine it seriously, and with the acceptance of Christianity.

Nevertheless, this standpoint *was* for Bonhoeffer a declaration of war against Fascism; even though it issued from an unrepeatable feudal and early bourgeois past and not from a will clearly to recognize and pursue the future. Even though the weapons of the past were rusty and weak (to recall Dietrich Bonhoeffer's image of Don Quixote)[5] compared with the shiny weapons of the future, they were nevertheless weapons which Bonhoeffer directed against Hitler. It was this alone which could justify these weapons. Bonhoeffer himself resolved the contradiction between his actual battle against Fascism and his historical understanding of himself as the restorer, when he exchanged these rusty weapons for shiny ones. In this way he took away any legitimacy from those who today would use the same rusty weapons in the service of those against whom Bonhoeffer used them.

There is a difference between a picture of Bonhoeffer, searching doubtfully for a battle-ideology against Nazism with the question, 'Who stands his ground?', and hitting upon the ideology of the Christian West which is itself reactionary, in order to turn this against Fascism – and a superannuated society making use of the same ideology in order to block the path of progress and to reorganize, in a 'democratic' and 'Christian' form, a Fascism which has already been irredeemably discredited in its Nazi form.

And yet, at the same time, this calling in question of the whole historico-theological outline which we have extracted occurs already in the *Ethics*. In thinking about the difference between ultimate and penultimate he really deals a death-blow to the synthesis of the ultimate and the penultimate, which is the history of the Christian West. Even more, the fact that the natural is recognized in its secularity by reason,

[5] An image used for the title of the first volume of selections from the German *Gesammelte Schriften : No Rusty Swords.*

that there is an ever-increasing current of rationalism in the *Ethics*, tells us that he begins to doubt that history can be dominated and interpreted by religion. Certainly all this may be interpreted from a Catholic perspective, as the relation between nature and grace. Certainly these parts (written partly in the monastery at Ettal) are enriched by Catholic theology as well – although this is done in such a way that Bonhoeffer, in seeking the unity of the Christian heritage, only comes again upon the source of the Reformation gospel when he looks at the Catholic tradition of medieval dogmatics. If we were to interpret these passages not as the progress of the Reformation but as the restoration of Catholicism, we would have to read the *Ethics* as a systematic unit incapable of development, in which the idea of the West, the notion of ultimate and penultimate, and the thought about the Natural mutually interpret one another. But this is impossible: Bonhoeffer's development moved further in such a way that the different statements of the *Ethics* appear to be pathways to a new knowledge. A static and systematic interpretation of the *Ethics* is rendered impossible by the further development in the letters. Surely Bonhoeffer himself felt how meagre the basis for his historico-theological conception was over against Fascism:

Over and over again, when a policy of Imperialistic conquest has been pursued amid contempt for law and justice and brutal mishandling of the weak there has come a gradual turning towards rightful order and peace, and even towards the happiness of those who had been the victims of violence, a change of course which has brought with it the healing of the wounds of guilt (E, p. 117ff.).

He is surely not thinking of the guilt of the Revolution, but rather that a victorious German bourgeoisie which has freed itself from Fascism can go on existing only on a foundation laid by Fascism – in spite of all the guilt clinging to it. Here a new qualification arises. Bonhoeffer noted in an unpublished fragment of the *Ethics* which is in the possession of Eberhard Bethge:

Lack of power can be guilt. Power too is an ethical qualification . . .
The exaggeration of the concept of law, as though the world could be
rescued through the law. Necessity for going beyond the law! Revolutionary.

In the *Letters and Papers from Prison* he speaks already of an
impending 'great historical turning' (LPP, p. 135), and it
sounds stronger than and different from the *Ethics* when he
can say:

To talk about going down fighting like heroes in the face of certain
defeat is basically very unheroic, because it does not look to the future.
The ultimate responsible question is not 'How can I extricate myself
heroically from the affair?' but 'How is the coming generation to live?'
(LPP, pp. 138–9: translation altered).

These sentences were written while the Battle of Stalingrad
was approaching its end. This reference to the defeat can be
related not only to resignation concerning the possibility of a
German bourgeois self-liberation. It is clearly also related to
the collapse both of German Fascism and of the bourgeois-
conservative opposition to it. So it has a different sound from
the discussion in the *Ethics* of rebuilding upon the wrong
ground, when he writes:

All the same, it remains true that historical success creates the only
basis for the continuance of life, and it is still a moot point whether it is
ethically more responsible to behave like Don Quixote and enter the
lists against a new age, or to admit one's defeat [in my estimation, the
internal and external collapse of the 20th July Movement is here
anticipated, H.M.] and accept the new age and agree to serve it (LPP,
p. 138).

How this new age is to be viewed as regards its content
may be seen in the 'Thoughts on the Baptism of D. W. R.' of
May 1944. These were written before the final miscarriage of
the plot of 20 July, but after the actual military collapse of
Germany: 'We may have to face events and changes which
run counter to our rights and wishes' – here is the anticipa-
tion of an anti-Fascist, democratic, social upheaval. And in
considering this perspective, he writes:

It should not be difficult for us to forfeit our privileges, recognizing the justice of history . . . If so, we shall not give way to fruitless pride, but consciously submit to divine judgement; and in generous and selfless participation in the whole of life, and in the sufferings of our fellow men, prove our vitality (LPP, p. 159: translation altered).

He was thinking not only of the social position of the individual, but also of the social position of the church, as one sees in the remark that 'the old country parsonage and the old town villa will belong to a vanished world' (LPP, p. 155). In this connexion he reflected upon the guilt of the church: 'During these years the church has fought for self-preservation as though it were an end in itself, and is not capable of finding the atoning and redeeming word to mankind and to the world at large' (LPP, p. 160: translation altered). The future duties of the church are seen anti-clerically: 'By the time you have grown up, the form of the church will have changed very much. We are not yet out of the melting pot, and every attempt to hasten it towards a new unfolding of . . . its power, will only delay the church's conversion and purgation.'

Then follows the reference to what he discovered at this time as the question of 'the non-religious interpretation of the biblical message' (LPP, p. 160: translation altered).

This point where Bonhoeffer's expectations intersect makes us aware of the revolution in his thoughts, when we remember his previous Western-Christian concepts in the *Ethics*. The observer of Bonhoeffer's development witnesses a truly dialectical journey. In the first period his interest centres on the church; clericalism of any kind is overcome in the interest of letting the church be the church and not a clericalized world. Then he looks at the world, but first in such a way that this world is to be clericalized after all through Christian criticism based on his earlier convictions. And then, in the final and highest stage, any clericalization is done away with, but at the same time responsibility for the world is maintained. From church ethics via Christian ethics to the human ethics of Christians!

Thus the liberation from the domination of the heritage of the middle ages proceeds by giant steps, as though Bonhoeffer knew how little time he still had to reach his goal. This heritage had assumed a power over Bonhoeffer which tied him down. The lack of freedom did not consist in Bonhoeffer's desire to oppose Fascism with a closed world view. It consisted in the fact that this world view left him with a two-fold contradiction. First, the ideology of the Christian West was Roman Catholic and clerical, and Bonhoeffer could only be a Protestant. He had to face the question of whether Jesus Christ really was the unity of the Christian West, the saviour from barbarism and war, the guarantor of the rebuilding of Europe and the counsellor for the new order of mankind. Is Jesus Christ, the founder of the West, still the crucified and powerless one? Has he not rather become one that can no longer save? The religious founder of the religion which unites the West, or even the personification of the idea of its unity?

Secondly, the ideology of the Christian West was reactionary. But Bonhoeffer wanted it to serve the future, the liberation from Fascism. He was bound to see this dilemma, and seek a non-religious, rational basis for the resistance against Fascism. This powerful heritage was expressed in a two-fold law which excluded the future. Because Christ had become for Bonhoeffer the history of the West, he was no longer the coming one, but the form of the inheritance, the past. In the ideology of the Christian West he was no longer present as the crucified, nor still to come as the resurrected one. He had become the form of reality, and therefore history had become a religious law. But at the same time, and not unrelated to this, this inheritance represented an historical bondage to a past and dying social order. It robbed the natural man of the freedom to dedicate himself openly to the future of earthly life; to find the criterion for the future not in the past, but in what is to come, and to find the criterion for historical tradition in the decisions he is called upon to make. A heritage which becomes the law and confinement and criterion of the present and future cannot be freely received. The present and the requirements of the future are rather the criteria by which the value of the historical inheritance is to be judged: it must serve them, or it is dead.

That Bonhoeffer now increasingly liberates himself from the domination of the Christian past is a turning-point, indeed a reformation. Here is the deeper reason why the later Bonhoeffer discovered afresh or accepted unconsciously so many of the earlier thoughts of Luther. This reversal is at the same time the liberation of faith from the legalism of a religious world view *and* the liberation of his world view from religious captivity. For Bonhoeffer, faith is now no longer, as it must appear, bondage to a Christ who is the unity of the West, a myth working itself out in history, but rather the participation in the messianic suffering of Jesus Christ (LPP, pp. 122–5: 18 July 1944). He who believes in this way, who shares the sufferings of God in the world, is set free to see the world beyond all religious and historico-theological categories: just as it is. That means that the believer is set free to see the world *etsi deus non daretur*, as though God were not given, freed for an atheistic world view.

In this way, through this change in his theology, Bonhoeffer becomes free to alter his view of history. But on the other hand, the change in his concrete historical expectation, the alteration of his political perspective, now results in that alteration in his view of history and the world, which forces his faith to seek and find a new expression. The change in his view of history may be seen as the *external* reason, as the cause of his theological reversal, and his reformation as the *internal* reason for the liberation to take up a new world view.

There are two main causes of the reformation in his last thoughts. First, there is the discovery that the Pauline question of whether circumcision is a prerequisite of justification has become today the question whether religion is the precondition of salvation. Secondly, there is the discovery that the New Testament does not preach the powerful God of other religions, the counsellor where human knowledge ceases, the rescuer where human abilities fail; but that the gospel is really the word of the cross, of the suffering and powerless God.

These discoveries have tremendous consequences. Religion is no longer a precondition of salvation; that means nothing less than that faith in Jesus Christ does not presuppose a religious conviction, religious consciousness, a religious world view. Belief and unbelief are in entirely different categories from theistic or atheistic world views. It is not the power but the powerlessness of God in the world which matters; that means nothing less than that all religions which recognize God as omnipotent and omniscient in the world and which think they can reckon with him in the reality of the world as though he were a reality of the world, become mere superstitions. True faith is nothing but participation in the sufferings of God in this world, in this – worldliness. Faith is the perseverance beneath the cross of him who is despised and powerless, with the apparently senseless hope of the resurrection of him who is dead and dying.

If one understands Bonhoeffer in his letters only abstractly, intellectually and individually as we have up to now, then one can receive the *Letters and Papers from Prison* only in a way which does not take in the full riches of Bonhoeffer's thoughts. If the collapse of the surviving social order in the face of its decay is anticipated and reflected in intellectual resignation (without the process of social transformation having been carried through or planned in a methodical and revolutionary way), and Bonhoeffer's conception is dissolved from its social connexion by means of an individual and intellectual reception, then it becomes topical merely as a way out of a theoretical crisis of faith, or rather of Christian self-consciousness. One should be warned against such a constriction by Bonhoeffer's ironical remark about the existential way out into subjectivism, about 'secularized methodism', in the irrational and pessimistic 'off-shoots of Christian theology' (LPP, pp. 107–8: 8 June 1944).

Bonhoeffer did not mean by his concept of the religionlessness of the future what some of his interpreters mean – intellectual sceptics with nihilistic overtones; he did not mean by religionless men those whose ideology reflects the decay of a society; but he meant a healthy, common, socially active, strong, optimistic, world-mastering atheism. Certainly he is thinking as little of Marxist atheism as he is of existentialism. But the atheism of Marxism which is completely non-nihilistic, which is not intellectual but positive, productive, and progressive, is closer to the religionlessness Bonhoeffer means than that secularized methodism which affects 'a small number of intellectuals, of degenerates, of people who regard themselves as the most important thing in the world' (LPP, p. 108). For it has to do with a social phenomenon rather than the individual anguish of the soul over the discrepancy between the *desire* for faith and the *necessity* for knowledge.[6]

[6] Although I value Ebeling's interpretation of Bonhoeffer (MW II, Munich, 1956, p. 12*ff.*) very highly, it does not seem to me that he has taken sufficient account of this social aspect of Bonhoeffer's thought (or by the way, of Luther's beginnings in this direction). In my opinion, Ebeling does not sufficiently show that the whole of Bonhoeffer's thought, especially the last period, is always related to the social content of theology. When Ebeling (rightly) interprets Bonhoeffer on the basis of the distinction between law and gospel, the social content of both concepts does not seem clearly enough indicated. It is certainly not by chance that Bonhoeffer develops his question (law and gospel) less in dependence upon Barth and more in direct dependence upon Paul, focusing on the *peritome* and thus upon a social category, according to the model of Jew *v.* gentile. He is concerned that the church once witnessed in fact and in existence to the dissolution of the law which separated and to the union of men; and therefore, in its existence, served as the witness to the reconciliation between those whom jealousy for God, misunderstood zeal for him, had torn apart. That we might be in spiritual unity with this church (so Bonhoeffer would go on to say), the church must today be the living and therefore reconciling union of religious and non-religious, theist and atheist. For religiosity

If we are aware of the whole breadth of its social and political implications, we can immediately see why Bonhoeffer's development has such vast consequences for himself. It clearly neither allows nor requires a religious way based on the history of theology – nor even an intentionally idealistic view of history (for all idealism bears its religious heritage within itself; even its atheism is religious). What is now possible, allowed, and called for by reason is a rational and optimistic atheism which is founded upon the freedom of faith, and is even now and then an original materialism recognizing an historical legitimacy which accords with human cognition; a view of history that is highly realistic at least in its intention.

We can trace clear beginnings of a secular historical understanding, even in the *Ethics*, when we read about the suitability of reason for the comprehension of the Natural: 'The Natural and reason are related to one another as the form of being and the form of consciousness of the preserved life' (E, p. 146), and again when the spontaneity of reason is rejected in a polemic against the Enlightenment (which therefore comes up against the idealism of Kant): 'Our view differs from the Enlightenment view in that it takes the Natural to rest upon what is objectively given and not upon the subjective spontaneity of reason' (E, p. 146). Of course, what the *Ethics* recognizes fluctuates to such a degree that it might also be interpreted Thomistically: the substitution of

---

is analogous to circumcision: it cannot be allowed to separate those who, on one side or the other, experience this reconciliation – the act of God which reconciles them one with the other. Thus the concept of law and religion enters that social reality which is the real concern. If we do not see this, then there enters into Bonhoeffer's interpretation an existential-intellectual and individual constriction which robs it of its *ecclesiastical*, i.e. its reforming, cutting edge. Then Bonhoeffer's much more sociological thoughts are not taken into account and, more important, the social intention of the word of God which Bonhoeffer discovered and pointed to (but did not invent) is not seen.

what I have called an original materialism for the naïve realism of a metaphysics postulating immaterial being.

In the letters this wavering is overcome. 'Laws' are spoken of, with which 'the world lives and manages in science, social and political affairs, art, ethics, and religion' (LPP, p. 107: 8 July 1944), and whose discovery has taken place since the thirteenth century. Thus, that apologetic interpretation which likes to view secularization as a Christian product of the Reformation, and hence under the control of Christianity, is abandoned; as well as that fashionable agnosticism founded by Dilthey, and others, which aims at separating the methods of natural science from those of the liberal arts. With the recognition of the laws which govern history, a break-through into the future is achieved, which only becomes the more apparent when we notice in studies of Bonhoeffer's ideas what energies are expended in order to eliminate this knowledge.

The general Christian view sees a legitimate process of secularization beginning with the Reformation, then taking an illegitimate turn with rationalism, the Enlightenment and the Revolution; whereby it slips away from legitimate Christian control. Bonhoeffer dates the beginning of secularization in the thirteenth century, which is historically more accurate, as this coincides with the rise of the bourgeoisie and the Western reception of Aristotle. This suffices to make the general Christian view invalid.

Thus it is that we encounter, as a basic feature of the last letters, a new picture of history – and therefore an implicit disavowal of that historical theology of the *Ethics*:

The movement beginning about the thirteenth century . . . towards the autonomy of man . . . has in our time reached a certain completion. Man has learned to cope with all questions of importance without recourse to 'God as a working hypothesis' . . . As in the scientific field, so in human affairs generally, 'God' is being more and more driven out of life, losing more and more ground (LPP, pp. 106–7: 8 June 1944).

God as a moral, political, and scientific working hypothesis is abolished and superseded. Equally as a working hypothesis for philosophy and religion (Feuerbach!). In the name of intellectual honesty these working hypotheses should be dropped . . . (LPP, p. 121: 16 July 1944. Translation altered).

Catholic and Protestant historians are agreed that it is in this development that the great defection from God, from Christ, is to be discerned, and the more they bring in and make use of God and Christ in opposition to this trend, the more the trend considers itself to be anti-Christian. The world which has attained to a realization of itself and of the laws which govern its existence is so sure of itself that we become frightened . . . Christian apologetic has taken the most varying forms of opposition to this self-assurance. Efforts are made to prove to a world thus come of age that it cannot live without the tutelage of 'God' . . . The attack by Christian apologetic upon the adulthood of the world I consider to be in the first place pointless, in the second ignoble, and in the third un-Christian (LPP, pp. 107–8: 8 June 1944).

Then, somewhat later he mentions, after the emergency exit from this problem in existentialism,

. . . the *salto mortale* back to the Middle Ages, the fundamental principle of which however is heteronomy in the form of clericalism. But that is a counsel of despair, which can be purchased only at the cost of intellectual sincerity (LPP, p. 121: 16 July 1944).

In comparison with the *Ethics*, we encounter here a wholly new, secular understanding of history, filled with that secular and optimistic 'Yes' to human development which we occasionally met in the *Ethics*. Seen from this point of view, the Western outlook of the *Ethics* must have appeared to Bonhoeffer to be a 'counsel of despair', the '*salto mortale* back to the Middle Ages', as clericalism. But Bonhoeffer receives the freedom to take up this new secularism from his theological discoveries:

And the only way to be honest is to recognize that we have to live in the world *etsi deus non daretur*, and this is just what we do recognize – before God! . . . God is teaching us that we must live as men who can get along without him. The God who is with us is the God who forsakes us (Mark 15. 34) . . . God allows himself to be edged out of the world and on to the cross. God is weak and powerless in the world and that is exactly the way in which he is with us and helps us (LPP, pp. 121–2: 16 July 1944: translation altered).

We feel that Bonhoeffer's development from its beginnings in the *Ethics* and through all its contradictions up to the final letters is a beginning, nothing more – but still a revolutionary beginning. Bonhoeffer's work itself has now become a heritage for us, confronting the church with the utmost urgency with the question of its *own* heritage. Will it find its future there, or its decay? Much will depend upon whether the church is willing to accept the heritage of Paul, of the early Luther and the later Bonhoeffer, the heritage of *ecclesia semper reformanda*, or whether it will cling to the heritage of early Catholicism, the apologists, the scholastics and orthodoxy, the romantics and their ideology of the Christian West. The deciding factor will be whether we shall be slaves to the tradition of church and middle class, and legalistically bind ourselves to a heritage which leads us into decay, or whether we shall find the freedom for the future within the heritage of the Fathers, in a spiritual and therefore also in a worldly sense.

It is not inheritance alone which determines the alternatives. The duties and alternatives of the present also determine the way the inheritance is received. I have attempted to show that within the comprehensive unity of Bonhoeffer's last period, the step is taken from the ecclesiastical to the worldly responsibility of the Christian. The step is a first step towards the assumption by the church of responsibility for the world. It is bound up with a hope that National Socialism will be overcome by the powers of the past, with the goal of reorganizing the Christian world in the light of Western tradition. Against it – contrary to Christian-Western heritage – the revolutionary heritage of the Reformation takes the field. The hope for a restoration is rent asunder, and the belief in the coming revolution breaks through. The second step is the renunciation of the ecclesiastical overtones, through loyalty to Christian responsibility for the world. Ecclesiastical responsibility becomes human responsibility. It is preserved by faith in the God who does not remove our history from us in order to make it himself, who does not hold himself aloof but who himself becomes a man in our history and this-worldly life, who is with us as a man in our secular existence, so that we in our world and our secularity may be with him. In discipleship we are drawn into the midst of his sufferings in this world and therefore, at the same time, we become for the first time really free for this world.

Unlike Luther, Bonhoeffer maintains his theology of the humiliation of the *ensarkos* – the humiliation which we witness to only in our own ecclesiastical powerlessness and lowliness – in such a way that his world view and his ethics never become nihilistic and pessimistic, but remain filled with an immanent optimism and rationalism – borne by a *theologia crucis*.

We are faced with the alternative of following Bonhoeffer's development and thus equipping ourselves for the complete secularity of coming social orders; preparing ourselves to witness to Christ as people who have come of age in a world come of age. Or we may twist Bonhoeffer's final insights into mere intellectual solutions to individual problems of faith. Worse still, we may renounce living through and carrying forward the development of Bonhoeffer's thought by using a transitory stage of his life as a key to understanding him (instead of leaving it behind as he did); devoting ourselves to the restoration of a Christian world whose collapse Bonhoeffer freely anticipated, through the freedom of his Protestant faith, and despite all his love for what was lovely in the past.

We are faced with the alternative placed before us by the splitting of the formerly united Confessing Church into two forces after 1945. On the one hand, we are left with that broad orthodox-positivist movement which fought for the clericalization of society against what was seen as 'the dechristianizing of our people' by National Socialism. This movement was victorious in 1945 with the help of Western allies, and has successfully, since then, carried out the reclericalizing of society and politics. On the other hand, there stands that small flock which thinks not only of an individual interpretation of the Sermon on the Mount, but also of an ecclesiological one, which thinks that the *abnegatio sui* is related not only to the individual Christian, but also and above all to the church. Bonhoeffer belonged to this small flock. But recognizing that the *abnegatio sui* of the church is not an end in itself but the way to that love which is possible only in the denial of self, he sought to go beyond the church to serve the world. At first – at the beginning of the final period – this service took the form of a well-meaning guardianship, comparable to that of enlightened monarchs who supposed they were the first servants of the state. At first, then, this service comes all too near to that broad front which furthers ecclesiastical lordship over the world. The new will to serve the world manifests itself in surviving inadequate forms of clericalism. But the *abnegatio sui*, as a social reality of the true church, is developed further. The problem of discipleship in the church, in the acceptance of the political responsibility of the Christian, is not solved by 'Inheritance and Decay'. This concept conflicts with the knowledge gained in *The Cost of Discipleship* of the unity of discipleship with the concrete tasks of citizens in the secular realm. He means that political ethics are fulfilled only in complete humiliation and self-denial, in discipleship to the one who suffers with us in the life of this world, the powerless one with whom we too may now suffer:

The church is the church only when it exists for others. . . . It must participate in the worldly tasks of *human* communal life; not ruling, but helping and serving . . . *Our* church will have to take a strong line especially with the vices of pride, worship of strength, envy and self-deception, for these are the roots of all evil (LPP, p. 166, My italics in the first sentence; Bonhoeffer's in the second. H.M. Translation altered).

Bonhoeffer's development is sufficiently stable and complete for us to decide how we shall receive his heritage rightly. That does not mean that we should stop where he stopped: the path which he entered on leads further than he went. We find in what he has left us many questions which have still to be solved. It seems clear that Christianity cannot be freed

213

World Come of Age

from religion the way contents are removed from a shell. The religion of Christianity cannot simply be interpreted non-religiously. The question arises whether religion is not part and parcel of the humiliation of Christianity, its second nature which cannot be eliminated but must be understood and endured as a stumbling-block. It seems clear that the preaching of the freedom of faith is related to religion as a preceding factor and that it leads to religion as a consequent factor. In Paul's controversy with the religion of the synagogue, pagans heard the gospel. Today it seems that the religionless world hears the gospel in Bonhoeffer's controversy with the religion of a false church. Might the open and public attack of the sovereign Word of God upon his church – which is fleeing to religiosity, restoration, and the past, or is itself attacking and ruling the world from this fortress – be the secret of non-religious proclamation, or, more correctly, the secret of the non-legalistic preaching of the gospel for the religionless?

Here is the beginning, it seems to me, from which to seek further and follow the path of Bonhoeffer – in its entirety, catching his meaning, though developing it critically.

214

VIII

The Cross of Reality?

Some Questions Concerning the Interpretation of Bonhoeffer

by Hans Schmidt

Bonhoeffer's writings have always caused 'a peculiar difficulty' to interpretation, which Karl Barth put down to the fact that Bonhoeffer was an 'impulsive, visionary thinker, who was suddenly seized by an idea to which he gave lively form and then after a time he called a halt (one never knew whether it was final or temporary) with some provisional last point or other' (page 89 f. above). With this primarily psychological characterization of Bonhoeffer's thinking (cf. p. 91: 'melancholy theology of the North German plain'), Barth relinquished his chance of pursuing Bonhoeffer's way of thinking. That way is certainly turbulent, long, and rich in stopping-points. But Barth did not ask whether one cannot point to a consistent tendency in it, in spite of all the apparent turning and winding. This tendency might be something like an expanding and deepening, but still constant, range of experiences and problems. And it might be something like a certainty of mission which endures all modifications of theological reflection. Did not Bonhoeffer himself express the hope that one might view in the 'fragment' of life 'how the whole was actually planned and laid out, and of which material it consists' (LPP, p. 153)? Are we not therefore, especially through the 'enigmatic utterances of his letters' (Barth, p. 90 above), exposed to the task of 'asking about the basic impulse which is persistent through all changes' (G. Ebeling in MW II, p. 17; cf. MW III, p. 69)? Church and theology cannot be satisfied with Barth's proposal 'to take the best from him . . . without searching for a deep meaning which he himself did not offer us, and perhaps had not even thought through himself' (p. 91 above). With that the impetus which Bonhoeffer gave would merely be weakened or even used to stabilize the old positions.

On the other hand, neither can one stop with Bonhoeffer, because his thought is fragmentary and therefore points beyond itself. A Bonhoeffer renaissance must therefore take care not to find in him premature solutions to problems, which eliminate his own sense that a problem does exist.

Nothing is more important for the interpretation of Bonhoeffer than finding a clue to the 'persistent basic impulse' of his thought and in the first instance pointing to that range of experiences and problems which was determinative for him. It is only by viewing this range that Bonhoeffer's new attempt to solve problems can be critically tested.

Let us ask first of all about the origin of Bonhoeffer's consciousness of the existence of a problem, in order to submit his own last attempt at a solution to a critical examination, and finally to consider what consequences could arise for the further interpretation of Bonhoeffer.[1]

---

[1] The investigation is to be understood as a contribution to the discussion and considers itself therefore indebted to the previous contributors. It has as its thesis that Bonhoeffer was unable to solve the problem of the relationship between the reality of the world and the reality of God which tormented him, that with the concept of the 'world come of age' he fell into a misunderstanding of the society which was freeing itself, and that this can be shown in his most important writings.

The conversation with the previous interpretation of Bonhoeffer must remain limited to allusions to begin with. For the same reason the

The Cross of Reality?

1. The origin of Bonhoeffer's consciousness of the existence of a problem

When Bonhoeffer turned to the study of theology, he set out to discover the church (cf. MW I, p. 27).

The theme of the church was given to him in Berlin by Troeltsch who had renounced a 'dogmatic' concept of the church and considered the Christian churches as the embodiment of the religious idea, and who had submitted them to an inner-worldly 'socio-typical' way of thinking, in order to determine whether they would have something useful and valuable to contribute to the mastering of the expanding tendencies of the development of the West and to the solving of the problem of socialism. For Troeltsch, therefore, the question of the church stood in the realm of the 'modern world' which had led to the dissolution of the traditional social structure.

And so through Troeltsch, who himself of course did not make modern society 'a theological theme of a social theory',[2] the question which was constitutive for Bonhoeffer's ecclesiology was posed, namely how the church as a social structure

[2] Trutz Rendtorff, 'Geschichte und Gesellschaft', in *Spannungsfelder der evangelischen Soziallehre*, Hamburg, 1960, p. 156.

question about the non-religious interpretation of biblical concepts (cf. MW II, pp. 12–73; G. Ebeling, *World and Faith*, London, 1963, pp. 98–161: and G. Ebeling, *Religion in Geschichte und Gegenwart*, III, p. 257) is intentionally postponed, because it is the opinion of the author that its answer is dependent upon the clarification of the understanding of reality. The dominant critical function of this contribution should however not conceal that Bonhoeffer's problem was like a temptation into which he came through obedience to his faith. As representative for others, he dealt with this world as the place to which faith is commissioned, and thereby subjected himself to the life of suffering of our responsibility for the world. The critique of Bonhoeffer's solution to the problem should stimulate a continuation in the certainty of mission to which he knew that he belonged and to which he knew he was responsible.

relates 'in principle from its very primary essence . . . to the modern social problem'.[3]

While Troeltsch arrived at the conclusion that the idea of the kingdom of God, which he considered the central Christian idea, is 'a completely universal utopia of the future', which could 'by no means be changed into a socio-philosophical or socio-theological theory of the present',[4] Bonhoeffer held 'the familiar separation . . . between the kingdom of God and the church to be . . . both theologically and sociologically "untenable"'; he viewed the church as 'the kingdom of God on earth' (sc, p. 236). To be sure, the church was 'not the same as the kingdom of God' for him, however much it was identical with the 'kingdom of Christ', which he designated as 'the kingdom of God which has been realized in history since the coming of Christ' (sc, p. 112). And so he could conceive of the church itself as the 'form of revelation', and accordingly, could give expression to the conviction that the church is the fundamental and directive social form, and must therefore also in its *form* proclaim 'Christ existing as community' (sc, pp. 97*f.*, 203).

The contrast to Troeltsch, for whom the important thing 'in the evangelical concept of the church was not the community, but only the Word', becomes clearly evident (cf. sc, pp. 102, 135, 203). Bonhoeffer opposed the 'characteristic indifference of the Christian idea to everything political and social',[5] which Troeltsch maintained. He tried instead to develop a dogmatic method out of a 'sociology of the church' in conformity with which he could speak of the church as a substantial social structure, while Troeltsch, following Johannes Weiss (*Die Predigt vom Reich Gottes*, 1892), thought of

[3] Ernst Troeltsch, *Die Soziallehre der christlichen Kirchen und Gruppen*, Tübingen, 1919 (1912), p. 2*f.*

[4] Ernst Troeltsch, *Die Sozialphilosophie des Christentums*, 1923, p. 7.

[5] Ernst Troeltsch, *Die Christliche Welt*, 1917, p. 146*f.* For Troeltsch history broke down into 'the actuality of the modern structures of reality, on the one hand, and the ethical content of Christianity which remained historical, on the other hand' (Rendtorff, *op. cit.* p. 157).

The Cross of Reality?

the kingdom of God strictly eschatologically, and therefore could speak only of the 'anticipated spiritual effects on the community which waits for the kingdom of God'.[6] Therefore Troeltsch could, in the face of the 'changing world situations',[7] speak only of a 'minimum of church' existing out of a 'common feeling and a consciousness of inheritance',[8] whereas on the other hand the young Bonhoeffer pressed for a 'maximum of church' from which he expected a wholesome penetration of 'the life of all human community and society' (sc, p. 199). He did not, however, expect to solve the problem of modern society posed by historicism with his 'belief in the people of God' (cf. sc, pp. 82, 194f., esp. 195f.). He simply ignored it, because the problem of *history* in all its depth remained hidden from him.[9] Otherwise he could not have called for an *essential* structure of the church on the basis of the observation that the Christian religion is distinguished from all other religions in that in it 'the idea of

[6] Troeltsch, *Die Sozialphilosophie des Christentums*, p. 6.
[7] Troeltsch, *Die Soziallehren der christlichen Kirchen und Gruppen*, p. 986.
[8] *Ibid.*, p. 983. Characteristically, Troeltsch quotes Richard Rothe.
[9] Despite his critique of the youth movement and *Lebensphilosophie*, Bonhoeffer remains under the spell of F. Tönnies's distinction between a complete and insoluble 'community' which is essential for man's humanity, and a purposeful and producible 'society' which no longer essentially concerns man (sc, p. 56f.). Cf. J. Moltmann, 'Die Rose im Kreuz der Gegenwart', *Monatsschrift für Pastoraltheologie*, 1961, p. 278, note 16. This extremely questionable sociological distinction, which contains a metaphysical value-stress, is also to be found in H. D. Wendland's attempt at an evangelical theology of society, when 'primary, organic connexions or formations' and 'secondary' functional systems can be spoken of. Cf. H. E. Tödt, 'Theologie der Gesellschaft oder theologische Sozialethik', *Zeitschrift für evangelische Ethik*, 1961, p. 228f. This critical questioning remains valid also in regard to H. D. Wendland's exposition, 'Über Ort und Bedeutung des Kirchenbegriffs in der Sozialethik', *Theologische Literaturzeitung*, 1962, pp. 175–82.
When Bonhoeffer speaks in sc (cf. p. 153) of the earnestness of historicity, he is thinking, as does dialectical theology, of the necessary recognition of the sin and incompleteness which is essential for the reality of the world.

219

community is essential' (sc, p. 92), as if the church, re-sembling a meta-historical formation, stands as a timeless guide in the midst of the total socio-political process.[10]

Bonhoeffer may have rightly refused to view the church, as Troeltsch did, according to socio-psychological motives and from socio-typical viewpoints, but in so doing he too hastily passed over problems which had stabilized themselves in Troeltsch's antithesis of relative and absolute.

Did he himself not conceal, through an ecclesiology which reminds one of A. F. C. Vilmar in its direct praise of the church,[11] the understanding of the 'historical revelation', with the help of which alone can be overcome the unsolved problem of history from which historicism suffers? Did he not bar access for himself to a theological understanding of modern society with his 'sociology of the church'? Did there not result from the 'inner connexion between the reality of the church and the whole reality of revelation' (sc, p. 93) which is basic to Bonhoeffer's understanding of reality, a non-historical, dogmatic construction for which even Bon-hoeffer's continuing experience of world-reality (and also therefore of the everyday reality of the church) was no match? How could categories, which are again to give a standard and goal to a world involved in a process of socio-political dis-

[10] Bonhoeffer ran the risk of supplying a Christian, Western con-ception of order, which had found its expression in the form of the church, with a value-stress which reached far beyond the justifiable limit; thus he erroneously bestowed upon it a normative and trans-historical meaning.

[11] Bonhoeffer's later studies in *Ethics* point, in many respects, back to A. F. C. Vilmar; cf. 'The Relation of Office and Congregation (from above and below)', E, pp. 222*f.*, 286*f.*, 294*f.*; 'The Judgment of the Revolution', E, p. 96*f.*, 99*f.*, 102*f.*, 142, and 291*f.*; 'The Four Man-dates', E, p. 207*f.* Bonhoeffer wanted to know that Vilmar's books were in a safe place in order to have them on hand again after the end of the war (cf. WE, the photocopy of an excerpt from a letter on the page preceding page 14, lines 7*f.*). Could not Bonhoeffer's evaluation of the Old Testament also be traced back to Vilmar's influence and, not least, even his ecclesiology (Christ existing as community)?

The Cross of Reality?

solution of the established orders, be extracted from a sociology of the church (sc, pp. 107, 111)? Is this understanding not similar to a morphological fundamentalism? Has the constitution of traditional society, which became involved in the crisis at the disintegration of the order of the state, not also been the substratum for the self-realization of Western Christendom; so that now the social structure of the church also has to enter into the crisis with the deeply-rooted alteration of the social situation? Did Bonhoeffer not pass too quickly over Troeltsch's awareness of the existence of a problem?

Otherwise how could he have expected, in spite of Troeltsch's insight that 'Protestantism has remained in its essential characteristics and forms a recasting of a medieval idea', that it can be attributed socio-historically to the Middle Ages and that therefore Lutheranism, as a social structure, had to decay and break down with the beginning of modern times,[12] in order to be in the position, with the help of a 'sociology of the church' and from the community-form of the church, to penetrate and thereby to reform 'all human life, whether community or society' (sc, p. 199; cf. p. 166)? Bonhoeffer shared Troeltsch's interest in a mastering of the expansive tendencies of Western development and in a solution to the socio-political problems associated with them, without however acknowledging Troeltsch's problem.

Bonhoeffer could therefore in no way be helped or served by Kierkegaard's protest against the existing church and by a corresponding non-objective theology of the Word in a time of dissolving and decomposing social structure (cf. sc, p. 106). Instead of saving himself in the 'category of the individual' and reducing the church to a pure Word-event, he took the church seriously as *the* reality of the revelation of

---

[12] Cf. H. Bornkamm, *Luther im Spiegel der deutschen Geistesgeschichte*, Heidelberg, 1955, pp. 71*f.* and 272*f.* H. Rückert, 'Die geistesgeschichtliche Einordnung der Reformation', *Zeitschrift für Theologie und Kirche*, 1955, p. 28*f.* E. Wolf, 'Schöpferische Nachfolge', in *Spannungsfelder der evangelischen Soziallehre, op. cit.*, p. 36*f.*

God. According to his conviction, not the so-called 'genuine movement' of the pure act of faith, but only the being-with-one-another and for-one-another in the concrete church frees men to be human (sc, p. 129). Were not the broken relationships renewed and the 'ethico-social connexion' concretized in the 'concrete social form' of the actual church? Was not the *kingdom* actualized in it, in faithful recognition of the Lordship of God in love (sc, p. 119*f.*)?

Already in these first inquiries Bonhoeffer's certainty of his task is manifest: he is concerned about the mission of the community of Jesus Christ for this world.[13]

At the same time the question about the correct understanding of church and world and their mutual relationship is posed anew, the question Bonhoeffer now had to engage in in the face of a modern revolutionary, post-revolutionary, revisionist society in process of emancipation. In this engagement he cannot avoid a concrete interpretation of history and he faces the task of interpreting the modern phenomenon of a society in process of emancipation and of showing anew the mission of the church of the modern world. The question is whether he was successful in this theological task.[14]

The actual historical contrast between the *Communion of Saints* and *antichrist*, which Bonhoeffer adopted in *Sanctorum Communio* from the Augustinian tradition of the Christian interpretation of history,[15] presupposes the idea of a 'double

[13] 'Only he who loves the earth and God in one . . . can believe in the kingdom of God', GS III, p. 270. 'God, brother and earth belong together', CF, p. 39. Cf. Chr. Hinz, 'Christliche Verkundigung angesichts atheistischer Anfechtung', *Monatschrift fur Pastoraltheologie*, 1962, p. 29*f.*

[14] This question, to which this investigation is limited, should be answered on the basis of *Sanctorum Communio*, *Act and Being*, *Ethics* and *Letters and Papers from Prison*.

[15] This real-historical contrast of the kingdom of God to the kingdom of the antichrist, under the aspect of which human society is considered as transitory and dualistic, and the eschatological statements of the New Testament are transformed into an apocalyptical-eschatological view of history, is also found in H. D. Wendland. Cf. H. E. Tödt, *op. cit.*, p. 236*f.*

historical process' (sc, p. 198*f.*), in which God's saving action had to appear as preserving action, whereas all changes had to be interpreted as perversions and destructions of the original, basic relations of social existence. Therefore for Bonhoeffer the Fall still stands at the beginning of human social history and the Last Judgement at the end, so that – in terms of a later, but nevertheless corresponding sentence in *Ethics* – the Creation is 'according to its origin' the indivisible whole of reality grounded and realized in God, while 'according to its goal' it is called the 'kingdom of God' (E, p. 193). Thereby Creation and kingdom of God threaten to remain limiting concepts so that history itself is understood as a mere episode which 'cannot bring the final solution', but which remains enclosed by Creation and the kingdom of God and therefore radically transcended. History is the time-in-between of the existing, but already perishing, world where the kingdom of God penetrates in the form of revelation – the church – but which becomes depreciated all the more to that which stands between protology and eschatology.

Consequently Creation is not, in Bonhoeffer's scheme, the etiology of the history of God with man and their world, for the sake of which the history of the saving acts of God can be antedated to Creation; rather it becomes an abstract primordial date and therewith a complete horizontal within which history appears only as a transitory force which produces nothing essentially new in all its movement, but only hastens to meet its end.[16]

Eschatology remains all the more the total horizon, both near and far, of a world which itself is no longer the place and content of God's saving deeds; rather it seems to be devaluated to a redemptive-historical no-man's-land. And so the history of this world-time moves for Bonhoeffer under a universal, apocalyptic aspect. In his opinion 'two basic

[16] Cf. G. v. Rad, *Theologie des Alten Testaments* I, p. 143*f.*

fundamental tendencies' are warring against each other, and 'both are destined to flourish in a constant increase of violence and power' (SC, p. 199).

'The one is the striving of the *sanctorum communio* to penetrate all human life, whether community or society' – the other is the power of the 'antichrist' which destroys all original forms of community and orders of Creation (SC, p. 199).[17]

The thought of a possible positive historical change of social 'givens', even a discovery and development of new possibilities of social realization being given as man's responsibility, is unable to emerge in this transitory, dualistic scheme of the social process.

Therefore where the desire for a better regulating of social problems broke forth, Bonhoeffer saw in it only contempt for the historicity of this world, a world which is and remains a world of sin and death (SC, p. 153).

However, in that Bonhoeffer, in his protest against the secularized kingdom of God concepts (Kant) and the socialistic kingdom of God expectations (Count St. Simon, Tolstoy, religious-social youth movement) separated the kingdom of God and history, he obligated himself to a redemptive historical scheme of *Creation* – (Fall) – *world-time* or history – (last judgement) – *kingdom of God*, within the framework of which he could no longer take history seriously – even when he called 'the history of the church . . . the hidden centre of world history' – because the presence of Christ in history was thought of thereby as analogous to an eternal presence of a timeless order, which in the struggle against 'human imperfection and sin' reveals itself, but is not itself history (SC, p. 154f.). To that extent Bonhoeffer's oft-emphasized 'seriousness of historicity' corresponds to the

---

[17] Cf. note 9 for the distinction between community and society. In addition, Bonhoeffer's concept of community is formally reminiscent of Hegel's.

'seriousness' of his 'Christian doctrine of sin',[18] not however to taking history seriously as a reality effected by God's Word.[19]

Just as in the Wisdom teaching of Israel, with the early Bonhoeffer everything created becomes transcendent towards God, without the phenomenon of history being of further interest.[20]

For example, by making use of Ranke's words about the immediacy of every epoch to God,[21] Bonhoeffer *theologically* (sc, p. 198) justified his sociological method for asking about the essential structure of the church, but in doing so he

[18] Cf. the early Barth's doctrine of sin, the consequence of which is that the sin of the individual is only an illustration of fundamental sin, which refers everything historical to the time-in-between, the time which stretches between the death of Adam and the resurrection of Christ as the world of man (of the merely human). Cf. G. Krüger, 'Dialektische Methode und theologische Exegese', *Zwischen den Zeiten*, 5th edition, 1927, p. 135*f*. Cf. sc, p. 145*f*.

[19] Cf. C. Westermann, 'Bemerkungen zu den Thesen Bultmanns und Baumgärtels', in *Problems alttestamentlicher Hermeneutik*, München, 1960, p. 102*f*.

Is not the history which we encounter the result of the developments and complications which arise from the fact that God, in *covenant* with man, manages history for the sake of the world? The histories in which we are involved every day remain therefore ambiguous and never speak for themselves; they always need interpretation which has to know more than the mere facts. We are therefore not able to secure for ourselves the meaning of history, and we cannot make it understandable simply on the basis of reason; we always start from the certainty of faith, if we are not to remain exposed, without promise, to the tragic question about the meaning of history.

[20] G. v. Rad, *op. cit.* 1, p. 447. Cf. G. Harbsmeier, 'Die nichtreligiöse Interpretation', in *Antwort: Festschrift für K. Barth*, Zürich, 1956, p. 558*f*.

[21] This conception of an immediacy of God corresponds to Ranke's ocular method. For Yorck von Wartenburg's and W. Dilthey's motives for rejecting Ranke as a historian, cf. Yorck von Wartenburg, *Bewusstseinsstellung und Geschichte*, Tübingen, 1955, p. 200, note 36. Erich Heintel, '"Wie es eigentlich gewesen ist"': Ein geschichtsphilosophischer Beitrag zum Problem der Methode der Historie', in *Erkenntnis und Verantwortung: Festschrift f. Th. Litt.*, Düsseldorf, 1960, pp. 207–30.

undoubtedly excluded the Hegelian method of 'giving an outline of its development from the point of view of the philosophy of history' (sc, p. 199) and, at the same time, confined himself within a concept of history; consequently, he believed it possible to find the saving answer in the non-historical question about the 'essential structure of the church' in the midst of a world-wide process of socio-political change and re-orientation.

But with its help he merely arrived – as the *Ethics* confirms – at a misinterpretation of the so-called secularization process, on the one hand, and of the venerable Western, Christian system of order, on the other hand. His contribution to a 'sociology of the church' threatened, in the guise of extreme piety, to give over the world as a world of godlessness. The tension between church and world, which Bonhoeffer thought he could still understand as analogous to Luther's doctrine of the two kingdoms as a 'polemical unity', threatened in the face of modern society to lead to the antagonism of a dualistic understanding of reality.[22]

This is all the more amazing, in that Bonhoeffer affirmed the church as 'God's new purpose for men' (sc, p. 103) in order to 'be able to take seriously the will of God in the concrete form of the other' and in this way to rejoice in the love and wisdom of God in the *midst* of the interpersonal relationships of everyday living.

Thus quite logically he attempted in *Act and Being* to designate the church as the 'place where existence is understood' in order to continue his critique of the disconnectedness of the proclamation of revelation from worldly reality and in order to reconcile both in an 'ecclesiastical way of thinking'.

However, with the endeavour to disclose, in the 'light of

[22] This corresponds to the antagonism of the double assurance of truth in the Greek tradition. Cf. W. Jens, 'Das Begreifen der Wahrheit im frühen Griechentum', Stud. Gen. 4, 1951, p. 240*f.*

ecclesiastical thinking', 'that the attempt at an autonomous understanding of existence fails *a priori*' (AB, p. 118), this 'ecclesiastical thinking' itself came under the spell of the conceptual system of this autonomous understanding of self and world.

Even if Bonhoeffer grasped act and being as the dialectic of belief and the community of Christ (AB, pp. 16, 125, 126*f.*), he still remained closely bound to that tradition from which the problem of act and being originates.[23]

In that he attempted 'to unite the concerns of genuine transcendentalism and genuine ontology in an "ecclesiastical way of thinking"', he spared himself further inquiry into the history of the origin of transcendentalism and ontology, as well as their latent antagonism.

And so the challenge of the act-being synthesis of an 'ecclesiastical way of thinking' was equivalent to the attempt to neutralize the problem of the *analogia entis* and the *analogia actionis* (i.e. *fidei*) in an *analogia ecclesiae*, in order to arrive, in this way, at an all-encompassing and illuminating understanding of existence.

Indeed the main point for Bonhoeffer was that God be

[23] Also in C. Ratschow, who, in opposition to Bonhoeffer, does not pose the question of act and being and want to see its solution in the church, but rather in Jesus as the event of God (*Der angefochtene Glaube*, Gütersloh, 1957, p. 102), the given conceptual horizon proves to be an obstacle to taking seriously the history of God with man and the world. Ratschow limits himself to the ever-new history of the Christian and, at the same time, to the question about the '*esse* of the Church' (*op. cit.*, pp. 313*f.* and 229, note 14).

Is not W. Pannenberg, too, in his endeavour at a complete understanding of reality, in spite of his distance from the 'inclusiveness of the essential orders of the world' which was still present in the Thomistic understanding of reality, entangled in the ontological problem of act and being, if he is willing to trust the 'historical basis of Western thinking' in order to ask anew about the structure of being, even if only emphasized 'in the sign of contingency' (cf. 'Akt und Sein im Mittelalter', *Kerygma und Dogma*, 1961, p. 218 and 'Die Krise des Ethischen und die Theologie', *Theologische Literaturzeitung*, 1962, p. 16)?

neither objectified nor relegated to obscurity, and so, especially in this work, his path diverged from the tendencies of dialectical theology, which he designated as theological transcendentalism.[24] He rightly emphasized that 'man *must be* placed into reality by God, so that room can remain in his thinking for reality' (AB, p. 89*f.*; cf. p. 117*f.*). However, from what kind of *understanding of reality* did he thereby *still* proceed if he thought he could examine the Christ-reality of the church for 'basic structures' and if he hoped to extract from them 'sociologico-theological' categories (AB, pp. 119, 122, 137*f.*), with the help of which 'all human community and social living' should be penetrated,[25] so that, in this way, 'the ultimate would lay claim to the penultimate once more' (SC, p. 198*f.* and E, p. 142)?

Did Bonhoeffer not come simply to a premature incorporation of theology, which as a function of the church, in analogy to Barth's 'positivism of revelation',[26] threatened to lead to a positivism of the church, and in analogy to Barth's Christo-centrism occasioned a possible pan-ecclesiology? In any case, the danger of an absolutizing of the empirical church was not to be prevented by establishing a careful distinction and therefore a safeguarding tension between 'Christ existing as community' and 'the heavenly Christ, whom we await' (AB, p. 121, note 2). For to the same extent that the church was removed from the changing of the times, its orders were attributed eternal validity. Did Bonhoeffer's categorial system of a socio-theology not therefore live from the negation of history (cf. AB, pp. 119, 139)?

[24] Cf. AB, pp. 70*f.*, 83*f.*, 86*f.* For Bonhoeffer, it is, for example, 'a fateful error on Barth's part to replace the Creator and Lord with the concept of the subject' (AB, p. 136). Cf. R. Prenter, 'D. Bonhoeffer and K. Barth's Positivism of Revelation', p. 124*f.* Bonhoeffer considers especially Barth's dialectic as a 'method inseparable from the heart of the matter' (cf. AB, p. 83*f.* and p. 119*f.* above). He is convinced that Barth's 'whole case stands or falls with it' (AB, p. 135, note 1).

[25] Cf. note 9.

[26] Cf. Prenter's essay, p. 93*ff.* above.

The Cross of Reality?

In spite of this, with his attempt at 'ecclesiastical thinking', Bonhoeffer did dare to have dealings with the reality of the world. He was therefore also very vulnerable to empirical reality and – this is without a doubt his advantage over against non-objective theology – he was also more easily shaken from his theological foundation.

He apparently tried too hastily to settle the problem of church and world, with all its epistemological questions, in an 'ecclesiastical way of thinking', so that Troeltsch's resignation was only apparently overcome and dialectical theology merely diacritically surpassed, without really breaking through its closed conceptual system. The maximum of his praise of the empirical, concrete, visible church was in conflict with a minimum of concrete, visible experience of the church. The 'reality of the church' nevertheless seemed to be still a long way from being synonymous with the concrete empirical reality of visible church communities. Otherwise how could that oft-quoted extract from the year 1931, the year *Act and Being* appeared, have been thinkable?

Could it be that our time is past and that the gospel is given to another people, perhaps preached with completely different words and deeds? What do you think about the imperishableness of Christendom in the face of the world situation and our own way of living? It becomes more and more incomprehensible that for the sake of the *one* righteous person 'the city will be spared ' . . . Who still believes? The invisibility ruins us. If we cannot see in our personal lives that Christ was there, then at least we want to see it in India, but this constant, senseless being thrown back on the invisible God himself – that no man can endure any longer' (GS I, p. 61).

The disintegration of state order had, as its result, the destruction of Western Christendom, in fact a new understanding of reality which seemed to get by without a religious *a priori*; this disintegration confronted a nearly nineteen-hundred-year-old tradition of proclamation and theology with its most difficult crisis to date.

Bonhoeffer was deeply shocked by the actual non-church

orientation of the present, and sensed already the religionlessness of the modern world. He was shocked by the extent of
the processes of the decay of the Christian West and undertook, in face of the increasing experience of a society in
process of emancipation, the resolute attempt to show the
church its task in the midst of a *corpus christianum* (E, p. 92), to
smooth out access to the proclamation of the Word for the
unchurched as 'preparation for the coming of grace' (E, p.
137), and to allow the ultimate to lay claim to the penultimate once more (E, p. 142); because of this he could not
relinquish the hope of working on the foundations of the
'reconstruction of a united West' (E, p. 12; cf. p. 119).

However, in his *Ethics*, which was to serve this purpose,
Bonhoeffer no longer presupposed the reality of the empirical
church as *the* reality of revelation, rather he spoke instead
much more carefully of 'God's self-revelation in Jesus Christ'
and of the 'realization of the reality of God's revelation in
Christ among his creatures' (E, pp. 193, 190). With that he
came very close to Barth, for example, when he called the
good, 'reality itself, seen and recognized in God, (E, p. 193)
and when for him – note the difference from the 'ecclesiastical
way of thinking' – only 'in Jesus Christ . . . the reality of God
has entered into the reality of this world'; therefore also the
'place at which the question about the reality of God, as well
as the question about the reality of the world, is given an
answer' can be designated only through the name, Jesus
Christ (E, p. 194).

For Bonhoeffer, in contrast to Kierkegaard's dialectic of
existence and dialectical theology, now as always the reality
of God in Jesus Christ actually *entered into* the reality of this
world and not merely into an absolute paradox with it. And
so he could ask, in his *Ethics*, 'about the realization of this
reality of God and of the world in our world which is given in
Jesus Christ' (E, p. 195), whereby for him 'the realization of
Christ with the reality of God and of the world are united in
one place'; this is the reason he no longer desired 'Christ

without the world or the world without Christ' (E, p. 197). But what did Bonhoeffer mean by this 'reality of Christ', since for him all 'concepts of reality' which neglect Jesus Christ remain 'abstractions' (E, p. 194)?

This may be shown in the differentiation of ultimate and penultimate which is characteristic of Bonhoeffer's ethics (E, p. 120*f.*), whereby one best proceeds from the 'two extreme forms' in which the relationship between the ultimate and the penultimate in Christian life '. . . unfortunately all too often . . . is dissolved' (E, p. 127):

1. '*The radical solution* sees only the ultimate, and in it only the complete breaking off of the penultimate.'

'What then becomes of the world is no longer of any consequence; the Christian bears no responsibility for it and the world must perish.'

2. '*The compromise*' separates the last word from all penultimate words. 'The penultimate retains its right in itself and is not threatened or endangered by the ultimate.'

'The world still stands; there are still penultimate things to be done in responsibility for this world which God created.'

Conclusion: 'There is no Christianity as such, for this would destroy the world; there is no man as such, for he would exclude God. Both are ideas. There is only the God-man Jesus Christ who is real, and through him the world will be preserved until it is ready for its end.'

It is an historically unmediated, dialectical union between God and man, Creation and salvation, time and eternity (cf. pp. 128, 130) which we find in this paradoxical relationship between penultimate and ultimate.

Therefore thinking in two realms is in no way overcome, rather only radicalized in the framework of a universal-apocalyptical conception, in that 'the ultimate leaves open a certain amount of room for the penultimate' (E, p. 133). Since Christ's resurrection an *old* perishing world of this *time* and a *new* approaching world of *eternity* overlap (E, p. 130*f.*) in the 'polemical unity' of a limited co-existence. The crucifixion of Christ is therefore 'not simply the annihilation of Creation', nevertheless Bonhoeffer understands it as the death sentence on Creation, so that only the execution of this judgement still remains, and man is therefore bidden in the name of the Crucified 'to live on . . . under the death-sign of the cross' (E, p. 132). For Bonhoeffer this comes to an intersection of two different, finally mutually exclusive realities in the Cross of Christ: the reality of the world and the reality of God.

This is a destructive dialectic of time and eternity which is only for a last short while held together by a reconciling dialectic of the reality of Christ. That is, the reality of Christ itself is synonymous with the strange paradox of a simultaneity of a separating and reconciling *dialectic* of time and eternity, Creation and salvation, so that 'the Christian life means neither a destruction nor a sanctioning of the penultimate' (E, p. 133).

So an extremely acute state of affairs results, which appears to take fully into account the situation of the *corpus Christi* in a broken *corpus christianum*, but nevertheless is untenable; a state of affairs the conceptuality of which Bonhoeffer had to disagree with, the more experience he had. That is to say, the unity of 'the reality of God and the reality of the world' which was for Bonhoeffer given in Christ, remained an extremely questionable notion. With its help Bonhoeffer wanted to overcome 'the conceptual pairs worldly-Christian, natural-supernatural, profane-sacred, reasonable-revelatory as the last static contrasts' of thinking in spheres. But did he really overcome them? Hardly![27]

[27] Bonhoeffer pursued the clarification of the problem of history and ontology very far, but at the same time he made the problem more acute. Cf. H. Schlüsser, 'Norm und Situation in der theologischen Ethik', *Zeitschrift für evangelische Ethik*, 1961, p. 165 *f.* There is still 'a natural-normative character to Bonhoeffer's concept of the mandates'; J. Moltmann, 'Die Wahrnehmung der Geschichte in der christlichen Sozialethik', *Evangelische Theologie*, 1960, p. 278, Cf. notes 9 and 11 above. With his teaching of the orders, Bonhoeffer does not succeed in

The Cross of Reality?

'The world, the natural, the profane, reason' were for him 'incorporated in God from the outset' (E, p. 198; cf. p. 133), because God's historical revelation happened, according to his understanding, in this world, but in the end was not related to this world; with this, Bonhoeffer merely sanctioned the *status quo* of an abstractly conceived reality of Creation for the *time* between the Fall and the Last Judgement, as the end of the reality of this world.

Actually, therefore, Bonhoeffer radically transcended the reality of this world-time in the name of the reality of God, although he did not want to draw the conclusions of dialectical theology and therefore strove to reconcile and unite the reality of God and the reality of the world in *history* (cf. E, p. 12), and although he himself was of the opinion that he had renewed with this 'polemical unity' of the reality of God and the reality of the world Luther's doctrine of the two kingdoms (E, p. 199). This allowed the 'ultimate to lay claim to the penultimate once more', as Luther had done, and thus to put a stop to the obvious disintegration of the system of order of the penultimate 'by a more emphatic proclamation of the ultimate' (E, p. 142). Bonhoeffer had, as little as Luther, applied the distinction between law and gospel to the understanding of history, although this should have been done long ago.[28] Consequently Bonhoeffer remained, as did Luther,

[28] 'The distinction between law and gospel . . . is with Luther and in the Reformation factually related to the doctrine of justification, as well as to the doctrine of scripture' (E. Wolf, 1523), but not to the problem of history, which is revealed but at the same time made insignificant by the liberation to 'creative discipleship' (cf. Gal. 4 and 5). Not by accident, the relationship between discipleship and commission into

his theological interpretation of modern society, which is released into its life of responsibility for the world. With it he remains obligated to the reformation social teaching, which is still connected to the social order of the Middle Ages. Cf. MW III, p. 65f. and note 12 above. To Bonhoeffer's tradition-bound exposition of Romans 13. 1–7 (E, pp. 339f., 342), cf. E. Käsemann, 'Röm. 13. 1–7 in unserer Generation', *Zeitschrift für Theologie und Kirche*, 56, 1959, p. 343.

caught in the old European system of thought, as if the 'kingdom' still existed and the appearance of its decay could be only the foreboding of the coming of the Day of Judgement.[29]

The Reformation, because of its conserving tendency towards the Middle Ages, had once more stopped 'a late medieval process of disintegration which, in the Renaissance and in humanism, stood directly before a break-through and in which the Western spirit already strove to free itself from its ties to Christian and church authority; it had subdued Europe once more for no less than two hundred years to the Christian norm.'[30] Therefore Bonhoeffer's neo-Reformation endeavours as the 'basis' for the 'reconstruction of a united West' (E, p. 12; cf. p. 196) were doomed to fail as an anachronism. The kingdom was long since broken and decayed, without the appearance of the 'dear Day of Judgement'. Instead, the experience of ongoing history under the impact of new social relations and industrial production standards made the historicity of this our world more clearly evident. Was it not the world-wide field of service for human recognition of the world, giving it form and thus changing it?

In his polemic against Troeltsch and later at the beginning of the church struggle, Bonhoeffer was too hasty in his

---

[29] Luther's view of history rested on the doctrine of the four monarchies, which was taken for granted well into the seventeenth century. Cf. H. Rückert, *op. cit.*, p. 48. In addition, *Weimarer Ausgabe* LIII, p. 1*f. Supputatio annorum mundi*. Further, cf. the chronicle of the world by Johannes Carion and Otto von Freising, which was published by Melanchthon in 1532, the chronicle which is, in historiography, the 'highpoint of the linking of "Translatio Imperii" and the teaching of the kingdom of the world of Daniel' (Goez).

[30] H. Rückert, *op. cit.*, p. 51.

---

the world (cf. Matt. 5. 1–16) remains hidden for Bonhoeffer, even though he sees that following Jesus brings 'the liberation of man from all human statutes' to 'single-minded obedience' (*Cost of Discipleship*, pp. 31, 33*f.* and 61*f.*). Cf. E. Wolf, *Schöpferische Nachfolge*, *op. cit.*, 26/27.

condemnation of the enlightenment and revolutionary tendencies generally, because of their hostility to the church, as the 'laying bare of the emancipated man' (E, p. 97) and saw in them the 'defection from everything existent' and 'the supreme development of all anti-divine powers' (E, p. 106); he therefore came to the conclusion that the West stood 'before nothingness . . . with the loss of its unity created by the figure of Jesus Christ' (E, p. 105*f.*). This is a conclusion which follows logically from Bonhoeffer's theological path, but which is no longer able adequately to follow the historical process of the Christian West.

So Bonhoeffer's redemptive-historical vision of a 'dualistic historical process' (SC, p. 199) arrived at its completion and its end in its interpretation of the 'end time' of the 'Western world' (E, p. 105*f.*). Bonhoeffer was unable to include his own experiences of the history of time and the growing knowledge of its possible pre-history in this traditional understanding of the process of history. He sensed a deep *aporia* which had to be connected with the end of a nineteen-hundred-year-old tradition of this Christian understanding of the world, and he was ready, in obedience to his faith, to engage in a new encounter with the world and interpretation of it.

As he found both the time and the necessary distance from events during his imprisonment to occupy himself anew with the 'inheritance and decay' of the West, he came to a new evaluation of the so-called secularization process (LPP, p. 120*f.*; cf. pp. 77*f.*, 122*f.*, etc.), whereby the Confessing Church came under his criticism because of its churchliness (LPP, pp. 109*f.* and 165*f.*) and he himself fell into a deep crisis of his own understanding of reality. Bonhoeffer's shock at the actual religionlessness of the world of today led to the query, what the church of Jesus Christ actually *still* means for this 'world come of age'.

What had the 'open church of Jesus Christ, which serves the world till the end' (E, p. 129), to do in a world which, with its autonomous reason, already seemed to be served for the best and, to all appearances, was also real?

Did the world not draft viable and functional social structures without needing to concern itself with the 'essential structure' of the social system of the church (cf. sc, pp. 92, 104, 111)? Did this world still need an *analogia ecclesiae* to understand itself (cf. AB, p. 117*f*.)? Was it not in the position to order all its concerns *etsi deus not daretur* – and could it therefore not forego the service of the church to the world? Had it not become a 'world come of age' and, at the same time, a religionless world (cf. LPP, pp. 121*f*., 122*f*.)? Indeed was it not high time for the church to deliver itself from its self-satisfaction and self-enclosed conceptions of order and to gain contact with the new understanding of reality? At the end of the long path which had proceeded from the experience of the church, with the effort to restore its lost centre to a broken social pattern in the social structure of the church, stood the phenomenon of the so-called 'world come of age' and with it the question whether and how 'to reclaim for Christ a world which has come of age' is still possible (LPP, p. 115).

Now, as always, the question was the relationship of the reality of the world to the reality of God. Only now the understanding of 'the reality of the world' had found its new and final interpretation for Bonhoeffer in the concept of the 'world come of age'. Bonhoeffer now saw the pre-history of the modern understanding of autonomous reason in a new light. He arrived at a new description and evaluation of the great secularization process (cf. LPP, p. 106*f*.). He also reached the question how, consequently, the being together of the reality of the world and the reality of God accomplished in Jesus Christ can be thought of. That is, he now interpreted the relationship of Jesus Christ to the world more and more from the new horizon of experience of the total reflection of autonomous reason. But was the concept of the 'world come of age' not identical with society's misunderstanding of its own history? Does 'intellectual honesty', within its closed conceptual system, not just mean the compulsion to abide strictly by the conditions required for the effort to achieve world-conquest?[31] Did Bonhoeffer, with his recognition of the need for unrestricted reflection on the concept of the 'world come of age', not merely fall prey to that tradition of thought from whose Greek-Catholic confirmation of truth[32] both ontology and transcendentalism drew their life; the tradition whose undisputed 'authenticity' gave life to Bonhoeffer's 'ecclesiastical thinking', because it only attempted to overcome the 'act-being synthesis' *dialectically*. The answer to these questions is decisive for Bonhoeffer's solution to the problem. The concept of the 'world come of age' cannot therefore be used uncritically. The methodical atheism given with this concept could, in its methodical energy, prove to be a last consequence of the metaphysical tradition of thought, in spite of all of its anti-metaphysical tendencies.[33]

Is Bonhoeffer's concept of the 'world come of age' not an unexplained misunderstanding of the man who is freed to be responsible for the world, a misunderstanding which lives from the denial of history and which prematurely justifies the reflection of the apparently autonomous reason? And is not Bonhoeffer's answer to his question about 'reclaiming the world come of age for Jesus Christ' inadequate to free men to the responsibility for the world, because a misleading understanding of the world lies at its very heart?

These appear to be the decisive questions for an interpretation of Bonhoeffer, from which every examination of the theology of the later Bonhoeffer and its long preparatory way must begin.

[31] Cf. G. Picht, *Die Erfahrung der Geschichte*, Frankfurt, 1958, p. 28*f.*

[32] 'Catholic', because the true must be the general *kath' olou* for this confirmation of truth. Cf. Picht, *op. cit.*, pp. 22, 13.

[33] Picht, *op. cit.*, p. 52*f.*; cf. p. 23. Picht, *Naturwissenchaft und Bildung*, p. 90*f.*

11. *Bonhoeffer's solution to the problem and a critical examination of it*

Let us first recall how, in the judgement of the later Bonhoeffer, 'Jesus . . . claims the whole of human life in all its manifestations for himself and for the kingdom of God' (LPP, p. 115), because in this connexion his emergent interpretation of the 'messianic suffering of God in Jesus Christ' (LPP, p. 123; cf. p. 164*f.*) not only throws a decisive light on his entire theological path, but also contains his answer to the crucial question about the mission and task of the church in this world.

Once again this is the problem of how to unite the reality of God and the reality of the world.

Is there still any room at all for God in this 'world come of age'? Was he not deprived of his justification for existence with the end of a 'nineteen-hundred-year-old Christian preaching and theology' which was based on a religious *a priori* (LPP, p. 91)? Why should the Western, Christian understanding of Christendom be only a time-bound 'garment of Christianity' (LPP, p. 91)? Could it not have been as easily concluded: 'If the cloak falls, so falls the duke' (Schiller)? Must not a religionless Christianity be a *contradictio in adjecto*?

Must not the reality of Christ, which Bonhoeffer could not give up for the sake of his belief, be hopelessly in conflict with the reality of the world, which he could not relinquish for the sake of his 'intellectual honesty'?

There is no easy answer to the difficulties. Bonhoeffer, now as before, was not prepared to yield to the realm of non-objectivity which was for him the last apparently storm-free zone; the zone into which, in his opinion, both Barth and Bultmann (each in his own way) had withdrawn in order to work 'essentially at restoration'.[34] Bonhoeffer himself had to reject the epistemological concept of transcendence in dialectical theology (LPP, p. 93) in order to let Christ remain

[34] Cf. for Barth, LPP, pp. 91*f.*, 95, 109, 110. Cf. for Bultmann, LPP, pp. 94, 110.

The Cross of Reality?

Lord 'even of those with no religion' in the midst of this world come of age (LPP, p. 91). Even now the important thing for him was the empirically-historical being-together of the reality of God and the reality of the world in Jesus Christ (cf. E, p. 197*f.*). But how could this have taken place, how was it to be realized, and hence how should the reality of God and the reality of the world be interpreted?

Bonhoeffer's crucial contribution to this question is found in his statements about Jesus himself being forsaken by God.

'. . . the only way to be honest is to recognize that we must live in the world – *etsi deus non daretur*. And this is precisely what we do see – before God! God himself brings us to this recognition. In this way our coming of age leads us to a true recognition of our situation before God. God teaches us that we must live as men who can get along quite well without God. The God who is with us is the God who forsakes us. The God who makes us live in this world without using him as a working hypothesis is the God before whom we are always standing. Before God and with him we live without God. God allows himself to be edged out of the world and on to the Cross; God is powerless and weak in the world, and that is the way, the only way, he can be with us and help us . . .' (cf. LPP, p. 122).

God is therefore, as the one who forsakes us, beyond in the midst of this world.[35] So Jesus appears as the first to transcend the world in this radicality, in that he unreservedly exposed himself to it and revealed all holy realms as only seemingly holy and all religious expectations as miracle-seeking and escapist. Therefore he appears, in contrast to the founders of religion, as the authoritative critic of religion and, at the same time, as the true precursor and pioneer of the autonomous understanding of reality, which has become possible, on Bonhoeffer's view, only through the reality of God revealed in Christ, and is therefore to be maintained only by reference to it.[36]

[35] Cf. LPP, pp. 93, 92 and G. Harbsmeier, *op. cit.*, p. 557.

[36] Thereby Bonhoeffer comes very close to Gogarten, who is no longer subject to criticism along with Barth and Bultmann in the *Letters*, as he was in *Sanctorum Communio* and *Act and Being*; he remains unmentioned, but begins to have something important to say about the

:off# World Come of Age

Thus Bonhoeffer encountered God's Yes and God's No to this world in the suffering and death of Jesus: the Yes and the No of a God who does not want to be without men, whom he nevertheless abandons, along with his world, 'for a short time', that is, and leaves man to himself and his autonomous reason.

Even if the knowledge of such God-forsakenness does clear away all false conceptions of God, does it not at the same time call in question the trust witnessed to in the history of Israel, trust in the God who reigns in the history of man and the world?

Does Bonhoeffer not merely swing from one extreme to the other in his unhistorical scheme of the reality of the world and the reality of God? Was his positive relationship to the apparently promising godlessness of the methodical atheism of total reflection (cf. LPP, p. 123) not premature? Was it not an exorbitant demand for autonomous reason to be responsible for the world (*etsi deus non daretur*)?[37] Was it not doing violence to the situation to make a virtue of obedient God-forsakenness out of the distress of godlessness, in order to solve the complications of a nineteen-hundred-year-old tradition of Western Christian culture?

In the *Letters and Papers from Prison* he wanted to free man, in reliance on Christ, to live responsibly 'on earth, before God',[38] victorious over despondency and arrogance (LPP, p.

[37] 'Natural-scientific knowledge does not exhaust a knowledge of man that would suffice to bear the responsibility for the world.' C. F. von Weizsäcker, *Zum Problem der Instrumentalisierung der Vernunft*. Cf., for example, A. Gehlen, *Urmensch und Spätkultur*, Bonn, 1956, p. 241.

[38] The expression 'before God' is an inadequate formulation for describing the relationship between God and man. It renders human existence too autonomous. It always happens 'with God' or 'against God' in that it engages in this world and its necessities, because no sufficient understanding of man and the world can be revealed to a methodical atheism.

interpretation of the 'world come of age'. Cf. H. Thielicke, 'Das Ende der Religion: Überlegungen zur Theologie Dietrich Bonhoeffers', *Theologische Literaturzeitung*, 1956, p. 323.

240

112), confident in his own work, cheerful towards this world (cf. LPP, p. 77), and therefore free from the obstinate, uncommunicative tragedy of all despisers and reformers of the world (cf. E, p. 127*f.*) : And he was undoubtedly instinctively on the track of the questions confronting us (LPP, p. 106*f.*).

However, the analysis of the age of reflection from which he proceeded and which he adopted with his concept of the so-called 'world come of age', was equivalent to a spurious construction of autonomous reason which would have needed a critical elaboration of the history of its origin. And so Bonhoeffer's trust in the self-sufficiency of autonomous reason was a fateful illusion closely bound to the modern superstition of the myth of belief in science.

Both prejudices were bound to deliver unconditionally the 'open church of Jesus Christ, which serves the world' (E, p. 129) and which is the church only 'when it is there for others' (LPP, p. 166) to the understanding of self, world and history of a methodical atheism, which is never neutral, whatever may be asserted to the contrary. They threatened to abandon men charged with responsibility for the world to the hopeless circle of abstract reason, or to secondary political causes.

The consequences which Hanfried Müller has drawn from Bonhoeffer's theology for a Christian community in a socialist society are therefore just as predetermined as they are false.[39] They abandon the socialist society, as well as the Christian community, to their own unexamined misunderstanding, and they renew the unhistorical thinking in two realms.[40] They

---

[39] Hanfried Müller, *Von der Kirche zur Welt: Ein Beitrag zu der Beziehung des Wortes Gottes auf die Societas in Dietrich Bonhoeffers theologischer Entwicklung*, Leipzig, 1961. Cf. p. *182f.* above.

[40] Bonhoeffer's surprising statement, that it is the cross of Christ itself which forces us to the recognition that we must live in a God-forsaken world, is usually uncritically received and adopted in the interpretation for Bonhoeffer as 'a new recognition of Christ'. Cf. J. Moltmann, 'Die Wirklichkeit der Welt und Gottes konkretes Gebot nach D. B.', MW III, p. 55*f.*, and Moltmann, 'Die Rose im Kreuz der Gegenwart', *op. cit.*, p. 287*f.* Also, Eberhard Hübner, 'Eine marxistische

sanction a totalitarian world 'in its being-closed-within-itself, in its inability to be transcended by man'[41] and speak to this world only of a 'negativity' of the cross[42] with the help of which the suffering of Christ is misused as a justification of the given state of affairs in this world.

This is to say no less than that Bonhoeffer himself was not in a position to reconcile the concepts which he regarded as the last great unhistorical entities of time and eternity, man and God, except in a paradoxical being-in-each-other of negative and positive dialectic. He was not able to bring them together in a dualistic thinking in spheres, or in a transitory and dualistic scheme of a double process of history.

Nevertheless, Bonhoeffer's leading intention, which was there from the beginning, is not disposed of. There is a clear line to be discerned: to a society which is freeing itself (and Bonhoeffer has different views about this at different times) the word of God should once more be so proclaimed 'that the world would change and renew itself' (LPP, p. 160). The ultimate must lay claim to the penultimate once again.

The question how God's revelation is related to Creation in its complete worldliness remains bound to this. This corresponded to Bonhoeffer's question about how the human and divine natures were related to each other in Jesus the Christ. Bonhoeffer was thereby – and here he came very close to the theological Wisdom of Israel – in search of the secret which God himself had planted in the world, without showing further interest in the phenomenon of history.[43] And so

[41] H. Müller, *op. cit.*, p. 379.
[42] *Op. cit.*, p. 376.
[43] G. v. Rad, *op. cit.*, I, p. 447*f*.

Bonhoeffer-Interpretation', *Kirche in der Zeit*, Düsseldorf, Okt. 1961, pp. 278–82. In his debate with H. Müller, the 'christological-soteriological beginning of Bonhoeffer's thought' which Müller has worked out, seems to him unquestionably above every criticism. *Op. cit.*, p. 380.

The Cross of Reality?

Bonhoeffer encountered the great temptation of a period for which contact with the reality of God in history had become the prevailing problem, with the conception of world history and redemptive history of a finally unhistorical Wisdom teaching, which directs an ultimate call to the responsibility of the individual. This call was bound to mean nothing, because the universal breadth of the implied conception was nothing but a theological abstraction.[44]

In fact Bonhoeffer was forced to proceed beyond the Wisdom teaching of the late Israel, which in its illusionless attitude towards the given[45] nevertheless understood the 'world' always as 'a supporting action of Yahweh', and for which the world *never* – in reference to God's decree – could be left to itself. Even for this Wisdom teaching, of whose efforts at 'interpretation'[46] Bonhoeffer's theology is reminiscent, Yahweh is always comprehensible only as the last 'limit' of a realm of the rational and empirical, which is given to man as his responsibility, in which what matters is mastering life with bold confidence, ready to fail with all its wisdom before God.[47]

With his attempt to lay claim to a religionless world for God's kingdom, Bonhoeffer returned to the 'non-redemptive-historical (*heilsgeschichtslos*) universal belief in Yahweh' of Israelite Wisdom, and to its 'pathos of recognition'.[48] His theology was the attempt of a middle class which, in the midst of the crisis of its own entire tradition, became conscious anew of its responsibility for the *whole* and tried to assume it;[49] but it remained subject to the current under-

[44] *Op. cit.*, p. 444.
[45] *Idem.*, p. 432.
[46] *Idem.*, p. 321.
[47] *Idem.*, p. 438.
[48] *Idem.*, II, p. 319.
[49] Cf. LPP, p. 68: '. . . it is a question of the *anthropos teleios* . . . Witiko does everything there is to be done by adapting himself to the realities of life, by always listening to the advice of those more experienced than himself, thus showing himself a member of the "whole".'

243

standing of reality in the prevailing culture-conscious-
ness.[50]

Bonhoeffer was here moving in the realm of assertions
about the reality of the world which, like the statements
about Creation of the Wisdom of Israel, 'should proclaim the
redemptive thoughts of God to the limits of their strength'.[51]
But this means that he abandoned the history of man and the
world to God-forsakenness. Especially the interpretation of
the commission of Jesus came under the increasing influence
of an understanding of world reality, the *aporia* of which is
reminiscent of late Israelitic scepticism as poetized in the fate
of Job.

The cross of Christ was misunderstood as an expression of a
double, overlapping reality, although it was the consequence
of mutually exclusive understandings of reality. Jesus was at
odds with the scribes and pharisees and therefore finally
brought to the cross by them, because he did not share the
late-Jewish conception of a distant God; he inaugurated
redemption in the midst of the present which, in pious
resignation, had been relegated to the end of history, and
thereby he went beyond the apocalyptic two-world theory,
broke through the barriers between sacred and profane, and
questioned deeply a self-sufficient, self-justified world of
order closed within itself. Jesus had to suffer from a world
which was not ready to allow itself to be concretely transcended by hopeful compassion and knowing love. It did not
want to be open and free for the Lordship of God which is
accomplished in the present in the midst of this world; rather
it waited, in deep resignation to an apparently real destiny
of this world-time, for the end of history, and surrendered

[50] Cf. notes 10, 11, 27, 28 above.
[51] G. v. Rad, *op. cit.*, I, p. 415.

We can never achieve this wholeness on our own; it can only be
acquired along with others . . .' Cf. what C. Hinz says about the
'Einwurzelung in Mitmenschlichkeit, Welt and Geschichte', *op. cit.*, p.
34*f.*

this world to God-forsakenness in the guise of extreme
piety. With this self-willed understanding of the world
Jesus did not agree. It is judged in the cross of Jesus, not
sanctioned, not even with time. And so the cross of Christ
cannot be understood as an expression of the so-called cross of
reality.[52]

Bonhoeffer suggested such a misunderstanding, because he
was too quick to approve the highly self-willed interpretation
of the world of entire reflection with his concept of the 'world
come of age', instead of submitting it to a theological critique
of reason. With the dialectic of his Christology of the cross he
was unable to escape the self-analysis of the age of reflection
which went back to Hegel via the anti-Hegelians Feuerbach,
Marx, Nietzsche and, not least, Kierkegaard; he remained
therefore under the spell of the tradition of thought of the

---

[52] Is not a misunderstanding of modern society reflected in the later
Bonhoeffer's understanding of the 'paradox of the cross' (MW III, p. 55)?
Indeed we must ask here 'in what way are Western evolution and
Christology related to each other' (cf. MW III, p. 55). But in contrast to
J. Moltmann's intention, this question ends in a critical query about
Bonhoeffer's dependence on an analysis of the present which, without
a doubt, goes back to Hegel (cf. J. Moltmann, 'Die Rose im Kreuz der
Gegenwart', *op. cit.*, p. 287f.). True Christianity does *not* stand in the
cross of reality, rather in that it engages in the currently existing society
in knowing love and active hope, it comes into conflict with its tendencies of self-preservation and self-assurance. Nor did Hegel engage in
history in the spirit of Jesus Christ; but he assured himself of it in the
spirit of the Greeks (Aristotle). His picture of the rose in the cross may
well be derived from Luther's coat-of-arms (he esteemed Luther very
highly), but his attempt to ally the Reformation to the revolution, so
that man would not fall prey to the horror of abstract freedom, failed
because of a misunderstanding of Christianity and his lack of understanding for the tradition of Israel.

Therefore especially G. Rohrmoser's thesis, that Hegel was the only
thinker who saw and understood the constitution of the modern world,
without concluding that Christian faith was conquered or destroyed,
should be called in question. Cf. note 54 below. For the uncritical
acceptance of Rohrmoser's thesis and its effects on the interpretation of
Bonhoeffer, cf. for example, W. D. Marsch's review in *Monatschrift für
Pastoraltheologie*, 1962, p. 125f.

Greek confirmation of truth.[53] And so, in his demand for a
religionless Christianity, Bonhoeffer is certainly aware of the
end of a nineteen-hundred-year-old tradition of Christian
preaching and theology. He is sure that what matters is to
free men for their responsibility for the world in a life of
suffering. But with the insight that the de-divinization of the
world presents an irreversible process, an understanding of
the world is still not achieved which can keep men from the
danger of making a self-willed picture of the world and from
falling prey to the logical screen of a metaphysical construction of reality, which can also result in religionlessness.

The question as to how mankind, which is released into the
freedom of its responsibility for the world, can be freed, still
remains open.

This question has been relentlessly posed anew by Bonhoeffer. But if we judge by the standard of this task of
reformation, he did not get beyond the beginning in his
attempt to allow the ultimate to lay claim to the penultimate.
To the very last he barred his own access to understanding
the crisis of tradition through his unhistorical scheme of the
reality of the world and the reality of God, derived from the
classical and Western tradition of the doctrine of the two
natures. He overlooked the problem, which had arisen with
the unveiling of man as free, of a society for which the world
had become history – had become the field of its thousand
possibilities, the race for the future, the system of security
against faulty constructions, had become fear in the face of
the open future of this world, and yet had become the field of
its unavoidable responsibility for the world.

For the interpretation of Bonhoeffer, we are therefore
bound to understand the expansion of the world and its

[53] The author hopes soon to be able to present the necessary basis for
this in a work on Hegel. Cf. W. Schulz, 'Das Problem der absoluten
Reflexion; Zur Auseinandersetzung mit dem Deutschen Idealismus', in
Einsichten: Gerh. Krüger zum 60. Geburtstag, Frankfurt, 1962, pp.
334–60.

The Cross of Reality?

connected crisis of devaluation from a theological standpoint. We cannot adopt, for the sake of 'intellectual honesty', its self-interpretation as documented in whatever is the current modern concept of society, as Troeltsch did – but also as Bonhoeffer did.[54]

III. *Consequences for the interpretation of Bonhoeffer*

The question is whether our world has been rightly interpreted by Bonhoeffer's concept of the 'world come of age'. Without a doubt Bonhoeffer was right in his demand that the Christian engage completely in this world in all its worldliness

[54] Because of the anti-Hegelian Hegelian, Kierkegaard, dialectical theology remained in Hegel's conceptual framework. Just as Kierkegaard only diacritically outdid Hegel with his 'armed neutrality', dialectical theology got round the problem of history. It therefore fell short of Hegel's consciousness of the problem in its critique of his solution, indirectly remaining bound to his conceptual system; this can be shown in an analysis of the section on Hegel in K. Barth's history of theology.

    G. Rohrmoser's critique of dialectical theology (*Subjectivität und Verdinglichung*, Gütersloh, 1961, p. 10*f.* and 'Die theologische Bedeutung von Hegels Auseinandersetzung mit der Philosophie Kants und dem Prinzip der Subjectivität', *Zeitschrift für Systematische Theologie*, 1962, pp. 89–111) should have a theological critique of Hegel's dialectical philosophy set alongside it. Both are necessary for gaining a sufficient understanding of history and society.

    Trutz Rendtorff's attempt to clear up the relationship of history and society remains bound to the conceptual system of Hegel's philosophy of society (*op. cit.*, pp. 161*f.*, 166*f.*) which was mediated to him by J. Ritter (*Hegel und die französische Revolution*, Köln, 1957). If one considers that Heidegger, in analogy to Kierkegaard, has leapt from the position of a particular consciousness into an 'image of the absolute, no longer Christian' (B. Liebrucks, *Idee und ontologische Differenz*, quoted in E. Heintel, *Hegel und die analogia entis*, Bonn, 1958, p. 52), one asks oneself how the course of biblical studies can be charted with this step backward into archaic thinking (cf. K. H. Haag, *Kritik der neueren Ontologie*, Stuttgart, 1960, p. 68*f.*), in order to allow Dietrich Bonhoeffer's call for a 'non-religious interpretation of biblical concepts' to find its answer. Cf. James M. Robinson, 'Heilsgeschichte und Lichtungsgeschichte', *Evangelische Theologie*, 1962, p. 138.

and therefore fall prey neither to a world behind the times, nor to a clerical reformation of the world (MW II, p. 75; III, p. 54). And so for the sake of the right relation to the world of the community of Jesus Christ, the correct understanding of the world was demanded, in order that, for the sake of the salvation of the world, the ensuing commission to the world[55] might not change 'into a mixture of fear of the world and victory over the world for the sake of the salvation of the church'.[56] Bonhoeffer had to give an answer to the question about the right relationship between 'worldliness and God' (LPP, pp. 118, 92, 122*f.*, 125; cf. MW II, p. 106*f.*). He still tried in his *Ethics* to interpret 'our world' from his understanding of 'God's entering into the world' in Jesus Christ (cf. MW III, p. 46*f.*). But in contrast to this, in the *Letters and Papers from Prison*, he apparently undertook the task of interpreting Jesus' life of suffering as 'the suffering of God in worldly life' and as 'the suffering of God in the godless world' on the basis of the self-understanding of the present age of reflection (LPP, p. 122*f.*). Therefore nothing is more important for an interpretation of Bonhoeffer than the examination of the conception of the 'world come of age'. For Bonhoeffer's own endeavours to discover the pedigree of the 'world come of age' and his conviction that the 'autonomy of man and the world' is not only 'the goal of thinking' everywhere, but is also the only appropriate understanding of the reality of the world, remain questionable (LPP, p. 121). Therefore it is important to investigate anew the history of the origin of the 'world come of age'. It refers back to Hegel's analysis of middle-class society in which the attempt was made, for the

[55] It is a matter of the reconciliation of the world, not only the proclamation of a reconciliation in the world. Cf. Romans 11. 15 and II Corinthians 5. 18*f.* Otherwise post-Christian history, which is a history with Christ, will be understood as a mere interval of patience for a possible proclamation and soul-saving and thereby devaluated into a redemptive-historical interval.

[56] G. Ebeling, 'Hauptprobleme der protestantischen Theologie in der Gegenwart', *Zeitschrift für Theologie und Kirche*, 1961, p. 133.

first time, to analyse the phenomenon of a society in process of emancipation and thereby to arrive at an interpretation of the world as history.[57]

In the world-shattering event of the French Revolution, Hegel was made aware of freedom as the historical realization of the *spirit*, which does not manifest itself once and for all in definite establishments, situations, customs, and necessities, but leaves the forms which have developed from time to time under its influence in order to enter new forms. This deprives the old institutions and orders of the power of their metaphysical and religious claims, freeing the world to be the field of historical realization and freeing men for responsibility for the world in history.

The thoughts which surged forth from the burden of existing conditions refused to let their expectations of a better world be diverted to hopes in eternity; they refused to be reconciled with the existing world as an indisputable order or as an emergency decree in expectation of the Day of Judgement.

Why should the social sphere remain closed to the world-changing power of progressing human knowledge, after it had successfully taken over and methodically promoted the investigation, discovery and advancement of the possibilities of life in the natural sciences? Once the human consciousness became aware of its possibilities there was no stopping the course of its reflection. It reflected about practically everything and therefore, sooner or later, it aimed to have everything in its power. The analysis of the existing world was followed by a synthesis of a possible new world, and the destruction of the hitherto existing conditions, by a construction of a possible future.

Should not even he who greeted the Revolution as the apocalypse of free men, in comparison to previous times of 'despotism', have been fearful at the thought of what these free men would now do or not do with their freedom? All

[57] Cf. J. Ritter, *op. cit.*, p. 10*f.*, 52.

designs of something new have not always been automatically constructive! How was one to protect oneself from false constructions? How could one protect oneself from the effects of those completely free? If the risk of history could be done away with neither by rational calculations nor by statistical estimates, then the question was posed – and it is Hegel's basic question – how a trust in history can be conveyed to men, a trust which frees them to engage in the developments and changes of this world in hope and love, in order to be able to serve the current necessities with insight and confidence. Without such an emancipation, a society was bound to fall prey to the horror of abstract freedom in which men seize their opportunities, through fear of history, of making sure of the future. This fear, if it does not come to a world-destructive race for the securing of the future, threatens to lead to more and more comprehensive preventive measures, which in the end would have to make sure of history by means of a world-wide system of security and a mesh of planning which would be the equivalent of a complete socialization of man and therefore a world-wide tragedy of freedom.

But what belief is in the position to disclose true freedom to history and so to guard mankind from the abstract freedom of an 'atheism of the moral world'?[58] In the name of what spirit is the trust in the 'right direction' (Hegel) of history to be conveyed to a mankind which is irrevocably released into a suffering responsibility for the world? What spirit has a task in history which it can bring to perfection despite all circumstances and resistance? What spirit has already matured in history and thereby proved itself for all time to be historically powerful? This question, which resulted from Hegel's analysis of the age of reflection, led him to a critical examination of the various facets of the tradition of classical and Western history. In his critique of existing Christianity and

[58] Hegel, *Grundlinien der Philosophie des Rechts*, Hamburg, 1955, p. 7. Cf. J. Ritter, *op. cit.*, p. 45*f*.

the related discrimination against Judaism he went back, under the influence of neo-humanism, to the spirit of the Greeks, thus finding reconciliation with the world and freedom for history.

As the Greeks once asked about the *logos* which rules the entire cosmos, so Hegel asked with the Greeks and, at the same time, beyond them, about the *logos* which rules the whole of world-history. The world-threatening fear of history was to be overcome by a contented consciousness of history. Just as the Greeks once secured themselves truth out of fear of possible error and deception, so now Hegel secured history.

He therefore had to carry out an operation of abstraction from everything which could deceive or err; and, because to err is human, and the world of appearances which we encounter can be deceptive, he had to construct an immense system of abolition of everything human and worldly, analogous to the Catholic tradition of the Greek confirmation of the truth, in order to make sure of the *logos* which reigns in history.[59] Threatened by the occurrences of history, he secured the meaning of history in a total logicalizing of history. Just as the negation of history connected with the Greek confirmation of truth had already once made history when the early church adopted classical tradition, so now it again threatened to make history, in the deepest crisis of this classical, Western, Catholic tradition, by way of the veneration of the Greeks in neo-humanism.

It is true that Hegel's philosophy of the spirit failed in its attempt to logicalize history. But did those who raised their voices against Hegel's attempt at a solution lead any further in the great crises of world-expansion and world-devaluation of modern times? Was it not precisely on the path via Feuerbach, Marx, Nietzsche and Kierkegaard – these anti-Hegelian Hegelians – that the national misunderstanding of civilization of neo-humanism, now more than ever, became an

[59] Cf. G. Picht, *Die Erfahrung der Geschichte*, pp. 8–23.

international misfortune?[60] Did these anti-Hegelians not hand the modern world over to the danger, from which Hegel wanted to save it, namely the threatening 'atheism of the moral world' – *etsi deus non daretur*? Even for Kierkegaard history was an inescapable mesh of human reflections in which true existence appeared no longer possible. And did not even dialectical theology and Bonhoeffer, who opposed the non-objectivity of its destructive dialectic, fail to escape from the thought-forms of this classical and Western tradition as revived by Hegel and the anti-Hegelian Hegelians?

To put it briefly: the first great crisis which early Christianity had to endure was the great world-expansion and world-devaluation of gnosticism. If it did not want to deny itself, it had to affirm that this world, living in the twilight of the gods, was the work of the one God and Father of Jesus Christ. But it did not affirm this by appealing to the prophets' testimonies to history (cf. II Corinthians 1. 20) as fulfilled and confirmed in Jesus as the Christ, to the world as the history of God with man; but it affirmed this world as the good and reasonable creation of God, with the help of Stoic ideas of the cosmos and their immanent teleology. In this way the world was re-naturalized to the order of creation and the redemptive action of God was supernaturalized as the order of redemption. And so the relationship between the two orders and natures, the natural and the supernatural, the reality of the world and the reality of God, became the decisive problem. Its solution shaped the conceptions and orders, the mentality and frame of mind of Western Christianity, which had to enter into the crisis to the same extent as the world inexorably confronted it as history. Did this crisis not reach its climax in the fall of the imperial order which was founded on the Catholic-paternal principle of classical and Western tradition?

Was not a renewed 'conversion to the world' needed (cf.

[60] Cf. F. G. Maier, 'Altertum', in *Das Fischer Lexikon*: Geschichte, 1961, p. 20, on the problem of neo-humanism.

Romans 12. 1*f*.), in order to affirm it for the sake of Jesus Christ, along with the prophets, evangelists and apostles, as the history of God with man? In contrast to this, did not Bonhoeffer's acknowledgement of the so-called 'world come of age' remain imprisoned, in spite of everything, in *the* tradition which, according to his own conviction, had already run its course? Certainly, Bonhoeffer did rehabilitate the Jews and he extracted the positive consciousness of the world from the Old Testament, in contrast to Hegel. But it was the unhistorical consciousness of the world of late Jewish Wisdom – and not the understanding of history which is found in the promise of the land of the old covenant and in the prophetic testimonies of history which Jesus consummated – which Bonhoeffer rediscovered and over-interpreted in the light of the age of reflection.

And so for Bonhoeffer the concept of the 'world come of age' was equivalent to the confession that in this empirical situation the claim of God cannot be realized and therefore the church can be *only* indirectly involved in the formation of this world, namely by its suffering in a God-forsaken world. A *theologia crucis* and an eschatological aspect were left in unconnected co-existence; history itself remained empty of all concrete expections of salvation.[61] The 'Cross of Reality' led to a misunderstanding of the cross of Jesus Christ. Because for Bonhoeffer this world appeared to be left to its own resources precisely through the word of God, God could no longer be thought of by him as the one who does his work in and with the world, but only as its last limit.

Bonhoeffer, who complained that theologians, in their embarrassment, usually exploited border-line experiences in order still to speak of God to people (cf. LPP, pp. 116*f*., 107*f*., 114*f*., etc.), in fact brought to fulfilment this attitude which

[61] In this connexion, a comparison of Bonhoeffer's theology of the cross with the meaning of suffering in Kierkegaard's picture of Christ would be of interest. Cf. S. Hansen, *Kerygma und Dogma*, 1956, p. 1*f*. on the latter; cf. LPP, p. 126*f*.

is only able to conceive of the reality of God as the completion or limitation of the reality of the world. And so even for him the testimony of the Jewish–Christian tradition which frees men to history remained hidden, and the reformatory task of freeing the emancipated world remained undone.

The fact that Bonhoeffer saw the end of a nineteen-hundred-year-old tradition of Christian preaching and theology coming in his thinking, which 'instinctively' sensed approaching questions (cf. LPP, p. 106*f.*): and that he dared to take stock of Christianity (cf. LPP, p. 163*f.*) and unmasked non-objective thinking as an evasion, shows what great tasks of self-conquest and renewed discovery of mission are faced by Western Christianity.

A critical interpretation of Bonhoeffer could be of great importance in the present situation of church and society, if one were to take up the task of which Bonhoeffer was aware. As always, the important problem is the interpretation of this 'our world', into the responsibility for which we are irrevocably freed, a problem which Bonhoeffer has investigated more thoroughly than anyone else. We cannot avoid giving an account of Christian, Western culture. In the life of suffering of our responsibility for the world we must look anew into the passion of Jesus and into the meaning of the way of the cross of Jesus Christ for our understanding of the world and our relationship to it. The way in which Jesus was involved in this world and therefore came into conflict with the lords (scribes and pharisees) of this world, contains the decisive interpretation of this world. This interpretation of 'our world' is the presupposition for the sending of the church into the world and, not least, for the possible co-operation of the churches in public life.[62]

---

[62] Catholicism can no longer be satisfied with considering the modern world in its plurality as merely the fragmentation of the former unity. It cannot, for the preservation of its self-realization, evaluate the new social relationships as signs of decay, merely because the old society was the substratum for the self-realization of the church.

The Cross of Reality?

Because we are invited for the sake of Jesus Christ to engage in this world in 'creative discipleship'[63] we are, at the same time, called not to place ourselves in agreement with the current self-understanding of the world, but rather to accept its interpretation as the task of faith which is bound to hope and love.

[63] Cf. E. Wolf, *Schöpferische Nachfolge, op. cit.*, p. 36*f*.

IX

The Idea of God and Modern Man

by Rudolf Bultmann

At the beginning of 1963 there appeared the book of the Anglican bishop John A. T. Robinson, *Honest to God* (honest to and about God).[1] In both England and Germany (as well as in America) it has provoked a somewhat heated debate. Articles appeared in the Hamburg newspaper, *Die Zeit*, with captions 'Is God a metaphor?', 'Is our image of God dated?', 'Is faith in God finished?' – questions evoked by Robinson's book. Some theologians rightly observed that the ideas advanced by Robinson were not new in contemporary theology. Now Robinson had not made this claim at all. He calls repeatedly on Paul Tillich, Dietrich Bonhoeffer and others[2]. But in the process of assimilating their thoughts, he sees that they add up to the following sum, so to speak: *a revolution is necessary*. For, since the traditional ecclesiastical image of God is no longer credible to contemporary men, *a new image of God* is required; the old one is obsolete.

It is understandable that for many readers – especially for readers among the laity to whom the book is directed – this thesis is frightening. With the disposal of the old image of God, is not faith in God and thereby also God himself finished? That this question forces itself upon men today is

---

[1] SCM Press (England), Westminster Press (U.S.A.), 1963.

[2] Professor Bultmann's modesty prevents him from mentioning that Robinson also calls frequently on him. [Trs.]

not signalized by Robinson's book alone. As early as 1961 there appeared the book, *The Death of God*,[3] by the American theologian, Gabriel Vahanian, which is a peculiar and admittedly theologically independent parallel to Robinson's book. The title of Vahanian's book comes from the famous pronouncement of Nietzsche: 'God is dead.'

The note 'God is dead' was struck almost a hundred years before Nietzsche by Jean Paul in his *Siebenkäs*, which appeared in 1796–7, and there is a ghastly vision: 'Discourse of the dead Christ from atop the cosmos: there is no God.'[4] This discourse is not a philosophical discussion of atheism. The import of the vision consists rather in showing that atheism is nihilism (in this respect also a precursor of Nietzsche): 'The whole universe is burst asunder by the hand of atheism and fragmented into innumerable quick-silver particles of I's, which twinkle, roll about, wander, flee together and from each other without unity and stability. No one is so very much alone in the universe as the one who denies God . . . Alas, if every I is its own father and creator, why can it not also be its own angel of destruction?'

Nietzsche permits the 'madman' to proclaim the message of the death of God in his work *Die fröhliche Wissenschaft* (1881). Martin Heidegger says in his essay 'Nietzsches Wort "God ist tot"'[5]: 'Nietzsche's word spells the destiny of

[3] G. Vahanian, *The Death of God. The Culture of Our Post-Christian Era*, New York, George Braziller, 1961. By the same author, 'Beyond the Death of God: The Need of Cultural Revolution', Dialog 1, 4, 1962, pp. 18–21.

[4] G. Bornkamm has reprinted the speech as an appendix to the second volume of his collected essays: *Studien zu Antike und Urchristentum, Gesammelte Aufsätze* II. (Beiträge zur evangelischen Theologie, Band 287, 1959, pp. 245–50). Hegel had also said that God was dead, namely the God of Church dogmatics. On this point cf. W. Anz, 'Tod und Unsterblichkeit' (in: *Einsichten. Festschrift für G. Krüger*, 1962, 11–35), p. 25. The 'atheism' of Hegel, however, is not nihilism in the sense of Jean Paul and Nietzsche.

[5] Heidegger, *Holzwege*, Frankfurt: Klostermann, 1950, 103–247. Cf. also K. Löwith, 'Nietzsches antichristliche Bergpredigt', *Heidelberger Jahrbücher 6*, 1962, pp. 39–50.

two thousand years of Western history.' This remarkable
assertion rests on the conviction that Western history has been
determined for two thousand years by Greek metaphysics,
through which the secularization of the world, brought to
completion in modern times, has finally been established. We
may here suspend judgement about the correctness of this
assertion. Explicit atheism, in any case, is a phenomenon of
the modern period, and Gerhard Ebeling has rightly said
that this atheism is a counter-movement against Christianity.[6]
It is also clear that the death of God for Nietzsche means the
death of the Christian God. 'But', Heidegger adds, 'it is
equally certain and is to be borne in mind in advance that the
names of God and the Christian God are used to designate
the supersensory world in general. God is the name for the
realm of ideas and ideals.'[7]

The 'madman' cries: 'What did we do when we unchained
this earth from its sun?', and continues: 'Where is it moving
to now? Where are we moving to? Away from all suns? Do we
not stumble all the time? Backwards, sidewards, forward, and
in every direction? Is there an above and a below any more?
Are we not wandering as through an endless nothingness?'
The consequence of the death of God is therefore *nihilism*,
as Jean Paul had pictured it.

We must guard against viewing *atheism* merely or even
basically as a consequence of natural science and its world-
view. To be sure, modern natural science has found the
hypothesis 'God' unnecessary, according to the well-known
dictum of La Place, and the atheism of natural science has
without doubt been widely influential, leading even to
absurdities in Russia, where as the result of a space-flight it is
given out that there was no trace of God in the space above
the earth. Nevertheless, even when there are natural

---

[6] G. Ebeling, *The Nature of Faith*, London, Collins; Philadelphia,
Fortress Press, 1961, p. 80f.; *Word and Faith*, London, SCM Press;
Fortress Press, 1963, pp. 135f., 343.

[7] Heidegger, *Holzwege*, p. 199.

scientists today who again hold the hypothesis 'God' to be possible and appropriate, atheism is not thereby contradicted. For it has far deeper roots.

Atheism, as Jean Paul and Nietzsche understood it, is indeed nihilism, and this is not necessarily a consequence of the way in which natural science understands the world. In this respect the loss of the supernatural could be and was replaced in the eighteenth and nineteenth centuries by the belief in progress and its accompanying optimism. The atheism of the natural sciences is a methodological procedure in so far as it subjects the world to an objectivizing way of viewing things. It must necessarily disregard God, because God, as the supersensory, cannot be the object of an objectivizing way of seeing.[8]

Atheism which ends in nihilism is rather the consequence of the *secularization of the world,* of which the objectivizing way of viewing nature is only a partial symptom. Secularization can be characterized simply as the world being conceived by man as an object[9] and thus delivered over to technology as its object.[10] This secularization takes place in every sphere of life, in morality, in law, in politics. For the relation of man to a transcendental power has been abandoned in all spheres of life. Heidegger calls this epoch in which the world has become an object the epoch of *subjectity.*[11] i.e. the era in which the

[8] Cf. Ebeling, *The Nature of Faith*, p. 81*f*.

[9] Cf. Heidegger, *Holzwege*, p. 236.

[10] Cf. LPP, p. 106*f*.: 'Man has learned to cope with all questions of importance without recourse to God as a working hypothesis.' Also on the process of secularization, cf. Ebeling, *Word and Faith*, pp. 128*ff.*; R. G. Smith, 'A Theological Perspective of the Secular', *The Christian Scholar,* 43, 1960, pp. 11–24, p. 18*f*.

[11] Heidegger, *Holzwege*, p. 237. Subjectity, of course, is to be distinguished from subjectivity. The latter refers to the subjective mode of the individual in his judgements (e.g. judgements of taste); the former refers to the disposition of an entire epoch to the world and history, a disposition which has achieved the status of self-evidentness. [The reader will perhaps excuse the neologism subjectity, which represents *Subjektität*; the form is drawn by analogy: *Subjektität* – *Subjektivität*: subjectity – subjectivity. Trs.]

259

world conceived as object is subjected to the planning of man as subject, a planning which is controlled by the values which man himself establishes.

And religion? One must first of all reflect that *Christianity itself was a decisive factor in the development of the secularization of the world* in that it de-divinized the world.[12] The Christian faith, by de-divinizing the world, allowed it to appear in its pure worldliness. It disclosed and evoked the *freedom* of man from the world, freedom from all powers which can encounter man from out of the world.[13] It is the freedom of which Luther said: 'A Christian is a free master over all things and subject to no one.' This consciousness of freedom is the presupposition of the secularization of the world; the latter follows, however, only when the continuation of Luther's remark is forgotten: 'A Christian is a servant in the service of all things and subject to every one,' or, to put it differently, when it is forgotten that *freedom* from the world is at the same time *responsibility* for the world.[14] This forgetfulness increases the more man becomes conscious of the possibility, in pure objectivizing

[12] Cf. Ebeling, *Word and Faith*, pp. 135*f*., 344; *The Nature of Faith*, p. 80*f*. Also especially F. Gogarten, *Verhängnis und Hoffnung der Neuzeit*, 1952; R. G. Smith, 'A Theological Perspective', p. 21.

[13] Cf. Gogarten, *op. cit.*, p. 8: (the most remarkable thing transpires in secularization) 'that the autonomy of man gains the radical sense which it has in the modern world only through the perceptions and experiences disclosed in the Christian faith'. *Ibid.*, p. 12: Secularization is the 'legitimate consequence' of the Christian faith, and in so far as it 'is grounded in the Christian faith', it 'makes the world the world (*Verweltlichung der Welt*)'. Cf. *Ibid*, pp. 93*ff*.

[14] On the interdependence of freedom from the world and responsibility for the world, cf. Gogarten, *op. cit.*, pp. 19, 24*ff*. Vahanian makes the same point, *The Death of God*, p. 61: 'Biblical thought considers the world as man's sphere of action and pre-eminence. Man's responsibility to God and his involvement in the world emerge as polar elements attesting to the original goodness of creation.' It is significant that both Gogarten and Vahanian make the distinction between a legitimate secularization (secularity) and a degenerate secularism (secularism). Cf. Gogarten p. 129*ff*.; Vahanian p. 60*ff*. Cf. R. G. Smith, 'A Theological Perspective', p. 21.

thought, of dominating the world through science and technology, of making it serve his purposes, values and plans.

This process plays the rôle, so to speak, which reason plays in life. Freedom from the world is at the same time responsibility for the world; that means, the world is delivered over to the reason of man.[15] For in order to be able to act responsibly, to come to decisions as they are required again and again, man must recognize the causal connexion of events in the world, must gain insight into causes and effects, and arrive at judgements about what serves the purpose and what does not. It is precisely for this purpose that he has his reason. Indeed, in the power of his reason he grasps the laws under which man's actions universally stand, i.e. the moral laws, whose force alone keeps the human community sound and whole. According to the myth of Protagoras in Plato,[16] Zeus sent reverence and justice to the earth by Hermes in order that political community might be possible. But rational judgements and plans, without which human work and community are not possible, are threatened by the danger that they will be placed in the service of self-seeking and that the authority of the moral laws will thereby wane.

The more reason is conscious of itself, the more the laws which regulate the community will no longer be simply derived from tradition, but will be understood as the moral laws which reason sanctions. And thus out of heteronomy arises *autonomy*. Autonomy is equivocal. In the genuine sense autonomy means self-legislation in the sense that the individual affirms the moral law as that in which he himself comes to win his authenticity.[17] But from the recognition that

[15] Cf. Gogarten, *op. cit.*, p. 88.

[16] Plato, *Protagoras* 322a–c.

[17] Cf. Kant, 'In this manner the moral law leads through the conception of the *summum bonum*, as the object and final end of pure practical reason, to religion, that is, to the recognition of all duties as divine commands, not as sanctions, that is to say, arbitrary ordinances of a

the rational man is a lawgiver in this sense, there arises the delusion that the individual as subject arbitrarily determines what is good and evil, as was the case already in the 'Greek Enlightenment' among the Sophists. And so today autonomy is unfortunately often spoken of as a self-legislation of the individual, and that determines value and valuelessness of itself. The outcome is nihilism.[18]

Religion was also drawn into the wake of 'subjectity'. That Christianity appears as a particular example of religion and is classified within the continuity of the history of religions (which, of course, is possible in any case) indicates that the decline has already set in. Moreover, if Christianity is acknowledged as the highest religion, then the capitulation to subjectity becomes evident at just that point. For the judgement about lower and higher religions can only be a judgement of the subject which evaluates. It is by no means the case that religion necessarily disappears in subjectity. If we consider the Western world, which has been a 'Christian' world for centuries, that world today is in general not anti-Christian, but a-Christian, partly in the sense that Christianity appears to it to be antiquated, and the questions to which Christianity proposes to give answers irrelevant; but partly in the sense that while the questions as such remain live issues, modern man himself now gives the answers. Thus ideologies arise, which assert that they are able to reveal the

[18] On autonomy cf. also R. G. Smith, 'A Theological Perspective', p. 18. Ebeling puts it well in *Word and Faith*, p. 113*f*.: 'But now, to the reality that concerns modern man there belongs . . . the discovery of the autonomy of the reason and accordingly the inescapable duty to make use of the autonomous reason – not, be it noted, to make autonomous use of the reason; for it is not man himself but reason which, rightly understood, is autonomous, whereas to confuse the autonomy of the reason with the autonomy of man results precisely in a new heteronomy of the reason . . .'

foreign will and contingent in themselves, but as essential laws of every free will in itself, which, however, must be regarded as commands of the supreme being . . .' (Kant's *Critique of Practical Reason*, tr. T. K. Abbott, London: Longmans, 1923, p. 226).

meaning of the world and history;[19] or doctrines of salvation are propagated, often from exotic religions, with the choice left to the subjectivity of the individual; or again – especially in the U.S.A. – the biblical hope of a millenium is secularized, that is, converted into optimism which seeks to renew the world through the 'social gospel'.[20] But above all, there arises a *religiosity* to which men flee from the claims as well as from the bitterness or tediousness of secular everyday life.

'In the last analysis, religiosity is an expression of subli-mated loneliness.'[21] The pressing problem for man in a world which has been cut loose from ties to the beyond is to find himself, to become certain of his own being. For with the loss of reference to the transcendent, man's certainty of know-ledge concerning himself has also been lost.[22] The question of God does not therefore die away; but the form of the question suggests 'that the deity is a missing link in man's unsuccessful attempts to grasp the meaning of his self and of the world'.[23]

The question by no means completely dies away in decided atheism either, provided that it draws back from the abyss of nihilism and does not risk laying hold of the ideas of the transcendent God and his revelation, but would still like to speak in some way of the divine as somehow immanent in the world, whether it be as the world's creative ground or as the spiritual life which lives and evolves in the world.[24] Indeed,

[19] Cf. R. G. Smith, 'A Theological Perspective', p. 19.

[20] Cf. Vahanian, *op. cit.*, p. 28*ff.*

[21] Vahanian, *op. cit.*, p. 4. Cf. also R. G. Smith, 'A Theological Perspective', p. 20*f.*; *The New Man*, London: SCM Press, 1956, p. 62*f.*

[22] Cf. Vahanian, *op. cit.*, p. 183. Also, Bonhoeffer, LPP, p. 164: 'Man (scil. who is threatened by today's organization) is thrown back upon himself. He is ready to cope with everything, but not with himself. He is able to secure himself against everything, but not against man. In the last analysis, however, everything depends on man.' LPP, p. 178. Also, R. G. Smith, 'A Theological Perspective', p. 12.

[23] Vahanian, *op. cit.*, p. 78.

[24] Cf., for example, what Robinson, *op. cit.*, pp. 127-9, says about Julian Huxley and Albert Camus.

one can say that such 'atheism' stands nearer the Christian understanding of faith than some institutional Christians who understand the transcendent God as the beyond which has retired from the world.[25]

Religiosity abandons precisely – at least according to the Christian faith – that upon which genuine religion is based: the relation of man to the transcendent God as that which stands over against him. Religiosity thinks from the point of view of the subjectivity of man. In this sense Karl Barth once fought against Schleiermacher and the theology of experience inaugurated by him, in which religion is understood as a province of the human spirit, as the feeling of absolute dependence. To what extent Barth's criticism of Schleiermacher was justified, I leave open.[26] In any case, it was justified to the extent that the relation to God was reduced to feeling. Vahanian takes up this battle against religiosity from the standpoint of the Christian faith with renewed vigour, as did Bonhoeffer before him. And they are followed by John Robinson.

Gone is *the relation of man to the transcendent* as that which stands over against man and the world and is not at their disposal, which is manifested only through encounter, only as gift, and cannot be reached by turning away from the world in a religious flight into a beyond. Now the word transcendence is ambiguous. It can be said that rational thought transcends all unmethodical and random thought. Reason is transcendent with respect to primitive-innocent opinions as well as arbitrary individual judgements and evaluations. But reason remains in the sphere of subjectivity, while religion,

[25] It is therefore understandable when Robinson, p. 127, produces a variation on Paul's formulation for 1 Corinthians 9. 20*f.*: 'I am prepared to be an agnostic with the agnostic, even an atheist with the atheists.' Likewise cf. R. G. Smith, *The New Man*, p. 109, on Feuerbach.

[26] On this point cf. C. Senft, *Wahrhaftigkeit und Wahrheit. Die Theologie des 19. Jahrhunderts zwischen Orthodoxie und Aufklärung (Beiträge zur historischen Theologie*, 22), 1956, pp. 1–46.

particularly the Christian faith, abandons this sphere.[27] The Christian faith speaks of a *revelation*, by which it understands God's act as an event which is not visible to the objectivizing thought of reason, an event which does not communicate doctrines, but concerns the existence of man[28] and teaches him, or better, enables him to understand himself as sustained by the transcendent power of God.[29]

In this, theologians like Tillich, Bonhoeffer, Ebeling, Vahanian, R. G. Smith and Robinson are one. But they are also agreed that *the transcendent* is to be sought and can be found not above or beyond the world, but *in the midst of this world*.[30] Allow me to quote some sentences of Bonhoeffer: 'The "beyond" of God is not the beyond of our cognitive faculties. Epistemological transcendence has nothing to do with the transcendence of God. God is transcendent in the midst of

[27] I leave it open here whether and to what extent it can be said that the existential life (e.g. in personal relationships) transcends the sphere of subjectity.

[28] Here I disregard the paradox, which involves the revelatory event being at once an historical as well as an eschatological event, both with respect to its origin, Jesus Christ, and with respect to its constant renewal in the church's proclamation.

[29] If one is persuaded that every man is basically moved by the question of God and that therefore the Christian proclamation may reckon with a pre-understanding, then one can ask whether this pre-understanding is not also concealed precisely in religiosity. Now H. G. Gadamer, in his book, *Wahrheit und Methode* (Tübingen: Siebeck, 1960), which is of greatest significance for theologians, has contested (in the context of the hermeneutical problem, p. 313*f.*) whether one can speak of a pre-understanding for the understanding of the biblical texts, namely, a pre-understanding that is given with the question of God that drives human existence. I am of the opinion that the pre-understanding is given precisely in that experience which Gadamer designates as the 'authentic experience', namely, the experience in which 'man becomes conscious of his finiteness' (p. 339*f.*). This experience is certainly not always realized, but it surely persists as an ever-present possibility.

[30] For R. G. Smith cf. 'A Theological Perspective', p. 15; *The New Man*, pp. 65–70, and especially pp. 94–112: 'This-Worldly Transcendence'. Ebeling, *The Nature of Faith*, p. 160*f.*

our life.' 'The transcendent is not the infinitely remote, but the nearest at hand.'[31] The 'death of God', according to Vahanian, takes place precisely in that the transcendent presence of God is lost if transcendence is conceived as purely other-worldly – just as in religiosity.[32] Or, to quote another formulation of Vahanian: 'Religious authority does not entail the eradication of personal autonomy for the sake of blind assent to a system of beliefs claiming sanction of absolute or divine authority. But religious authority . . . symbolizes a synthesis of subjective truth and objective reality . . . Faith is an attempt to reconcile subject and object, subjective truth and objective reality, without overwhelming either one of the terms.'[33]

Faith permits the world to be the world; indeed, it gives back to the world its authentic worldliness; faith 'recognizes the hidden unconditional ground even in the most autonomous of human pursuits. It needs to welcome those pursuits not for the hope that they may be violently "baptized" into Christ, but for their own sake'.[34] Dietrich Bonhoeffer formulates the discernment of faithful relation to the world very pointedly: 'And we cannot be honest without recognizing

---

[31] LPP, pp. 165, 163. On Bonhoeffer cf. especially R. G. Smith, *The New Man*, pp. 96–106; Ebeling, 'The Non-religious Interpretation of Biblical Concepts', in *Word and Faith*, pp. 98–161.

[32] Vahanian, *op. cit.*, p. 44.

[33] *Op. cit.*, p. 164*f.* Cf. 11: 'Now, as then, today and always, the Christian problem is to correlate the truth of Christianity with the empirical truths men live by, without confusing them: man cannot live by one or the other kind of truth alone,' p. 169: 'On the contrary, even as the meaning of existence lies outside existence, in the dialectical relatedness implied by the polarity between Creator and creature, so also the meaning of history lies above and beyond history.' The formulation of Tillich, quoted also by Vahanian, is in substantial agreement: 'Theology moves back and forth between two poles, the eternal truth of its foundation and the temporal situation in which the eternal truth must be received' (*Systematic Theology*, Vol. 1, Chicago University Press, 1951, p. 3).

[34] R. G. Smith, *The New Man*, p. 69.

that we must live in the world – *etsi deus non daretur*. And this is just what we do recognize – before God! God himself drives us to this recognition.'[35] This is precisely what Robinson designates as the necessary revolution: the God above the world having become the God beyond the world, today it is a question of finding God in the midst of the world, in the present. The contrast between here and beyond, and thus the contrast between naturalism and supernaturalism, must be overcome. God must be recognized as the unconditional in the conditional.

It is surprising how such theological perceptions are also taken up by sociologists. Eckart Schleth says in his book, *Der profane Weltchrist*: 'The unity of Christ and world is found in the "nevertheless" of the believer for the world, in his imperceptible eschatological existence here and now, in his freedom from the world, in the world and for the world.' Also 'Life in faith, the character of which is to be permanently in process of fulfilment, is life in the "ultimate reality", which is always here and now and identical with everyday things.'[36]

The relation of faith and worldliness is a dialectical relationship, as R. G. Smith especially has emphasized.[37] I will try to make the meaning of this dialectical relation clear by means of an analogy. The loving look into an eye which is loved and loving is fundamentally different from the objectivizing look with which an ophthalmologist examines the eye of a patient. But when the doctor who has to treat the diseased eye is also the one who loves, the two ways of seeing stand in a dialectical relationship; he has to examine the eye of the other in an

---

[35] LPP, p. 121f.

[36] E. Schleth, *Der profane Weltchrist. Neubau der Lebensform für den Industriemenschen*, 1957, pp. 114, 159. Cf. p. 8: The author is of the opinion 'that the church as "eschatological phenomenon" occurs where Christians without reservation take the profane world seriously, because only in the "solidarity of faith and unfaith" can the new creation in Christ be recognized and the world served by it'.

[37] *The New Man*, p. 106f., also pp. 58–70; 'A Theological Perspective', p. 22.

objectivizing way precisely in his love. The objectivizing way of seeing enters into the service of the one who loves. Robinson endeavours, following Tillich, to make clear the relation between faith and worldliness in the dialectical relation between engagement with the world and withdrawal from the world. To this dialectic corresponds the dialectic in the relation of man to God, namely, as the relation between personal freedom and utter dependence, between ultimacy and intimacy.[38]

He who has understood the dialectic of the relationship between worldliness and faith in relation to the transcendent God, also sees that the recognition of God as the nearest at hand, as he who is in the midst of worldly life, does not imply pantheism.[39] For the dialectic is missing in pantheism, and it avoids the paradox that is given to man to conquer by grasping the unconditional in the conditional in every *now*: that means, not in a theory, but in existential comportment, in the conscious or unconscious decisions of life.

The contrast can be made clear by saying that faith in the transcendent presence of God can be expressed in the phrase 'transformations of God'. Ernst Barlach chose this phrase in order to say that the paradox of the presence of God in the world takes shape in ever new form, just as God himself wishes to give expression to the supra-real and infinite in his works perpetually in new forms.

Ernst Troeltsch once also spoke of the 'transformations of God', since he sought to hold on to the idea of God in his philosophy of history in view of the 'pluralism of reality and its movement' *vis-à-vis* changes in the knowledge of truth and ideals.[40] These changes depend upon an 'inner life-know-

---

[38] Robinson, *op. cit.*, pp. 100, 130*f*.
[39] R. G. Smith, 'A Theological Perspective', p. 16, also emphasizes this point.
[40] E. Troeltsch, *Der Historismus und seine Probleme*, 1922. The formulations in question, to which reference is made above, are collected by Gogarten, *Verhängnis und Hoffnung der Neuzeit*, pp. 112–14.

ledge of the All or the Divinity', upon a 'life-process of the Absolute', a 'becoming of the divine Spirit'.

Troeltsch saw the problem, but he sought to solve it not on the basis of the historicity (*Geschichtlichkeit*) of human existence, but from a standpoint which views history from the outside and speculatively postulates a transcendent deity, which always has its life beyond my historicity.[41]

Hans Jonas represents the opposite extreme in his essay 'Immortality and the Modern Temper'.[42] in which he projects, so to speak, the historicity of man into God himself and speaks of the destiny of the deity for which man is responsible.[43] We men are experiments of eternity, as it were, and God's own destiny is at stake in our decisions, in the universe to which he has given himself up. God's being at the mercy of the world does not mean his immanence in the sense of pantheism. Rather, there is the paradox that the deity has chosen a destiny which consists in the continuous elevation out of immanence into transcendence, for which we men are responsible. In such a process, in the succession of surrender and deliverance, the deity becomes itself.

Schubert M. Ogden understands God's being as historical being in another way.[44] God's eternity is not to be conceived as his timelessness following the metaphysical tradition, but rather as his eminent temporality, his historicity.[45] God is a God who acts, as he is known in the Bible; his self must

[41] For criticism of Troeltsch, see Gogarten, *op. cit.*, pp. 114–16.

[42] *Harvard Theological Review*, 55, 1962, pp. 1–20.

[43] Jonas, of course, also sees the dialectic between the relation to the world and the relation to God, and says that we encounter the eternal in the temporal, especially in the decisions in which eternity and nothingness meet in one in that the now of the decision is always to be understood as the final moment of time granted us. That means in fact to understand the end in a light from beyond time.

[44] *Journal of Religion*, 43, 1963, pp. 1–19.

[45] Cf. M. Heidegger, *Being and Time*, tr. J. Macquarrie and E. Robinson, London, SCM Press, 1962, 499, n. xiii: 'If God's eternity can be "construed" philosophically, then it may be understood only as a more primordial temporality which is "infinite".'

therefore be conceived in strict analogy with the human self, and anthropological language about God is entirely appropriate. Just as man is not an isolated I, neither is God. Without the universe, without the world, his creation, God is not. To this extent he not only stands in relation to the world, but is dependent upon it. But this dependence is actual, i.e. it is actualized in his own free decisions as well as in the free decisions, which correspond to his own, of the creatures that constitute his world. Decisions arising from unbounded love as answer to God themselves contribute to God's self-creation.

This all certainly sounds astonishing at first hearing. For is not God, as we learned from Psalm 90, he who was there before the mountains were brought forth and the earth and the world created, God from everlasting to everlasting? Indeed he is! But we understand Ogden when we comprehend how he endeavours to free the idea of the eternity of God from the metaphysical conception of God as the unmoved mover, the *causa sui*,[46] and to conceive the eternity of God as historical without giving up thinking of God as creator. If, according to the biblical tradition, God is a person, so is he historical. In support of the view that God is not, apart from the world, the creator is not, apart from the creation, Ogden is able to invoke John 1. 1–3, that remarkable assertion that in the beginning was the word, and the word of creation at that, through which everything came into being. This word in the beginning was with God, indeed the word was God. That is no different from what Ogden intends to say. And when we reflect on the word 'before' in the psalm, it is to be said that already for the psalmist the meaning of 'before' is not exhausted in the chronological sense, but that it means the creative superiority, the creative origin. This origin did not occur once as *prima causa*, out of which world history then unfolded in time; on the contrary, the origin is always present.

[46] Cf. M. Heidegger, *Identität und Differenz*, 1957, p. 70*f.* (*Essays in Metaphysics: Identity and Difference*, tr. Kurt F. Leidecker, New York: Philosophical Library, 1960, p. 64*f.*)

The Idea of God and Modern Man

With this we come back to the assertion that for modern man the idea of God above or beyond the world is either no longer viable or is distorted into a religiosity which would like to escape from the world. By no means! Only the idea of God which finds, which can seek and find, *the unconditional in the conditional*, the beyond in the here, the transcendent in the present at hand, as possibility of encounter, is possible for modern man.

It then remains to keep oneself open at any time for the *encounter with God in the world, in time*. It is not the acknowledgement of an image of God, be it ever so correct, that is real faith in God; rather, it is the readiness for the eternal to encounter us at any time in the present – at any time in the varying situations of our life. Readiness consists in openness in allowing something really to encounter us that does not leave the I alone, the I that is encapsulated in its purposes and plans, but whose encounter transforms us, permits us to become new selves again and again. The situation can be heartening just as well as disheartening, can be challenging as well as requiring endurance. What is demanded is selflessness, not as a pattern of moral behaviour, but as the readiness not to cling to our old selves, but to receive our authentic selves ever anew. This can be a questioning readiness, but it can also be completely unconscious. For, surprisingly, God can encounter us where we do not expect it.[47]

[47] That is evidently also the intention of Herbert Braun, whose avoidance of the word 'God' in his delineation of what the New Testament has to say to me (*Gesammelte Studien zum Neuen Testament und seiner Umwelt*, Tübingen: Siebeck, 1962, p. 297) has offended and evoked criticism (cf. especially H. Gollwitzer, *Die Existenz Gottes im Bekenntnis des Glaubens*, 1963, pp. 26 9). Braun's purpose is to emphasize, over against atheism with a world-view, that God is not 'the one who exists for himself', but rather is 'the whence of my being driven around' (*op. cit.*, p. 341). This being driven about is understood by Braun as determined by the 'I may' and 'I ought'. It might be asked how this dialectic (if it may be called that) relates to the dialectic between worldliness and a believing relation to transcendence. But, in any case, the relation to transcendence is understood in the New Testament,

We have thus perhaps come to an understanding of what is meant by the 'transformations of God'. All of us are probably acquainted with sagas and legends, pagan as well as Christian, in which the profound idea of the transformation of God has been concealed in the mythological representation of the metamorphosis of the deity or of gods, who visit a mortal incognito and unrecognized. How the one visited receives the god determines his destiny.

The New Testament contains the most striking proclamation of the 'transformations' of God, and oddly enough in the picture which Jesus sketches of the last judgement (Matthew 25. 31–46). The judge of the world assembles all men before his throne, some to the right, some to the left. To those on the right he says: 'I was hungry and you gave me food, I was thirsty and you gave me drink, I was a stranger and you welcomed me . . .' And when those so addressed inquire in astonishment, 'When did we do all this?', the Lord will answer, 'What you did to one of the least of these my brethren you did to me!' The dialogue with those on the left runs correspondingly 'I was hungry and you gave me no food, I was thirsty and you gave me no drink . . .' And when they ask,

---

according to Braun, as an event, and indeed, as he formulates it, as an 'unexpectable' event (p. 275). The believing self-understanding awakened in such an event is not theoretical knowledge, but 'an event which occurs again and again' (p. 277). The truth of the relation to transcendence understood in this sense is 'bound to its being perpetually proclaimed anew' (p. 277) and to its being heeded (p. 297), to its being heard (p. 298), respectively. The self-understanding awakened by such hearing is actualized in concrete human community. Braun is thus able to put it very sharply: 'Man as man, man in his community with man, implies God.' – R. G. Smith also emphasizes the importance of the community, 'A Theological Perspective', p. 22: 'Man is (scil. man) in so far as he receives. He is (scil. man) only so far as he is whole. And this wholeness is found only in relation to others. Man's being is being in relation. This simply cannot be arranged or planned. It happens, it is an event in which man's being is disclosed in the presence of the other.' The problem of the relation of law and gospel also belongs here; see, e.g. Ebeling, *Word and Faith*, p. 143*f.*

'Lord, when did we see thee hungry or thirsty . . and did not minister to thee?', then they must face the answer, 'What you did not do to the least of these, you did not do to me either!' This picture thus contains the two doctrines which belong together, of the 'transformations' of God and of the presence of eternity in time.

INDEX

Index

Index

'Biblical concepts already have a meaning' (*see also* Non-religious interpretation . . .): 101

Biblical references: *Old Testament*: II Chronicles, *xx, 12,* 39, 42, 43; Genesis *ii, 8–17,* 172; Isaiah, *xxviii, 21,* 163; *liii,* 153; Jeremiah, *xlv,* 154; Numbers, *xi, 23,* 17; Psalms, *iv,* 163; *v, 12,* 162; *xxxi,* 179–80; *lxxxvi,* 179; *xc,* 270; I Samuel *ii, 6,* 164; *New Testament*: Acts, *viii,* 153; *x,* 153; Colossians, *iii, 3,* 108; I Corinthians, *i, 18 and 23,* 163; *ix. 20,* 264; II Corinthians, *i, 20,* 252; *i, 23,* 17; Hebrews, *xii, 11,* 163; John, *i, 1–3,* 270; *i, 14,* 11; *i, 29,* 153; *i, 47,* 153; Luke, *vii,* 153; Mark, *xv, 34,* 19, 149, 151, 168, 210; Matthew, *viii, 17,* 149, 153, 168; *xvi, 17,* 107; *xviii, 3,* 149; *xxv, 31–46,* 272; Philippians, *iii, 20,* 108; Revelation, *ii, 4 ff,* 39; Romans, *i, 4,* 106; *ii,* 16, 116; *ii, 17–25,* 113; *iii (opening verses),* 110; *iii, 1–2,* 113; *iii, 2,* 110; *iii, 2–4,* 110–11; *iii, 3,* 114; *iii, 21,* 109, 113; *iii, 22,* 107; *iii, 27,* 113, 117; *iii, 28,* 108; *iv, 17 b,* 108; *v,* 163; *v, 12–18,* 118; *v, 30,* 114; *vi, 4–5,* 108; *vi, 5,* 114; *vii,* 111; *viii, 1–2,* 108; *ix, 111–12,* 117, 118; *ix, 13,* 118; *ix, 24–9,* 118; *xii, 1 f,* 253

Biblical terms and concepts, non-religious interpretation of: see Non-religious interpretation . . .

Biographica (by periods): first, 27–32; second, 45–9; third, 66–70

Blut und Boden (doctrine): 51

Bodin: 148

Bonhoeffer, Dietrich: his contribution to modern theology, 9–10, 23–4; his chief concern, 12, 16; his life, 12–13; his writings, 13–21; his problem, 14, 217–37; his narrowing audience, 22; and publicity, 23; his high standard, 23, 29; his transcendence, 23–4; his eschatology, *see* Eschatology; his challenge, 24–5; the martyr, 24, 66, 69, 73; the theologian, 24–5, 28; his 'periods', 25–88 (I, 26–43; II, 44–65; III, 65–88); in America, 26, 29, 47, 50, 66–7; and his contemporaries and other theologians, 27–8, 82–8, 149*n*, 152; his intellectual honesty, 28; and Barth, *see* Barth; his relaxations, 30, 63; his development, 31–43, 44–65, 65–88, 203, 211; and the church, 33–9 *et seq.*, his ecclesiology, *see* Ecclesiology; and ecumenical meetings, 39–40, 41; and reality, 42; his sermon on Gideon, 46; and conscription, 46, 47; in London, 47; his *Bruderhaus*, 47, 58–65; and ordinands, 47, 60–1; his 'retreats', 47–8; 'would not compromise', 48–9; and Aryan discrimination, 49; a turning-point in his thought, 49; his loneliness, 53, 64; concentrated on a small community, 58; and education for the ministry, 60; his 'secret discipline', *see* Secret discipline; and seminary for ordinands, 60–1; and Oxford Group, 62, and Zinzendorff, 63; and heretics, 64; widely known, 64; his changes, 64 5, 69, 144–5, 188–92; and 'otherness', 64–5, in Encyclopædia Britannica, 65, 87–8; and separation from the church, 67; forbidden to preach, 67; 'V-man', 67, 68; and Hitler's war machine, 68; and Visser't Hooft

277

Index

Bonhoeffer—contd.

68; and plots to kill Hitler, 68 (*see also* Hitler); his engagement, 68; betrayed to Gestapo, 68; tried and condemned to death, 68–9, 153; hanged, 69; his change from passive to active resistance, 69; and the Bible and religion, 70–1; his new discovery, 75–8; his views on religion, 78–82; and Kant, 77; shocked at things he says, 87; in Barth's letter to Herrenbrück, 89–92; and the *kerygma*, 91; and Barth's 'Positivism of Revelation', 93–130; moves on only one front at a time, 145; and the young Luther, 161–81; his theologies of the Word and of the Cross, 162–81 *passim*; reception and interpretation of, 182–214, 215–55; his 'last period' (1940–45), 184–5; his final theological utterances, 184*n*; and the Christian West, *q.v.*, 187, 188, 191–2; his intellectual ideas clarified, 188; his heritage, 182, 189–211; foresees future sociological changes, 190; his social status, 190–1; his view of history, 191–211, 235; his 'liberation' and 'reformation', 204–5; his 'religionless future', 207; his consciousness of a problem, 217–37; his solution, and a critical examination of it, 238–47; his leading intention, 242; consequences for the interpreter of D. B., 247–55

'Bonhoeffer and the Young Luther' (Prenter, essay): 19

'Bonhoeffer's Thought on Church and Preaching in World Come of Age' (Schoenherr): 137*n*

Bornkamm, G.: 257*n*

Bornkamm, H.: 221*n*

Bourgeois liberalism and revolution: 195–8 *passim*

Braun, Herbert: 271*n*

Brethren Councils of the Confessing Church (1934): 45, 46, 58

Brethren House (D. B's): 47, 58–65

'Brown Synod' (Sept. 1933): 45

Bruderhaus, D. B's: 47, 58–65

Brunner, Heinrich: 42, 51

Bruno, Giordano: 148

Bultmann, Rudolf: vii, 10–11, 14, 65, 83–5, 90, 92, 100, 104, 105, 132, 139, 140, 159, 238, 239*n*, 256*n*

Buren, Paul van: 14, 21

Calvinists: 36; neo-Calvinists, 90

Camus, Albert: 263*n*

Canaris, Admiral: 13, 67, 69

Cape Town, Archbishop of: 64

Catholic, Catholics and Catholicism (Roman): 73, 74, 199, 201, 204, 251

'Characters of Love, The' (Bayley): 131

Christ (*see also* Jesus): today, 14, 16–21, 43, 134, 149; as a community (the church), 33–8 *passim*, 218, 228; 'the man for others', 35, 43, 76, 157; lives in his followers, 56; the Lordship of, *see below*; and the World, 73; the crucified, 77–8, 81, 171–2 (*see also Theologia crucis and* God, a suffering); humanity of, 86; the message of, 88; as congregation, 125, 129; the centre of life, 142, 143; (the sinless) bears our sins (literally), 143, 176; and our humanity, 176; and the newly matured world, 147; our justification and our judgement, 167; the presence of, 176, 177–8

278

Index

Christ, the Lordship of God in (*regnum Christi*): 40 42, 51, 72–8 *passim*, 97, 98, 102, 123, 142, 152, 155–6, 222, 238–9; 'not of triumph and completion but of suffering and humiliation,' 156, 159; and secularity, 159

Christendom, the imperishableness of (?): 229

Christengemeinde und Bürgergemeinde (Barth): 127

Christian: apologetic, 210; life, self-contained, 65; settlement (Siedlung), 59

Christianity: today, 14, 16–21, 43; without religion, 43; 56, 65–6, 96, 238, 246; the narrow pass for, 44; not an end in itself, 74; as 'religion', 97; religious interpretation of, 98–9, 155, 169, 175; non-religious interpretation of, 132, 134, 138, 155, 172–3, 175 (*see also* Non-religious interpretation . . .); what it is (*quotation*), 134–6; suited to the time, 178; feudalization of, 193, 194; humanistic-humanitarian, 198; and religion, 213–14, 260; a religionless, 246; and secularization, *q.v.*, 260

'Christians and Unbelievers' (poem): 87, 155, 170

Christokrator: 76, 82, 157

Christology, D. B's: 42, 44, 51, 54, 71–8 *passim*, 142–3, 145, 152, 157; and ecclesiology, 37; right and wrong, 55; of the Cross, 245 (*see also Theologia crucis*)

Christology (D. B's lectures): 30, 38, 144, 173n, 176 and *n*, 193

Christ's word: 56

Christus praesens: 56

Church, the (the Body of Christ, or Christian Community): 50; Christ as, 33–5, 37, 38, 43; its

word of authority, 38; and immanence and transcendence, 38; and the World, 40, 72, 82, 96, 100–1, 103–4; must declare the Word of God *now*, 41; its social position and character, 49–50, 54, 203; the 'new man', 55; Barth's view of, 111–12; its unifying function, 207n; which heritage will it adopt?, 211; *abnegatio sui* of, 213; hiddenness of, 137 and *n*; its guilt, 203; as form of revelation, 218

Church Committees in Germany (*Kirchenausschüsse*), Hitler's: 45

Church of the Cross: 174–5

Church of the Union of Prussia: 46

Clergy, remuneration of the: 102

Clericalism and clericalization: 210, 212, 213

Coming of Age of the World, The: 145–52; Christian apologetics and, 147; two aspects of, 186

Commentary on the Epistle to the Romans (Barth): 104, 106–22 *passim*, 125, 148

Communism: 200

Community of pastors (*Bruderhaus*), D. B's: 47, 58–65

Concentration (D. B's second period): 44–65

Concrete message to the world: 38–43

Concrete nature of Christian message: 32 8, 52

Concreteness, the attribute of revelation: 33–8; what it includes, 38

Concretion, problem of: 40

'Confessing Church', the: 13, 25, 26, 54, 58, 128, 235; meeting of (1936), 22; Brethren Councils of, 45, 46; split and weakened, 45, 212; and heretics, 64;

279

Index

Index

Index

Index

Index

Index

Index

Weizäcker, C. F. von: 240*n*
Weltanschauungen: 57; Christian and Marxist, 44
Weltflucht, no: 52
Wendland, H. D.: 219*n*, 222*n*
West, the Christian: 187–94 *passim*, 197–203 *passim*, 211, 230, 235, 254; its ideology, 204–5; D. B's aim at uniting, 234
Westermann, C.: 225*n*
'Wisdom' teaching (of Israel): 225, 242, 243, 244; late Jewish, 253
Wolf, E.: 84, 221*n*, 255
Wolf, Hugo: 23
Word and Faith (Ebeling): 15
Word of God, the: 36, 56, 141
'Word of God and the Word of Man, The' (Barth's address): 119

World Alliance for International Friendship through the Churches, Youth Commission of: 30
World, the: autonomy of, 17–18, 52, 146–8, 248; centre of, 172–4
Worldliness ('this-worldliness'): 33, 70–1, 78, 133–4, 153–4, 158–9; first formulation of D. B's idea of, 132–4
Worship, proper uses of: 82; in a religionless world, 102

Yahweh and the world: 243

Zeit, Die: 256
Zinzendorff's writings: 63
Zoellner, General Superintendent: 45

288